Understanding violent crime

Stephen Jones

Open University Press
Buckingham · Philadelphia

Open University Press
Celtic Court
22 Ballmoor
Buckingham
MK18 1XW

email: enquiries@openup.co.uk
world wide web: www.openup.co.uk

and
325 Chestnut Street
Philadelphia, PA 19106, USA

First Published 2000

Reprinted 2011

A catalogue record of this book is available from the British Library

ISBN   0 335 20417 1 (pb)   0 335 20418 X (hb)

Library of Congress Cataloging-in-Publication Data available

Typeset by Type Study, Scarborough

Printed and bound in Great Britain by
CPI Antony Rowe, Chippenham, Wiltshire

This book is dedicated to my father,
Clifford Jones (1913–1977)

Contents

Series editor's foreword

Stephen Jones's book is the latest contribution to the Open University Press Crime and Justice series, which provides relatively short but challenging introductory textbooks on important areas of debate within the fields of criminology, criminal justice and penology. All the books are written by experienced lecturers and researchers who set out to give undergraduates and postgraduates both a solid grounding in the relevant area and a taste to explore it further. Although aimed primarily at students new to the field, and written as far as possible in plain language, the books are not oversimplified. On the contrary, the authors set out to 'stretch' readers and to encourage them to approach criminological knowledge and theory in a critical and questioning frame of mind.

Stephen Jones's main focus is upon the perpetrators of 'criminal violence' – that is, of the kinds of assaultive acts that are normally recognized and responded to by the police and courts as offences against the criminal law. He uses examples from the UK, USA, Canada, Australia and elsewhere to show that definitions of criminal violence vary considerably across time and space, and that measurement of the extent of violent crime is by no means a straightforward exercise. He is also careful to point out that the general term 'violence' can be applied to many other kinds of activity (by individuals, groups, corporations or the state), some of which are less clearly illegal and less likely to attract police attention. Nevertheless, his core interest is in questions about violent offending: why some individuals commit serious physical assaults on others and, in particular, why some do so repeatedly. He explores the main biological, psychological and sociological explanations which have been put forward in answer to such questions. He also looks at the possibilities for reducing interpersonal violence, including a chapter on recent developments in the field of cognitive-behavioural offender programmes. There are further chapters on the victims of violent crime and on recent trends in sentencing – the latter, again, covering developments in several countries besides England and Wales.

Other books already published in the Crime and Justice series – all of whose titles begin with the word 'Understanding' – have covered penological theory (Barbara A. Hudson), criminological theory (Sandra Walklate), criminal statistics (Clive Coleman and Jenny Moynihan), youth crime (Sheila Brown) and crime prevention (Gordon Hughes). Others in the pipeline include texts on white collar crime (Hazel Croall), criminal justice (Mike Maguire), prisons (Kathryn Chadwick, Margaret Malloch and Phil Scraton), policing (Simon Holdaway), crime and social exclusion (Loraine Gelsthorpe), punishment in the community (Peter Raynor and Maurice Vanstone), risk (Hazel Kemshall) and race and crime (Colin Webster). All are major topics in university degree courses on crime and criminal justice, and each book should make an ideal foundation text for a relevant module. As an aid to understanding, clear summaries are provided at regular intervals, and a glossary of key terms and concepts is a feature of every book. In addition, to help students expand their knowledge, recommendations for further reading are given at the end of each chapter.

Finally, I must record my gratitude to the staff of Open University Press for the original suggestion that I become involved in editing this series, and for their help in bringing it to fruition. Most of all, I thank the authors, who have made my job as series editor both simple and pleasurable.

Mike Maguire
Professor of Criminology and Criminal Justice, Cardiff University

Preface

Violence and violent images permeate nearly every part of life from its very beginning. In some societies, the first event a new born baby experiences is to be hit by a midwife to make it cry. As it grows older, the infant may come to realize that the biblical instruction 'spare the rod and spoil the child' is still alive. On reaching school, it may experience bullying. If the child is a boy, he will soon be socialized into 'rough and tumble'. After school, children are increasingly likely to be collected by a parent (it is not safe to walk alone) to go home and play violent computer games. Eventually, the child will start to watch news items about bombing and war. As young adults venture into the world, they will encounter the pub and club, with the accompanying threat of violence. The workplace may hold its own dangers, especially for women. The men may play rugby football or stay at home to watch the boxing on television. Babies will be born and the whole cycle will start again.

Allusions to violence are common in everyday speech, especially in sporting or competitive contexts. The British are particularly fond of this: expressions such as 'being thrashed by', 'taking a lot of punishment' and 'taking stick' are still commonly used, particularly in a sporting context.

Several countries have established major enquiries to consider violence. America has had two: the National Commission on the Causes and Prevention of Violence, established following the assassinations of Martin Luther King and Robert Kennedy; and the Panel on the Understanding and Control of Violent Behavior (Reiss and Roth 1993). The Australian federal government set up a National Committee on Violence in 1988 (Chappell *et al.* 1991). In Britain, the Economic and Social Research Council (ESRC) Violence Research Programme has commissioned 20 research projects, which are due to report by 2002 (ESRC 1998).

The idea of a *cause* of violence must be treated with care. Zimring and Hawkins (1997) have pointed out the difference between the usage of the word in common parlance, which generally indicates a single or sufficient factor, and its usage in a scientific sense, which may refer to one of several contributory or necessary factors. In this respect, an event can be said to have several causes, perhaps with different degrees of proximity. It is therefore possible for a consideration of factors which are claimed to be *related* to the infliction of violence to be undertaken, and their strengths and weaknesses highlighted. Such claims may be evidenced by anything from general observation, through participants' accounts, to highly complex statistical analyses of the behaviour of groups of individuals. A large amount of research evidence is referred to in this book. Although no single finding 'proves' anything, it will become apparent that, in some areas, the bulk of the evidence does point towards certain conclusions. My own view is that psychological explanations, although unfashionable in certain quarters, still have an important role to play.

During the writing of this book, a search for the word 'violence' was made in a computer database which purports to contain the titles of books and articles in the leading periodicals. Around 6000 entries were recorded for the previous five years alone. This provides some indication of the vast scope of the subject, and the impossibility of covering all its aspects in a work of this size. As Chapter 1 shows, this has been dealt with by adopting a broadly legal definition of violence based on either the personal infliction or threat of physical force. Rape and indecent assault are therefore considered, but not other sexual offences which are based on activities which appear to be consensual (although it is conceded that the consent may be spurious). Length restrictions have also precluded discussion of bullying and violence in the workplace as specific topics, although much of the discussion will also be relevant to these areas. Extensive references are provided throughout the text, together with some suggestions for further reading at the end of each chapter.

An unusual feature of the book is that some information is provided on the way violence is dealt with in several other countries. Once again, shortage of space has proved a constraint, but references occur throughout to data from Australia, Canada, New Zealand and the USA. These countries receive particular attention in Chapter 1, which considers legal definitions of violence, and Chapter 9, which deals with sentencing. To assist the flow of the text, the detail of the non-English law relevant to these chapters has been placed in an Appendix. Unless otherwise stated, references to government policy or statistical data relate to the United Kingdom.

We live in a world where people increasingly wish to be credited for their contributions, but (thanks to the influence of lawyers) are not prepared to take any responsibility for them. On this basis, it is appropriate to mention Mark Berger, Simon Bronitt, Chris Clarkson, Catherine Creamer, Geoff Hall and Sue Pettit for providing me with information, and Katie Steiner for helping with the research. Fiona Brookman, of the University of Glamorgan, has kindly allowed me to look at her doctoral thesis, and this has provided additional insights into certain aspects of violence. The series editor, Mike Maguire, has made a wide range of useful suggestions and reminded me not to overlook the interests of sociologists. Finally, thanks are due to Filomena Jones and all my family for their continuing support.

Stephen Jones
Barlaston

part one

The phenomenon of violence

chapter one

Definitions of violence

In this chapter, alternative definitions of violence will be considered. The main English non-fatal offences against the person will then be outlined. Those who wish to compare these with the corresponding provisions in Australia, Canada, New Zealand and (to a limited extent) the USA can find this information in the Appendix. The problems arising from the defences of consent, self-defence and corporal punishment will be discussed.

General definitions of violence

The term 'violence' does not have a standard, fixed definition. Notions of what constitutes violence can vary not only between different societies, but also between different groups within the same society at different times and in different contexts. What would have been considered as routine corporal punishment of children in the nineteenth century might now be viewed as violent and illegal conduct. The men of the Yanomamö society of South America, reputedly among the most violent in the world, routinely beat their wives severely and hold glowing sticks against them. Yet the women gauge their husband's devotion in terms of the number of minor beatings they receive. Heelas (1982) asked whether an act can be considered violent if an observer adjudges it to be so, regardless of the views of the participants. In most societies, a violent act could not amount to a criminal offence unless at least some observers considered it to be unjustified (van Eyken 1987).

Context can also be important. Whereas most of the respondents in a study by Blumenthal *et al.* (1972) considered that student demonstrations against the Vietnam war constituted violent behaviour, few thought that violence had been perpetrated when the police hit the demonstrators.

Most people think of violence in terms of the infliction of physical injury by force. In recent years, the legal definition of assaults in some countries has been extended to include serious forms of psychological harm. It has been claimed that oppression (for example, resulting from racism or sexism) should be defined as violence (Howitt and Owusu-Bempah 1994). From a feminist perspective, Adams (1988: 191) has defined violence as 'any act that causes the victim to do something she doesn't want to do, prevents her from doing something she wants to do, or causes her to be afraid'.

There is also the question of whether violence should primarily be defined in terms of the *moral blameworthiness* of the actor (was the harm caused intentionally, recklessly or accidentally?) or the suffering of the victim. Blameworthiness is usually a determining factor as to whether criminal liability exists, but Howitt and Owusu-Bempah (1994) argued that their wider definition of violence should include the unconscious behaviour of the aggressor. They asserted that '[b]y reducing the essence of violence to a moral issue, for instance, such definitions serve to legitimize state and institutional violence and oppression' (Howitt and Owusu-Bempah 1994: 36).

Some writers classify violence as either 'instrumental' or 'hostile'. Instrumental violence is used to effect a particular purpose, such as a robbery. The attacker will probably be acting in a calm and calculated manner. 'Hostile' or 'expressive' violence involves the spontaneous showing of angry feelings and will not be premeditated. The notion of control is important here: violence is either instrumental in order to achieve control, or hostile as a result of a loss of control. However, other people have questioned the distinction: Katz (1988), for instance, claimed that many robbers also obtain a 'high' from their activities.

In certain situations, the use of violence is legally permitted. Non-consensual violence may be inflicted against the enemy in times of war and in the execution of capital and corporal punishment. All these occurrences are, in differing degrees, controversial. The use of violence in self-defence would be accepted by most people. On the other hand, consensual violence with the capacity of resulting in more than trivial harm is usually only lawful if it is considered justifiable on the grounds of 'public policy'. This elastic term generally includes boxing and wrestling, but excludes consens masochistic activity.

The word 'aggression' is sometimes used interchangeably with violence. In fact, it is a wider term although it can have a specific meaning: for example, psychoanalysts consider aggression to be a basic human instinct which needs to be channelled into constructive activity in early childhood (see Chapter 4). In common usage, however, aggression is often referred to as a desirable attribute in social life, particularly in sport and increasingly in business, with reference to such practices as 'aggressive sales techniques'. This is clearly very different from a physical attack, but it suggests that – whether or not they are called instincts – aggressive tendencies develop in many people to some degree and, in an increasingly competitive world, this is encouraged in a growing number of situations. Both violence and aggression are attempts to impose dominance. Total destruction (that is, killing) is rarely necessary to achieve this and, indeed, could be counter-productive (Gunn 1993).

Zillmann (1979) defined aggressive actions as those which aim to inflict injury or harm on a person who is motivated to avoid it. If non-fatal harm does result from such actions, this becomes similar to the working definition of violence which is adopted in this book. (Consideration of homicide is omitted for reasons of space.) Such a definition emphasizes both the importance of culpability on the part of the perpetrator (in the sense that the violence was intended) and the lack of consent on the part of the victim. This is not to deny that the argument of Howitt and Owusu-Bempah has merit: it is simply that the confinements of space do not allow a discussion of wider definitions based on notions such as pollution, racism and sexism, even though it is clear that such behaviour can have very serious consequences. For example, Levi (1997) cited data showing that in 1989 British residents were 100 times more likely to be killed in the oil and gas industries than by homicide.

Legal definitions of violence

In this section, a brief outline is presented of the main non-fatal criminal offences involving violence in England (whose legal jurisdiction includes Wales). For historical reasons, Scotland did not adopt English common law, although some of its criminal law is contained in statutes passed by Parliament in Westminster. An account of the comparable legal provisions in Australia, Canada, New Zealand and the USA, whose legal systems are based on English law, is contained in the Appendix.

Criminal law in England and Wales is a mixture of what is termed the 'common law' (decisions in legal cases) and statute law (laws made by Parliament). The main distinction among the different non-fatal offences broadly results from the amount of harm caused. Interestingly, the word 'violence' does not appear in the definitions of any of the main crimes.

Assaults

'Assault' is the intentional or reckless causing of another person to anticipate the immediate application of physical force (however slight) to the body. The term 'reckless' refers to the taking of an unjustified risk – in other words, where a person realizes that their actions may have a particular (undesirable) consequence, but still decides to proceed. The legal definition is therefore wider than the one given to violence throughout this book, which is restricted to an *intention* to cause harm.

The crime of assault is infrequently prosecuted on account of its generally trivial nature. Confusingly, the word assault is often used to describe what is technically the separate crime of 'battery' – the intentional or reckless *application* of force (however slight) to the body. Assault and battery are the lowest-level crimes, and are sometimes also referred to by the (non-legal) expression 'common assault'.

The next most serious is the statutory offence of 'assault occasioning actual bodily harm' (Offences against the Person Act (OAPA) 1861, section 47). Despite what has just been said about the distinction between assault and battery, for this provision to have any effect the distinction has to be overlooked, and the word 'assault' has to include 'battery'! The statute does not define 'actual bodily harm', although in recent years guidelines have been issued for prosecutors. Bruising and minor fractures or breaks would be included in the definition.

The next level of non-fatal harm that can be caused is either 'wounding' or 'grievous bodily harm'. The latter expression has been defined in a case as simply meaning 'serious bodily harm'. Although many people refer to a crime of 'grievous bodily harm', there are broadly two distinct offences in English law, one of which is considered far graver than the other. The distinction does not result from the amount of harm caused; it depends on whether the perpetrator intended the harm caused to be serious, or whether some lesser degree of harm was intended or envisaged, but serious bodily harm still resulted. The more serious offence is contained in OAPA 1861, s. 18. A person who wounds or causes grievous bodily harm with intent to cause grievous bodily harm is liable to a maximum punishment of life imprisonment. The less serious offence of wounding or inflicting grievous bodily harm (but without the specific intent) is contained in s. 20. This carries a maximum punishment of five years' imprisonment. Finally, the most serious of the non-fatal offences is attempted murder, for which there must have been an intention to kill.

It was decided in *Ireland; Burstow* [1997] 4 All England Reports 225 that psychiatric illness could constitute either actual or grievous bodily harm, depending on its severity.

The current definitions of non-fatal offences against the person are contained in Victorian legislation and are nowadays considered defective, in that they overlap and provide an inadequate gradation between the different degrees of blameworthiness and harm. The Offences against the Person Bill 1998 has been published, which replaces the present structure with three new main offences: intentionally causing serious injury; recklessly causing serious injury; and intentionally or recklessly causing injury. Old-fashioned terms such as 'battery' and 'grievous bodily harm' will disappear, as they have in several other jurisdictions (see Appendix).

Indecent assault and rape

The main sexual offences against the person which may involve violence are indecent assault and rape. An indecent assault is an assault or (usually) a battery which is committed in circumstances where the average person would consider the act to be indecent. This effectively leaves the issue to be decided either by the magistrates or jury who are trying the case.

Rape, historically a common law offence, was defined in the Sexual Offences Act 1956 as sexual intercourse (whether vaginal or anal) with a person who at the time of the intercourse does not consent to it. In an amendment to the law in 1994, the offence was extended to cover victims of anal rape, whether male or female (although such behaviour already constituted the common law offence of buggery). For this purpose, 'intercourse' requires a degree of penile penetration – neither full penetration nor emission are necessary. Non-penile penetration (for example, by a finger or object) cannot amount to rape, although it may constitute an indecent assault. Consent must be real and not obtained from a person who is intoxicated, mentally deficient, or too young to understand; or where it was obtained by force, fraud or mistaken identity. Since the case *R v R* [1991] 4 All ER 481, a husband can be convicted of raping his wife, whether or not they were cohabiting at the time.

However, even where there is no proper consent, an accused can only be guilty of rape where intercourse was intended and the accused either knew that the victim did not consent or was reckless as to whether there was consent. This means that, in theory, defendants could avoid a rape conviction by convincing the jury that the possibility that the victim was not consenting had never occurred to them. Not surprisingly, this has proved controversial but, in practice, it is unlikely to be a serious impediment to conviction if the circumstances are such that lack of consent was blatantly obvious – in such cases, the jury will simply not believe the accused.

In some of the countries considered in this book, far more extensive changes have occurred in relation to violent sexual offences. For example, the Canadian Criminal Code has abolished the distinction between sexual and non-sexual assaults. Some jurisdictions have created crimes such as 'serious sexual assault', which usually include penetration by objects in addition to penile penetration. Such behaviour would have amounted to a criminal offence previously (indecent assault), but these legislative changes are designed to emphasize the gravity of the conduct. Where the crime of rape still exists, it can usually now be committed against a wife and, in some jurisdictions, against a man (see Appendix).

Defences to crimes of violence

In addition to the obvious defence that the accused did not commit the crime intentionally or (where relevant) recklessly, the criminal law provides a range of legal defences that can be raised. Some of these apply to all crimes. For example, most countries have a minimum age of criminal liability (in England and Wales it is 10). Most societies also allow mental disorder as a defence to a criminal charge, although the nature of the disorder required varies considerably. Intoxication and the influence of drugs may amount to a defence in certain circumstances. Three defences that are particularly relevant to acts of violence will be considered here.

Consent

Perhaps the most interesting defence to non-fatal offences against the person is consent. In the jurisdictions considered in this book, the consent of the victim can never be a defence to a charge of murder or manslaughter. The sanctity of human life, together with the dangers of abusing such consent, has hitherto been sufficient to ward off the legalization of euthanasia. With assaults, however, the situation is different: all the jurisdictions effectively allow consent as a defence in certain circumstances (see Appendix).

The consent of an adult victim can be a defence to any charge of assault, battery or rape. Consent must have been freely given and not obtained as a result of threats, force or deception. However, if actual bodily harm is caused, consent can only be a defence in certain situations. These were discussed in the case *R v Brown* [1993] 2 All ER 75. One is 'properly conducted games or sports' such as boxing and wrestling. Another is 'reasonable surgical interference': this would cover virtually all operations nowadays, although female circumcision is prohibited by statute (Prohibition of Female Circumcision Act 1985). It appears from *Brown* that tattooing and body-piercing for cosmetic reasons are considered lawful. However, the actual decision in the case itself was that flagellation and body-piercing for sado-masochistic reasons are unlawful, despite the consent of all the participants, as being contrary to public policy.

In Australia, the position is broadly the same as in England and Wales for non-sexual assaults. The common law statements of what does not amount to consent in rape cases are now found in statutory or code form in all the jurisdictions and, in some instances, a wider definition is used. In Victoria, for example, a person who is 'affected by alcohol' may be considered not to have consented.

The Canadian Criminal Code provides a list of circumstances where consent cannot amount to a defence to a charge of assault. For sexual cases, this includes where the victim is incapable of consent; where the accused took advantage of a position of trust or authority; where the victim expresses, by words or conduct, a lack of agreement; and where the victim withdraws consent after initially giving it. In *Cuerrier* [1998] 2 Supreme Court Reports 371, the Supreme Court held that the non-disclosure of HIV-positive status vitiates consent to sexual intercourse. Consent in non-sexual cases cannot be a defence if it was obtained by force (actual or threatened), fraud or the exercise of authority. As in England and Wales, consent cannot generally be a defence where actual bodily harm results. Although there are similar exceptions to this rule, they again do not include sadomasochistic activity (*Welch* (1995) 101 Canadian Criminal Cases (3d) 216). However, unlike in England and Wales, the exceptions appear to include street fights: in *M (S)* (1995) 22 Ontario Reports (3d) 321, the Ontario Court of Appeal held that the consent of the victim to a fight could be a defence to a charge of assault occasioning actual bodily harm.

In New Zealand, English law applies in issues concerning consent to non-sexual assaults. An important change in the law – and a reversal of the position still applying in England and Wales – means that a person can be guilty of sexual violation (which includes rape), even if the person mistakenly believed the victim consented, unless a reasonable person would have made such a mistake in the circumstances. However, on a charge of indecent assault, the accused's subjective belief that the victim was consenting will still suffice; there is no requirement here that a mistaken belief as to consent should have been reasonable.

In the USA, the situation in many states with regard to consent appears to be generally the same as in England and Wales. The American Law Institute's 'Model Penal Code' (the provisions of which have increasingly been adopted in the various state criminal codes) provides that such a defence only applies where 'the bodily harm consented to or threatened by the conduct is not serious' (2.11(2)(a)). Courts in several American states have rejected defences of consent where more serious harm has been caused by sadomasochistic activity.

Defence of person or property

The legal provisions are framed in general terms. A person may use such force as is reasonable in the circumstances in self-defence or defence of another, the defence of property or the prevention of crime. A person is also allowed to strike first to ward off an apprehended attack. Once the issue has been raised in a case, it is for the prosecution to prove that the use of force was unreasonable. This involves two questions: whether the use of any force was reasonably necessary in the circumstances; and whether the amount of force used was excessive. If the reasonableness test in either question is not satisfied, the defence fails. However, the courts have stated that the question of reasonableness should be determined on the basis of what the reasonable person would have done in the circumstances as the accused believed them to be. Under English law, this is an 'all or nothing' defence; there is no partial defence (involving conviction for a less serious charge) based on the use of excessive force.

The law on the use of force in self-defence and the protection of property in Australia is broadly the same as in England and Wales. There are similar provisions in the Canadian Criminal Code (s. 37), the New Zealand Crimes Act 1961 (s. 48), and most American states, although some provide that self-defence is not a permissible defence for the original aggressor, and others deny the defence if its need has arisen during the performance of criminal activities.

Corporal punishment

In all the states considered here, the common law rule that parents do not commit a criminal offence by using reasonable corporal punishment on their children still prevails. At common law, this rule also applies to school teachers, but some jurisdictions, including England and Wales, have introduced statutory provisions forbidding the use of corporal punishment in schools.

Together with boxing, corporal punishment is a legalized form of physical violence which gives rise to considerable controversy. One of the major claims made by abolitionists is that its use can result in a continual cycle of physical abuse and violence committed in later life by the original 'victim' (see Chapter 4). The large amount of flagellant pornography available in shops and on the Internet should perhaps also alert society to other dangers that can arise from this form of discipline.

The situation in England and Wales has been affected by judgements made under the European Convention on Human Rights, which is now incorporated in domestic law under the Human Rights Act 1998. In *A v United Kingdom* (1999) 27 European Human Rights Reports 611, the European Court of Human Rights held that a nine-year-old boy, who had been beaten with a garden cane by his stepfather, had not been protected by the state from 'inhuman or degrading treatment or punishment' in violation of Article 3. (The stepfather had been acquitted by a jury of assault occasioning actual bodily harm.) The Government was ordered to pay £10,000 in damages and undertook to change the law. In a consultation paper (Department of Health

2000), it is suggested that blows with an implement or to the victim's head should cease to be considered 'reasonable', but that 'smacking' should otherwise still be permitted.

Conclusion

Together with the Appendix, this chapter illustrates how the English criminal law relating to violence, which is still rooted in nineteenth-century legislation, lags some way behind the developments that have occurred in several of the other jurisdictions considered in this book. Legislation has been proposed in England and Wales to provide a clearer distinction between the different levels of crime.

Most of the jurisdictions have created offences, or widened existing ones, to cover situations where psychological harm is caused to the victim. The definition of recklessness in English law (see above), which historically prevailed, is increasingly being abandoned in the other countries, so that an accused who claims they did not foresee the consequence of their actions can still be held criminally liable if a jury considers that they *should* have realized the consequence, in that a reasonable person would have realized it. This issue has been important in rape cases, where defendants have argued that they did not appreciate that the victim was not consenting.

Some jurisdictions – in particular, Canada and some Australian states – have made sweeping changes to their sexual offences law, including the abolition of the term (but not the crime) rape or its extension to cover non-penile penetration. It seems likely that similar changes will occur in England and Wales.

There is greater similarity on the main controversial issues surrounding physical violence. The fact that boxing is still lawful – and, indeed, a multimillion dollar business in America – shows that consensual violence is still acceptable to many people, not only on the grounds of tradition or to encourage 'manliness', but because it does not pose the threat of a stranger–victim attack. This is not the case, however, if such violence is used for sexual gratification: another type of threat is perceived here, and the behaviour is deemed in law to be immoral and contrary to public policy.

Corporal punishment is still allowed for the 'training' of children, although the position in English law has been challenged under the European Convention on Human Rights, and its use is now illegal in schools and under threat in the home. Given that physical abuse is often explained away as legitimate corporal punishment, and that the evidence suggests that such abuse is often connected to violent crime (see Chapter 4), this could yet prove to be the most significant of all the legal developments discussed in this chapter.

Further reading

Understanding Criminal Law (Clarkson in press) provides an excellent introduction to the major principles underlying English criminal law, and is also relevant to a consideration of other common law jurisdictions. For those wanting a detailed discussion of the English law, the leading textbook has for many years been *Criminal Law* (Smith and Hogan 1999). A more radical approach can be found in *Reconstructing Criminal Law: Critical Perspectives on Crime and the Criminal Process* (Lacey and Wells 1998).

Australian common law jurisdictions are covered in *Outline of Criminal Law* (Murugason and McNamara 1997). The codes in Queensland and Western Australia are dealt with in *An Introduction to Criminal Law in Queensland and Western Australia* (Kenny 1999). In Canada, one of the best-known criminal law textbooks is *Mewett & Manning on Criminal Law* (Mewett and Manning 1994). For New Zealand, *Principles of Criminal Law* (Simester and Brookbanks 1998) provides a comprehensive account. Finally, *Understanding Criminal Law* (Dressler 1995) is a good introductory text to the general principles of criminal law in the USA.

chapter two

The extent of violence

In order to try to understand criminal violence, it would be useful to have some idea of the frequency with which it occurs, as well as information about other surrounding circumstances. Sociologists sometimes use the medical term 'epidemiology' to describe this form of knowledge. It is clearly preferable to have reliable data on these questions than to rely on pure speculation. In this chapter, consideration will be given both to official and other sources of information about violent crime. However, it will become apparent that what may at first appear to be the straightforward task of obtaining such data is, both in principle and practice, far more complex.

Official criminal statistics

An obvious starting point is official, government figures on the extent of crime. In England and Wales, 'crimes made known to the police' were included in the judicial statistics for the first time in 1856. The main compilation used nowadays, *Criminal Statistics England and Wales* (hereafter *Criminal Statistics*), was first published in 1876 and appears annually. It broadly comprises crimes reported to the Home Office by each of the 43 police forces and the nature of the punishment imposed on conviction. (The Scottish version is entitled *Recorded Crime in Scotland*.) There are also supplementary volumes providing more detailed information, and the Home Office issues regular updating statistical bulletins. Figures from local areas within police forces are now published. The corresponding information for the USA can be found in the *Uniform Crime Reports*, which have been compiled by the Federal Bureau of Investigation (FBI) since 1929 and are based on data obtained from the local police. Canada has published annual official crime figures through the Uniform Crime Reporting system since 1962. In Australia, national data are compiled by the Australian Bureau of Statistics. Information for New Zealand is published by the Ministry of Justice.

Most acts of violence amount to criminal offences. As such, it might be expected that most would be recorded in official crime statistics and that the perpetrators, if apprehended, would be prosecuted and punished on conviction. However, in practice a series of hurdles exists at every stage of the process, which means there is a high attrition rate, with only a small proportion of violent incidents resulting in either recorded offences or successful prosecutions.

Crimes made known to the police

The annual *Criminal Statistics* compilation is divided into two parts: court statistics, containing details of the sentences passed by the courts; and offences known to the police. It is this second category which is particularly problematic. The first difficulty that occurs is that many cases of violence either never come to the attention of the police or are not taken seriously by them. This phenomenon of unreported data – a common problem in all the social sciences – is known as the 'dark figure'.

Some idea of the extent and nature of the dark figure of crime has become apparent through the use of victim surveys. It is particularly large for violence perpetrated in the home. There are several reasons why this is often unreported. The commonest explanations given by respondents in the 1998 British Crime Survey (see below) for not reporting violence were that the matter was private or had been dealt with by the victims themselves, or that the incident was too trivial and had resulted in no loss (Mirrlees-Black *et al.* 1998). The victim (usually a woman) may fear that intervention will only exacerbate the situation. The occasional beating may be tolerated if the perceived alternative is the break-up of the family or the battered partner and children being rendered homeless.

In some communities, there may be cultural expectations that women accept physical and sexual abuse without complaint. For instance, Choudry (1996) found that Pakistani women in London are under considerable pressure to succeed in their marriages, and that failure would result in dishonour both for them and their families. These women usually live with their husband's relatives, who are likely to support him in any dispute and condone any violent behaviour towards his wife.

The disincentives for the victims of domestic violence to report incidents to the police were documented in an unusual project carried out in Bristol by Cretney and Davis (1995). The researchers closely examined the cases of 93 assault victims who had visited the casualty department at the Bristol Royal Infirmary. The in-depth interviews that were conducted provided an interesting source of data as, although all the victims had suffered injuries they considered worthy of immediate medical attention, some of them – particularly in domestic cases – had no wish to involve the police. (Similar research has been conducted at a hospital in Sydney: see Cuthbert *et al.* 1991.) Fear of reprisals, coupled with a realization that they would have to continue cohabiting with the aggressor, formed the main reason for this reluctance. As Cretney and Davis (1995: 51) put it: '[T]he fleeting intervention of police and courts can never be sufficient in itself to free a woman from dependence upon perhaps the only source of support and companionship which she knows and, in some limited sense, can rely on'.

Surveys of victims have confirmed that fear of reprisals accounts for a proportion of unreported cases. In the 1998 British Crime Survey (BCS), this reason was given for 14 per cent of unreported cases involving mugging; 14 per cent involving domestic assaults; 9 per cent involving acquaintance assaults; and 3 per cent involving stranger assaults. The American National Crime Victimization Survey reported that 4 per cent of victims offered this as a reason for not reporting a serious assault, although this figure doubled in relation to more serious cases (Hindelang *et al.* 1975). The Bristol researchers also found a significant number of cases that were not reported for fear of reprisals in situations where individuals shared a common social environment – such as a pub – or were members of the drugs underworld.

A Law Commission report on domestic violence (Law Commission 1992) suggested that many victims are not mainly interested in punishment: what they want is a public condemnation of their assailant and a vindication of themselves. Research by Hoyle and Sanders (2000) found that many calls to the police from domestic violence victims were simply requests for immediate help in a particular instance. Only just over half wanted their partner arrested, and many of these did not want the matter to go any further. This explains why some women, having reported the attack to the police, are unwilling to give evidence in court. They may feel that bringing the matter to the attention of the police is sufficient in itself.

There may also be a belief among victims that the police will not be interested in pursuing 'domestic' incidents. The 1998 BCS found that 9 per cent of domestic violence victims who did not report the attacks to the police gave this as a reason. There may be a fear that the police would conduct their investigations with such a lack of sensitivity as to make the complainant feel that they are the real criminal. Indeed, there is clear evidence that this last view is justified: some police officers have admitted that they do not consider domestic incidents to be 'real' crimes (Reiner 2000).

Some people may not bother to report an attack because they think that the police could do nothing about it. The 1998 BCS found that this depended on the context of the assault: it was given as a reason for 27 per cent of the non-reported muggings, but only 9 per cent of the domestic attacks. The police may also be mistrusted, as it seems they are in sections of the black and Asian communities on the basis of the 'institutionalized racism' that was identified in the inquiry into the killing of a black teenager, Stephen Lawrence (Macpherson 1999). However, the 1998 BCS found that dislike or fear of the police was offered as a reason in only 1 per cent of cases where violent crime had not been reported.

Shah and Pease (1992) discovered that the police are more likely to be notified of assaults alleged to have been committed by non-whites (although this applied mostly to assaults where there was no injury). It has been suggested that middle-class and better-educated victims are more prepared to report assaults to the police than working-class victims (Mayhew *et al.* 1989). The Bristol research noted that the local police appeared, in practice, to make a distinction between the *reporting* of a crime and *complaining about* a crime. For the police, 'making a complaint' meant that the victim was prepared for the case to go all the way to court and give evidence, if necessary.

The decision to record

On receipt of information, the police may decide to take no further action. They may disbelieve the person who reported the crime, especially if the individual comes from a section of society they consider unreliable as witnesses, such as women, children or the mentally unstable. This can be significant, as members of the public alert the police to over 80 per cent of recorded crime (Bottomley and Pease 1986). The police may decide that the alleged crime is too trivial or too old. Police forces have long been judged by their 'clear-up rate' and there may be little interest in recording a crime which there is no prospect of solving. Overall, it has been calculated that only about half of all the crimes reported to the police are recorded (Mirrlees-Black *et al.* 1998).

'Notifiable offences' are those which chief constables have to list in returns to the Home Office and which are reported in the *Criminal Statistics* as crimes known to the police. They do not include most 'summary' offences (those triable only by magistrates).

The decision to prosecute

If the police find a suspect and their investigation suggests there may be grounds for prosecution, a file on the case will be sent to the Crown Prosecution Service (CPS) and it is there that the decision whether or not to prosecute will be taken. The CPS is subject to a code drawn up by the Director of Public Prosecutions (Crown Prosecution Service 1994) which emphasizes considerations such as cost, public interest and likelihood of obtaining a conviction: the CPS should not proceed unless a conviction is more likely than not. The willingness of the victim and other witnesses to give evidence is a vital element in the decision, and many cases collapse at this stage because the prospect of facing the aggressor in court is too daunting. A survey of victims in London by Sparks *et al.* (1977) discovered that nearly a quarter of assault and wounding cases were 'written off', usually because the victim did not wish the offence to be prosecuted. Most of these cases involved family disputes.

An initial classification of a crime by the police, which is then included under *offences known to the police*, may not correspond with the resulting conviction, which will appear under the court statistics. For example, it is quite common for a charge originally brought under section 18 of the Offences against the Person Act 1861 to be reduced to either a section 20 or a section 47 offence (for definitions of these crimes, see Chapter 1).

A case that has survived this far still has to confront the hurdle of being heard and adjudicated in court. In 1998, 49 per cent of defendants tried for violent offences in the Crown Court pleaded guilty and, of the remainder, 33 per cent were convicted (Home Office 2000). Thus, there is a good chance that a contested trial will result in an acquittal.

The 'clear-up' rate

Most people probably assume that 'clearing up' a crime means that a person has been convicted of its commission. In fact, the term has a considerably wider meaning in the *Criminal Statistics*. If a person has been charged with, or cautioned for, a crime, it is considered as having been cleared up. If a particular offence could have been charged separately, but has been merely 'taken into consideration' by the sentencing court in a list of other offences, it is also counted as cleared up. A crime admitted to by a person in prison for another offence is similarly treated, as are cases where the victim is unwilling or unable to give evidence; the offender is below the age of criminal responsibility; or the case does not proceed because the defendant or a vital witness is ill or has died.

Trends in crime

Further problems with the *Criminal Statistics* arise when attempts are made to make comparisons between figures for different years. Not only is the situation complicated by the creation of new crimes, or changes in the definition of existing ones (such as the definition of rape in 1994: see Chapter 1), but even the counting rules are sometimes altered. For example, in 1998 the practice of recording only the most serious of a chain of offences in one incident was replaced by recording one crime for each victim. This had the effect of increasing the amount of recorded violent crime from 352,873 cases in the year ending March 1998 to 605,803 cases during the next 12 months. However, had the old counting rules still applied, the recorded level would have *fallen* to 331,843 cases (Povey and Prime 1999).

The amount of formal cautioning – particularly for juvenile offenders – has increased considerably since the 1970s. A caution should only follow an admission of guilt, and it is possible that some people have been prepared to admit to offences they did not commit in order to avoid the possibility of prosecution.

Moreover, the 43 police forces of England and Wales not only vary demographically (ranging from central London to rural Wales), but often target their resources on different offences at different times, usually as a result of perceived local or national public opinion. There is little doubt that the rise in sexual offences found in the *Criminal Statistics* in recent years is largely (if not wholly) explicable by both victims' increased reporting and a change in attitude by the police. Mayhew *et al.* (1993) found that the police were more willing to record violent offences in 1991 than they were a decade earlier.

A good example of an extreme regional variation can be seen in the recorded figures for violent offences in England and Wales between April 1997 and March 1998. Whereas Essex showed an increase of almost 4 per cent during this period, the nearby county of Kent showed a fall of over 17 per cent (Povey and Prime 1998). It seems highly unlikely that these figures reflect the real differences in the level of violence between these areas.

Thus, it can be seen that the *Criminal Statistics* do not provide an accurate picture of the amount of violent crime that occurs. Moreover, the information mainly relates to the nature of the offence and provides very little detail about the offenders or the surrounding circumstances. For homicide, the method of killing, the age and sex of the victims, and their relationship to the suspects are made available, but no such detail is provided for other violent offences (except those involving firearms). A picture is provided but, in the phrase of Maguire (1997), it is created through painting by numbers.

The tables of crime statistics are heavily influenced by the attitudes of both the victim and the police, and the court statistics reveal only what emerges at the end of a lengthy process where cases fall away at every stage.

Alternative sources of information on crime

The shortcomings in official crime statistics have encouraged researchers to look for alternative sources of information to provide a more accurate picture of the level of crime – in other words, to cast more light on the dark figure of crime. The result is that particular attention is now given to victim surveys and, to a lesser extent, self-report surveys.

Victim surveys

These involve a representative sample of the population being questioned as to their experiences of being victims of crime. They were used in the USA by the President's Commission on Law Enforcement and Administration of Justice, which reported in 1967. One of the surveys, conducted by the National Opinion Research Centre, found that there were five times the number of rapes and eight times the number of assaults shown in the official records.

The National Crime Victimization Survey (NCVS) has reported in the USA every year since 1973. It now consists of a nationwide representative sample based on addresses, where all the occupants over the age of 12 are interviewed about their experience of victimization. The crimes investigated by the NCVS were based on the eight most serious categories of crime as found in the official crime statistics. For the first time, a large amount of information about victims could be considered. Earlier speculation as to why people do not report crimes to the police could now be replaced by hard evidence.

Other countries have introduced victim surveys. The first national crime victims survey in Australia was carried out in 1975. Such are now conducted by the Australian Bureau of Statistics, which also organizes state surveys.

Although some small-scale victimization studies were carried out in Britain during the 1970s, it was not until 1983 that the Home Office published the first British Crime Survey. There have been six subsequent reports, the latest being in 1998. Changes in the methodology have occurred over the years. For example, before 1992 the sample was taken from the electoral register. However, poorer people are less likely to register to vote and the sample is nowadays drawn from the Postcode Address File. There are now plans to extend it to an annual survey of 40,000 households. In 1982 the sample was 10,000: in 1998 it was almost 50 per cent higher. The response rate in the 1998 survey was 79 per cent. Scotland now has its own survey, the latest report being for 1996 (MVA Consultancy 1997).

Respondents, who must be aged 16 or over, are asked if they have been the victim of any of a range of crimes since 1 January of the previous year. Additional information is sought on several other issues, including fear of crime and lifestyle. Some self-report questions (see below) have also been included. Fewer offences are covered than in the Criminal Statistics, and it is only in respect of these that any comparison can be made with the official figures. The survey divides crimes into 'personal offences' and 'household offences'. The former category includes assaults, robberies and sexual offences.

The first BCS report found that more crime was revealed than shown in the official statistics in every category of offence it considered except theft of motor cars. The number of woundings, albeit relatively small, was five times higher than officially recorded. Overall, the 1982 report showed four times more crime than for comparable offences in the *Criminal Statistics*. This difference has remained fairly constant through subsequent BCS reports.

Although the BCS reports have generally revealed more crime than is officially recorded, most of the additional offences are relatively minor in that they involved much lower levels of harm than those classified as made known to the police. Given the sifting process operated by the police which is outlined above, this was to be expected. The police may not record a crime if they consider there is insufficient evidence: the BCS researchers will record as a crime any incident which satisfies the legal definition of the offence. The BCS has also shown the commonest reason given by victims for not reporting crimes to the police to be that they considered that the incident was too trivial. This raises the question of whether society should be concerned with technical breaches of the criminal law which are considered so unimportant by the victims that they do not bother to report them.

Victim surveys do not inevitably disclose the same trend in either the growth of, or decline in, crime rates as found in official statistics. In America, although the FBI-compiled *Uniform Crime Reports* showed that recorded offences against the person more than quadrupled between 1960 and 1990, the NCVS found a decline in the same categories between 1973 and 1992 (Zawitz *et al.* 1993). The 1998 BCS disclosed a 17 per cent decrease in the number of woundings since the previous report, whereas the recorded crime figures revealed an 18 per cent increase over the same period (Mirrlees-Black *et al.* 1998). These differences largely result from variations in the reporting and recording practices discussed above.

The early BCS reports were subject to a number of criticisms. The 1982 report in particular seemed keen to emphasize that a 'statistically average' person was extremely unlikely ever to be the victim of a crime, being liable to an assault resulting in an injury once a century, and a robbery once every five centuries. Left realist criminologists, who claim to take crime and its victims 'seriously' (see Chapter 8), were concerned about the lack of social and geographical focus in the reports. They claimed that the emphasis of the BCS on street crime suggested that women had the least cause to be afraid of violent crime because they are less likely than men to go out at night, and that their fear was therefore irrational and unnecessary. Left realists also alleged that the BCS had paid insufficient regard to the fact that victimization is unequally distributed throughout the population, both geographically and in terms of sex. Men were more likely to be victims of violence because they spend more time on the streets. Moreover, some people are better able to withstand the impact of crime than others.

Several of these critics underlined their arguments by conducting local victim surveys which indicated that residents of deprived inner-city areas were particularly likely to be victims of certain crimes. For example, the first Islington Crime Survey (Jones *et al.* 1986) showed that one-third of the households in that area of London contained people who had been sexually abused during the previous year, and that young white women were 29 times more likely to be assault victims than women aged over 45.

Other writers criticized the early BCS reports for being unable to uncover sexual crimes and domestic violence against women. The fact that each of the first two reports disclosed only one unreported attempted rape was taken to illustrate this. In America, National Family Violence surveys have been conducted periodically since 1975 using questions that were specially formulated to deal with the sensitive nature of the subject. The local British surveys included carefully worded questions to cover such issues, and the interviewers were provided with the appropriate training. As a result, the first Islington Crime Survey revealed much higher levels of sexual assault, and over 20 per cent of all assaults were described as 'domestic' – a far greater figure than in the BCS.

However, the local surveys also have their drawbacks. Most of them were based on small samples. Some were commissioned by local authorities, which perhaps had their own agendas, and consequently some people may question whether the research was completely independent. Although their findings have a personal, sometimes intimate feel, the apparent preoccupation of these small surveys with domestic violence and sexual attacks against the urban poor raises doubts about the wide-ranging conclusions drawn by some left realist criminologists.

Nevertheless, in response to the findings of the smaller surveys, the BCS researchers adapted their methodology to be more sensitive to issues of domestic violence. The 1998 report included a new computerized self-completion element designed to give a more accurate picture of the extent of such incidents (Mirrlees-Black 1999). Some reports have used a boosted sample of minority ethnic groups in order to allow a separate analysis of their victimization. Although the 1994 report included a self-completion element on sexual victimization (Percy and Mayhew 1997), the BCS researchers are now very wary of their findings in this respect: the 1998 report states that 'due to the small number of [sexual assaults] reported to the survey estimates are not considered reliable' (Mirrlees-Black *et al*. 1998: 5).

Self-report surveys

Another source of information on the extent of violent crime is the self-report survey, in which individuals are asked to report their offending behaviour. These have generally been less popular than victim surveys, as researchers believe there will be a high level of under-reporting, particularly for more serious crimes.

The early American self-report studies appeared to show a much higher middle-class involvement in crime than was apparent from official data, or than was predicted by the prevalent criminological theories of the day. However, later research indicated that most of the under-reporting was on the part of lower-class individuals (Hindelang *et al*. 1981). Moreover, self-report surveys have usually concentrated on juveniles, with the result that there has been an over-representation of 'street' crimes and an under-reporting of crimes committed in the more private domain of the home or office (Braithwaite 1979). A further problem is that some of the American studies used the term 'delinquency' to encompass behaviour which, although antisocial, is not illegal. Even the criminal behaviour was often of a level of triviality that would have resulted in a total lack of interest from the police (Hindelang *et al*. 1979).

The best-known example of a self-report study in Britain, the Cambridge Study in Delinquent Development, has managed to overcome some of these difficulties. Unlike the usual cross-sectional study which takes a 'snapshot' of the situation at a particular time, this is a 'longitudinal' study which followed 411 males from a working-class area of London from the age of 8–9 through to adulthood. Enquiries by researchers into the subjects' self-reported involvement in delinquency were made on several occasions. In addition to using questionnaires, the researchers have checked the subjects' criminal records (Farrington 1989). Findings from the Cambridge Study suggesting a link between child abuse and subsequent offending are discussed in Chapter 4.

In America, several large-scale longitudinal studies were being conducted by the 1980s, including the National Youth Survey which has periodically reported on a representative sample of American youths aged 11–17 (Elliott 1994). An example of a longitudinal study in New Zealand is the Christchurch Child Development Study (Fergusson *et al*. 1992). Such research can also have methodological problems: it has been claimed that interviewing the same group of people over a long period of time can result in a reduction in their willingness to admit to offending (Thornberry 1989).

Self-report studies have always been more popular in America than in Britain. Coleman and Moynihan (1996) suggested that this is because in the

USA a stronger interest has remained in the offender. In Britain, on the other hand, concern about the causes of crime has declined, and the relative popularity of the victim survey reflects a greater interest in the impact of crime on the victim (see Chapter 8).

Problems

The main problems that victim and self-report surveys share are unwillingness to report and forgetfulness. It is obvious that people who have committed very serious offences are highly unlikely to admit them to a researcher. Sparks *et al.* (1977) found that more female victims of violence refused to be interviewed than male victims. It is apparent from most surveys that women are reluctant to disclose cases of domestic violence or sexual assault. Even the Merseyside Crime Survey, which was supposed to be more sensitive to such issues than the BCS, did not discover any cases of sexual offences against women (Kinsey 1984). Crawford *et al.* (1990) reported a greater likelihood that individuals who declined to complete the questionnaire for the Second Islington Crime Survey had recently been victims of violent crime than those who cooperated.

Forgetfulness is clearly a distinct possibility. There is also the phenomenon of 'telescoping', where respondents with inaccurate recall move events forwards into the survey period or backwards out of it. However, it appears that, in most cases, these two possibilities are likely to cancel each other out (Sparks *et al.* 1977). Although the American NCVS has sought to deal with this by conducting its interviews at six-month intervals, a considerable increase in cost ensues and most other surveys adopt the 12-month recall period used by the BCS.

The BCS has found that better-educated people are more likely to report being the victims of violent crime. Hough (1986) has suggested that the educated middle class may have a lower tolerance threshold of minor threatening and violent acts. Sparks (1981) pointed out that middle-class individuals are more likely to have the verbal skills to provide full answers to the researchers' questions.

The extent of violence

What do the above sources tell us about the level of violence? The 1998 *Criminal Statistics* show about 503,000 recorded offences of non-fatal violence against the person, forming 9.8 per cent of all recorded crimes. This underlines how violence forms only a small percentage of recorded crime. Offences classified as 'endangering life', such as wounding or attempted murder, form about 9 per cent of this total. The remainder mainly consist of common assaults, assaults occasioning actual bodily harm, less serious wounding and grievous bodily harm, and possession of offensive weapons. In 1998, the national average for all notifiable violent offences was 963 offences per 100,000 of the population. There were 7139 recorded rapes of women, 502 rapes of men, and 19,463 indecent assaults on women. Sexual offences comprised 6 per cent of all recorded violent offences and 0.7 per cent of all notifiable offences.

The 1998 BCS provided a rather different picture. The report estimated that there were 714,000 woundings (involving 'more than trivial injury') and 2,276,000 assaults (involving 'physical assault or attempted assault with at most slight bruising') during 1997. About 45 per cent of these incidents were reported to the police and, of those, about 63 per cent were recorded. No information was provided for sexual assaults. The 1998 BCS disclosed a 17 per cent drop in violence between 1995 and 1997. In the 1993 Australian crime survey, six out of ten victims of personal crime during the previous 12 months had not reported the most recent incident to the police (Australian Bureau of Statistics 1994).

Unlike the *Criminal Statistics*, the BCS is able to provide some background information on its data. Most violent crime occurs between people known to each other: in 1997, 43 per cent involved acquaintances and a further 25 per cent people in a domestic relationship (defined as partners, ex-partners, household members and other relatives). The researchers considered that these figures may still be an underestimate, but pointed out that they were still more reliable than those provided by the police. Men were more likely to be the victims of violent attacks (60 per cent), particularly by strangers (over 80 per cent). Women were the victims in 70 per cent of domestic incidents. The average risk of violent crime is low: 4.7 per cent of adults were victims of violence, generally of common assault (3.2 per cent). Only 1.3 per cent were the victims of stranger violence. However, the risk is not equal. Young adults are the most likely to be victims of violence, as well as the single, the unemployed, and those who go out most evenings, especially to a pub or wine bar. People living in London face the highest risk of violence, even though there is no more than an average likelihood of their being victims of burglary and vehicle-related thefts.

International crime comparisons

Official data

There are considerable difficulties in comparing the official crime statistics of different countries. The problems inherent in the compilation of any criminal statistics, discussed above, will apply in varying degrees in all jurisdictions. There will also be differences in the legal definitions which make it very doubtful whether like can ever truly be compared with like (Zimring and Hawkins 1997). The International Criminal Police Organization (Interpol), has produced comprehensive statistics for more than 80 countries, and adopts its own broad definitional categories in an attempt to overcome this problem. The United Nations Crime and Justice Information Network also publishes wide-ranging international statistics.

It has been argued by Archer and Gartner (1984) that the only reliable use of such figures is to note the apparent trends in criminal behaviour for each country, on the assumption that any distorting features in the compilation (such as political interference) will remain reasonably consistent over the years. Some researchers are prepared to accept the validity of comparative data on homicide rates, arguing that, as most incidents are recorded, the statistics are therefore far less likely to be subject to the usual inaccuracies. However, this premise seems rather dubious: there may well be political reasons for not recording homicides in some countries.

The International Crime Victims Survey

Another way of obtaining comparative international data is by administering a victims survey. The International Crime Victims Survey, which first reported in 1989, has now published information on more than 50 countries. The third and latest of its reports was based on data compiled in 11 countries in 1996 (Mayhew and van Dijk 1997). As the questions were formulated by researchers, there was less danger of the findings being corrupted by different legal definitions. Interviewing was generally conducted by telephone. In the category of 'assaults and threats', respondents were asked the question: 'over the past five years [have you] been personally attacked or threatened by someone in a way that really frightened you'. In reply, the US sample revealed 10 incidents per 100 population; England and Wales 9.8; Scotland 7.3; Canada 7.1; and Northern Ireland 3.8. Information for 1992 was provided for New Zealand (9.7) and Australia (8.1). However, this question typifies a problem in such surveys: in an attempt to avoid legal terminology, the question is imprecise and could be interpreted in different ways. (For example, is it the attack or the threat that has to be really frightening – or both?)

The International Self-Report Delinquency Study

This has developed since the late 1980s as a way of investigating self-reported delinquency in several countries for a range of offences committed by young people aged 14–21 (Junger-Tas *et al*. 1994). The questions had to be formulated to cover different jurisdictions and languages, and most of the problems concerning self-report studies discussed above also apply here, in particular the concentration on youthful offending. The age range in England and Wales was extended to 25 for some categories of response. The information was collected in self-completion booklets, but the non-completion rate in England

and Wales was fairly high, especially among minority ethnic groups (Graham and Bowling 1995).

Conclusion

Official statistics suggest that the amount of violent crime has increased considerably over the past forty years. Despite the problems involved in accurately recording this information, the extent of the increase makes it fairly safe to conclude that some growth in particular kinds of violence has occurred. The difficulties arise when attempts are made to obtain precise quantifications or measure short-term trends.

It seems clear that some of the increase in violent crime rates (including rape) is due to a greater willingness to report such incidents. This is attributable to various changes in society's attitudes and the different approach adopted by the police. In the 1950s, the success of a police force was measured by its 'clear-up' rate, and it therefore made little sense to record minor crimes which were unlikely to be solved. Crime then increasingly became a political issue, and it appeared to the police that greater funding could ensue from a rise in recorded crime levels (Coleman and Moynihan 1996).

Although criminal statistics attempt to provide a measure of the *quantity* of crime, they can say very little about its *impact* (Coleman and Moynihan 1996). Violent crime forms only about 5 per cent of recorded crime, but the effects on its victims are likely to be far greater than those of, say, criminal damage. This is discussed further in Chapter 8.

The purpose of comparing the rates of violent (or any other) crime for different countries can be questioned. Even if the information provided were wholly accurate, is it really possible to draw conclusions from comparing data from, say, Dubai and the USA? Furthermore, the stark way in which the findings are usually presented provides no information on the likelihood of victimization in different parts of a country.

Why, then, with all these drawbacks, is it felt necessary to measure rates of violent crime at all? There are several good reasons. Crimes that are recorded as increasing can be targeted by government and law enforcement agencies. It is sometimes claimed that crime statistics provide a 'moral barometer' of the state of a society (Sparks *et al.* 1977), and they are thus invoked by politicians to support their own arguments. Government ministers, who nowadays like to set attainment targets for public bodies, have a ready source of information which they can use to judge police performance.

However, it is arguable that the political agenda for criminal justice policy is increasingly being set not by official crime statistics, but by the popular mass media. Politicians are less likely to respond to changes in recorded crime rates than to lurid press stories. The role of vested interests can also be important. For example, there is evidence that stricter gun control would reduce the level of violent crime in America (Zimring and Hawkins 1997), but politicians are afraid that introducing such measures would lead to a loss of support from the gun lobby (and political fund donors).

Further reading

The best recent book on crime statistics is *Understanding Crime Data* (Coleman and Moynihan 1996). *The 1998 British Crime Survey* (Mirrlees-Black *et al.* 1998) is the latest in the series of national victim surveys conducted by the Home Office. There is also an excellent chapter, 'Crime statistics, patterns and trends: changing perceptions and their implications', by Mike Maguire (1997) in *The Oxford Handbook of Criminology*.

An example of a left realist local survey is the *Second Islington Crime Survey* (Crawford *et al.* 1990). *International Comparisons of Criminal Justice Statistics 1998* (Barclay and Tavares 2000) and the International Crime Victims Survey (Mayhew and van Dijk 1997) provide data for a number of countries although, for the reasons explained above, caution should be exercised in making comparisons between different jurisdictions.

Crime is Not the Problem: Lethal Violence in America (Zimring and Hawkins 1997) makes the interesting point that violent crime rates in countries such as Australia, Canada and New Zealand are similar to those found in the USA: it is where violence results in death that the American figures soar ahead of other industrialized societies.

A large amount of statistical (and other) information about crime can now be found on the Internet. In Britain, the Home Office Research and Statistics Directorate website at www.homeoffice.gov.uk includes a link to the British Crime Survey. The American Uniform Crime Reports can be reached on a link from www.fbi.gov and the Canadian statistics are at www.statcan.ca. For Australia the address is www.statistics.gov.au and for New Zealand www.justice.govt.nz.

part two

Explanations of violence

chapter three

Biological influences, mental disorder, drugs and alcohol

The theme linking the issues considered in this chapter is that some instances of violence may be related to the state of a person's body or mind, such that aggressors may not have complete control over, or awareness of, their actions, or may be predisposed to behave violently. In this sense, 'mind' refers to the workings of the brain, whether affected by internal physiological or external environmental factors. For policy reasons, most legal systems (including the ones considered in this book) base their test of criminal responsibility at such a level that many of the situations discussed below would only excuse offenders from liability if they were almost completely unaware of what they were doing. Thus, it is not the case that the mentally disordered or the intoxicated will usually 'get away with it' on appearing before a court; nor will a genetics-based defence that the assailant was descended from a long line of criminals be successful.

In particular, the chapter will consider whether a proneness to act in an antisocial way has occurred through evolution or is transmitted through genes; the effects of the physical constitution on behaviour; the relationship between mental disorder and aggression; and the widely assumed connection between the ingestion of drugs or alcohol and violence.

Evolution

Before the implications of genetics began to be understood, the suggestion was made that a proneness to act violently could be located in humans' close relationship to apes. Initially, this belief was pursued by studies of the shape and size of the human body. In the immediate post-Darwin era, this view became popular among certain writers who argued that, as humans were just a more developed species of ape, people whose appearance seemed to bear certain characteristics of lower primates (such as excessive body hair and very long arms) were suffering from a depravity caused by atavistic reversion. One of the main exponents of this argument was Cesare Lombroso (1876), and his experimental findings are nowadays generally ridiculed. Nevertheless, more refined versions of Lombroso's explanation have appeared in the work of later writers. Sheldon (1949) concluded that delinquents have distinctive body shapes (generally large, muscular and athletic) and Cortés (1972) claimed to have replicated this finding.

However, not only is the methodology used in this sort of research very suspect (imprecise bodily measurement and self-evaluation of temperament), but it ignores certain common-sense explanations. Body shape can be linked to diet and physical manual work. These factors are in turn related to class, and lower-class individuals have always been over-represented in official criminal statistics. Moreover, the finding that large muscular types engage in aggressive acts to get their own way can be explained on the basis that they discovered at an early age that they could do this successfully. This may, at least in part, explain research by Raine et al. (1998), which concluded that three-year-old children (boys or girls), who were just half an inch taller than their peers, had a greater than average chance of becoming classroom bullies and ultimately violent criminals. The researchers alleged that the differences could not be explained by any socio-economic factors such as family income or parental education.

Ethology and sociobiology

After the early attempts to explain violent humans as being grotesque throw-backs to their ape ancestors, it became increasingly apparent to researchers that a sufficient number of people are liable to act violently to render the argument of the 'occasional reversion' hardly tenable. Nevertheless, not wishing to abandon Darwin's explanation of evolution by natural selection, some authors have tried to explain certain aspects of human behaviour by reference to ethology – the study of animal behaviour. Animals are assumed to be innately aggressive, and humans are just a more developed form of animals. One of the best-known writers to put forward this view was Konrad Lorenz, in his book *On Aggression* (1966). For Lorenz, aggression is an instinct which ensures the survival of the individual and the species. His opinions have been adopted and developed by more recent writers, some of whom have emphasized the inevitable supremacy of men over women that such an explanation provides. For example, Anthony Storr (1968: 88) claimed that '[i]t is highly probable that the undoubted superiority of the male sex in intellectual and creative achievement is related to their greater endowment of aggression'.

The term 'sociobiology', which was popularized in the 1970s by Edward Wilson, is basically a development of Lorenz's argument. Instead of a narrow concentration on the evolutionary importance of an individual's ability to survive and procreate, sociobiologists claim to incorporate a consideration of other ways in which people can maximize the likelihood of their genes being transmitted to future generations. In fact, these 'other ways' comprise all forms of human behaviour, which sociobiologists analyse in terms of their functionality in spreading genes. Everything humans do is considered as selfish; altruism does not exist. According to Wilson (1978), all humans have an inherited potential for aggression, but cultural factors determine its outlet and the form it will take. Aggression will occur when it is in aggressor's interest for it to do so, with the important proviso that 'interest' is here defined in terms of the need to enable oneself to pass on one's genes.

The problem for such writers is that the evidence does not clearly support their arguments. Animals typically resort to violence either to protect themselves against a real or perceived threat; to protect their family or community (which involves protecting their territory); or, in the case of carnivores, to obtain food. Animals rarely engage in random violence through boredom or for purposes of revenge. Moreover, when animals do resort to violence, their response is dependent on sensory input. Research on the neurological centres of the brain which are involved in attacking behaviour by mammals has shown that animals consider immediate environmental factors before engaging in violence. Delgado (1971) found that rhesus monkeys would not attack other monkeys if a socially superior monkey were present. This finding provides an important illustration of why it is crucial to remember the difference between angry and aggressive feelings and the physical manifestation of violence. There are clear physiological changes which are observable in both human and non-human primates as a result of rising anger, but it would be wrong to assume that these translate directly into violence without the presence of other influences.

A difficulty with the sociobiologists' thesis that human aggression is inevitable is that it is possible to identify both particular species of animal and human societies that exist without resort to violence. For example, the bonobo chimpanzees of the Congo (formerly Zaire), with a genetic make-up which is about 1 per cent different from humans, seldom resort to violence, preferring to maintain group harmony and deal with disputes by way of extensive and varied sexual behaviour (de Waal 1989). In a survey of 90 pre-literate and peasant societies, Levinson (1989) identified 16 where family violence is almost unknown. Sociobiologists might reply that these must be societies where cultural requirements have rendered the *use* of violence unnecessary. This argument, however, appears questionable. If people's entire *raison d'être* is to transmit healthy genes, as claimed by sociobiologists, it is difficult to envisage circumstances where the use of force against weaker members of the group would not be beneficial.

Biological influences on violent behaviour

Genetics

Genetic influences relate to the blueprint of people's appearance and behaviour that is contained in their chromosomes. The chromosomes contain deoxyribonucleic acid (DNA), the genetic material which is inherited from biological parents. It has long been understood that individuals' *physical appearance* is affected by their DNA: what is nowadays increasingly exercising geneticists is the question whether people's *behaviour* can be influenced by it as well. The problem, however, is in measuring this in such a way that any similarities in behaviour between parent and child cannot simply be explained by common environmental experiences. The so-called 'nature versus nurture' argument has proved a difficult one to settle.

Twin studies

One method of trying to bypass the effects of the environment and socialization has been the study of twins. There are two types of twins: monozygotic (MZ) twins result from a single fertilized egg that has divided, and dizygotic (DZ) twins come from the simultaneous fertilization of two eggs. MZ twins share the same genetic structure, whereas DZ twins have no closer genetic relationship than any two siblings. One difficulty is that any similarity in offending behaviour manifested by twins may be a consequence of their common upbringing. A further problem is that there are not many twins available to study. Only about one in every 70–90 births results in twins and only a quarter of these are MZ twins. The ideal scenario would be a study of MZ twins who were brought up separately from birth but, given the very small numbers involved, this would be very difficult to achieve.

In a study of 6000 Danish twins, Christiansen (1974) found that 35.8 per cent of the male MZ twins both had a criminal record, compared to 12.3 per cent of the DZ twins. (The figures for females were 21.4 per cent and 4.3 per cent, respectively.) Similar results were discovered in his later study of twins from the Danish islands (Christiansen 1977). However, Christiansen still suspected the influence of environmental factors behind these findings. Researchers in the Ohio Twin Study have found that people seek out the most favourable environment in accordance with their genetically based personality, and that this explains why MZ twins are more likely than DZ to choose similar friends and participate in similar activities, including delinquent ones (Rowe 1990).

O'Connor *et al.* (1998) studied the co-occurrence of depressive symptoms and antisocial behaviour (including violence) in a sample of 720 same-sex adolescent siblings, including 93 pairs of MZ and 99 pairs of DZ twins. The researchers discovered that around half the variability could be attributed to genetic factors. In a study of male twins who had served in the US military between 1965 and 1975, Lyons *et al.* (1995) found that shared environmental factors may have a stronger influence on antisocial behaviour for juvenile offenders than for adults.

Adoption studies
Another way of trying to assess the effect of heredity on crime is to study the behaviour of adoptees. If a child adopted soon after birth and removed from a 'criminal' parent grows up in a 'non-criminal' home, and comes to behave like its biological rather than adoptive father, this provides some evidence of genetic influence. Adoption studies provide a better (although not perfect) control of environmental influences than other research methods such as twin studies.

Mednick *et al.* (1987) studied all adoptions in Denmark between 1924 and 1947 where the child was not related to the adoptive parents. The adopted children were more likely to be convicted of crimes, both violent and non-violent, when their natural father had a criminal record. However, if the adoptive father also had a criminal record, the likelihood became even greater, suggesting that there is an environmental factor which cannot be ignored. This conclusion was supported by Walters (1992), who analysed 38 of the twin and adoption studies. He found a small correlation between genes and crime; a larger one where there was one particular shared environmental factor; but the greatest one (up to 65 per cent) where there were environmental factors specific to the individual subject.

There are potential difficulties with more recent adoption studies. Nowadays, adoptive parents are selected on the basis of being particularly suitable, which reduces the likelihood of certain problems arising during the child's upbringing. In the absence of longitudinal studies, it may be hard to differentiate the parents' effects on the child from the child's effects on the parents (Rutter 1997).

Chromosomal abnormalities

There is some evidence that a proneness to violent behaviour can not only be genetically transmitted from one generation to another, but also be connected to genetic mutations which occur at the time of conception. Researchers have become particularly interested in chromosomal abnormalities. Chromosomes are the structures in both animal and plant cells which govern the individual characteristics of the organism. Each human cell contains 23 pairs of chromosomes, one of which is the sex chromosomes. A normal female has sex chromosomes of a similar size which are known as XX. A normal male's sex chromosomes are referred to as XY, as each is of a different size and shape. On very rare occasions, an abnormal cell division occurs before conception, so that the resultant embryo contains an unusual number of sex chromosomes.

When cases of XYY sex chromosome complement were discovered in the 1960s, speculation arose that the extra Y chromosome may be an indication of increased 'maleness' and a greater tendency to resort to violence. This was fuelled by reports from hospital doctors describing such individuals as dangerous. However, later research into a sample of XYY men found that they were no more likely to have been convicted of violent offences than a control group (Witkin *et al*. 1976). The fact that XYY men are extremely tall and that their alleged involvement in crime has been sensationalized by the popular press may have encouraged some courts to order their detention in institutions. This could be exacerbated by the apparent intellectual inferiority of XYY males. In any event, even if XYY men were prone to acts of violence, it would hardly have a major impact on society, as estimates suggest that they comprise no more than 0.15 per cent of the population.

Neurotransmitters

In recent years, there has been a growing interest among biologists and psychologists in the significance of neurotransmitters in human behaviour. Neurotransmitters are the chemicals through which electrical impulses in the brain pass. They are therefore of crucial importance in the origins of all human behaviour, including violent behaviour. The illness schizophrenia is believed to be partly caused by the levels of neurotransmitter chemicals. The question then arises whether such levels can affect a propensity to act violently. Some research suggests a relationship between impulsive violent behaviour and considerably lower levels of the neurotransmitter serotonin than are found in non-violent people (Virkkunen and Linnoila 1993). However, the connection does not appear to be a strong one. Serotonin levels are genetically determined, but they can be subsequently influenced by external environmental factors such as diet, stress, alcohol or drugs. Medication can be used to enhance the level.

Hormones

Whereas neurotransmitters, which are very fast messengers, only work within the brain and spinal chord, hormones, which operate much more slowly, are chemical messengers which are distributed throughout the whole body.

Developments in biochemistry have resulted in speculation that an imbalance in hormonal levels may have adverse consequences on human behaviour, including an increase in aggressiveness and possible recourse to violence. Particular interest has centred on the male sex hormones, known as androgens. Starting from the assumption that men appear to be more aggressive than women, some researchers have investigated whether men with unusually high levels of the male sex hormone testosterone are more likely to engage in violent crime. During puberty, the level of androgens increases dramatically – as does the level of inter-male violence. Many cat owners are aware that castration, which significantly reduces androgen production, can almost completely eliminate aggression towards other male cats.

Olweus (1987) studied the effects of testosterone on a group of young men. He noted a distinction between provoked aggressive behaviour, which was usually a verbal response to another's aggression, and unprovoked aggressive conduct. The provoked aggression was clearly related to the level of testosterone, indicating the additional requirement of a particular environmental setting. Olweus also discovered that a greater likelihood of aggression resulted when an increased level of testosterone was combined with a low frustration tolerance, which itself is usually associated with a child's upbringing. In childhood, a low frustration tolerance does not usually result in aggressive behaviour, but this becomes more likely with the increased levels of testosterone with the onset of puberty.

In a more recent study by van Goozen *et al.* (1994), observation was made of a group of female to male transsexuals, who required a large dose of male sex hormones as part of their sex change process. The researchers found that the androgens did increase anger proneness, but did not have a direct effect on aggression.

However, Raine (1993) has pointed out that any association between increased testosterone level and violence does not prove the direction of a causal link: it may be the aggressive behaviour itself which causes the increase. Research by Bjorkqvist *et al.* (1994) found that, where individuals expect a substance to make them more aggressive, it generally does, even when the substance is a placebo.

Consideration has also been given to whether the wide variations in hormonal levels at the time of menstruation can be related to antisocial behaviour. A review of the research by Fishbein (1992) showed that a small percentage of women show greater hostility during fluctuation in their hormonal levels. This, of course, does not necessarily result in criminal behaviour: estimates suggest that up to 40 per cent of women suffer from severe pre-menstrual symptoms, but it is inconceivable that four out of ten women offend as a result.

The hormone adrenalin has also been related to violent behaviour. The increase in its level, which usually results when a person feels under stress, leads to heightened cortical arousal manifested by a moistening of the skin and an increased alertness. It has been suggested that violent offenders may take stronger stimuli to arouse them than is required for other people. Olweus (1986) found that aggressive behaviour by persistent bullies was unaccompanied by an increase in adrenalin, and Magnusson (1988) arrived at a similar conclusion in a study of hyperactive boys. Baldwin (1990) considered that criminality among young men peaks at a certain age through a combination of cortical arousability and environmental factors. Adolescents may feel an increasing urge to seek out greater forms of excitement. For many, this can be channelled into acceptable outlets such as sport. Others, however, may resort to antisocial activities including violence. By the time young people enter their twenties, these environmental pressures will have declined and this will be accompanied by a fall in their urge to seek new stimuli.

It has also been claimed that violent behaviour in male children and adolescents may be associated with low saliva levels of the stress hormone cortisol. In one study, clinical and peer evaluations of the behaviour of 38 boys found that those with low cortisol concentrations were identified as three times more likely to show aggressive symptoms (McBurnett *et al.* 2000)

External factors

The above discussion relates to biological factors which are, at least to some extent, innate or based on heredity. However, it has also been suggested that a tendency to act violently may arise from changes to the physical constitution caused by wholly external factors, such as diet or damage to the central nervous system. (Alcohol and drug use also come into this category, but they are considered separately below.) The idea that antisocial behaviour can be related to nutrition has a long history, but there is little supportive evidence. Some research has suggested a link with hypoglycaemia (low blood sugar). Claims have been made concerning substances such as monosodium glutamate, caffeine and some chemicals found in chocolate (Curran and Renzetti 1994). However, many of the findings in this area have been criticized on the basis of their methodology (Kanarek 1994).

There is some evidence of a relationship between high levels of lead and violent behaviour. A study of lead levels in bones showed a significant correlation between the concentration of lead and violence (Needleman *et al.* 1996).

However, even here environmental considerations cannot be ruled out: the higher levels of lead that are found in boys than girls (Taylor 1991) may have been exacerbated by children's behaviour (for example, boys may play outside more frequently).

Early attempts to study the electrical processes of the brain through electroencephalograph (EEG) testing indicated that a significant proportion of violent offenders had abnormal brain patterns. Subsequent, more sophisticated research has also found a relationship between violent behaviour and brain damage. Mednick *et al.* (1982) took EEG recordings from a group of Danish boys born between 1959 and 1961. Those who were later convicted of violent offences had generally good neurological and physical reports during pregnancy and at birth, but these had significantly worsened by the end of their first year of life. Neuropsychological tests involve verbal or visual assessments which measure sophisticated brain functions such as learning and memory abilities. They have been administered to violent offenders, and the results show that minor brain impairments are often present. In one study, a low score on a neuropsychological frontal lobe test predicted aggressiveness among 72 males (Giancola and Zeichner 1994). There is also evidence that people with poor neuropsychological functioning are more aggressive when provoked (Lau *et al.* 1995).

Such findings raise the possibility that the brain functioning may have been related to the later violence, although environmental factors could clearly operate as well (for example, the children in the Danish study may have been physically abused by their parents). Complications during birth could also be relevant. In a sample taken from the same Danish study, Kandel and Mednick (1991) found that 80 per cent of those convicted of violent offences experienced greater than average complications at delivery.

Summary

This is an appropriate point to take stock of what has gone before. The general thrust of the preceding discussion is that a propensity to act violently or antisocially may be genetically transmitted and/or affected by biological factors within the body. These approaches do not receive universal approval; sociologists are particularly sceptical on the grounds that social context often appears to be overlooked. Although the early research often contained considerable shortcomings, more recent offerings are far more sophisticated, and this is clearly a rapidly developing area.

Mental disorder

From at least the time of the ancient Greeks, writings have associated mental disorder with violence. This tradition is continued in the present day by the media. Taylor (1993a) cited two pieces of American research: one showed that, on prime-time American television, the mentally disordered are portrayed as violent almost twice as often as the mentally healthy; and the other indicated that 86 per cent of all newspaper stories printed about former mental patients are based on their having committed a violent crime.

The legal definitions of mental disorder are contained in the Mental Health Act 1983. Section 1(2) states the four categories: mental illness; arrested or incomplete development of the mind; psychopathic disorder; and any other disorder or disability of mind. 'Mental illness', which is not defined in the Act, includes psychoses (such as schizophrenia), anxiety states, affective disorders (such as depression) and hysteria. A psychosis is a mental disorder which results in severe disruption to a person's mood, reasoning processes and practical functioning. The mental functioning of psychotics is so badly impaired that they are generally unable to meet the routine demands of daily living.

Two different methods have been used to assess the level of mental disorder in offenders: the study of disorder among convicted criminals and the analysis of criminal behaviour in a psychiatric population. There is clear evidence that psychological problems are common among prisoners (although the findings are not confined to violent offenders). Birmingham *et al.* (1996) reported that 26 per cent of remand prisoners at Durham jail were suffering from one or more mental disorders. Four per cent of this total were diagnosed as psychotic. In a sample of just under 10 per cent of the male unsentenced prison population, Brooke *et al.* (1996) discovered that 63 per cent were suffering from some form of psychological disorder, including substance abuse. Singleton *et al.* (1998) also found evidence of extensive mental disorder in a large sample of inmates from the entire prison population. For example, clinical assessment showed that 63 per cent of male remand prisoners had an antisocial personality disorder, and 14 per cent of female prisoners were psychotic.

However, such evidence does not prove a causal link between mental disorder and crime. Mentally disordered offenders may have a higher chance of being caught through their ineptitude. Once apprehended, they could be more likely to plead guilty in the hope of obtaining treatment. Alternatively, some prisoners might develop mental disorders as a result of their incarceration.

Research into the crime rate of psychiatric patients has been less conclusive. Several studies have indicated that the prospects of such people offending on their release from hospital are related to their arrest record prior to entry (see, for example, Steadman *et al.* 1978). However, the research does not make it clear whether these individuals were still affected by their earlier condition on release.

Schizophrenia

Of all the disorders, schizophrenia appears to be the one most closely related to acts of violence. This illness involves such symptoms as difficulty in associating different thoughts, the hearing of voices, and the experiencing of strong and inappropriate emotional responses. Physical manifestations include strange facial grimaces and gestures, and disturbances in motor behaviour.

There is evidence of some connection between schizophrenia and violent crime, including homicide. Taylor (1986) found high levels of schizophrenia among life-sentence prisoners in London. A longitudinal study of discharges of schizophrenic patients from Swedish psychiatric hospitals by Lindqvist and Allebeck (1990) discovered that their rate of subsequent violent offending was four times higher than that of the general population. However, most of the violence involved minor assaults and no one was killed. Despite her earlier research findings, Taylor (1993b) has endorsed the view that, as a group, schizophrenics are unlikely to commit serious violent offences. Appleby *et al.* (1999) found that only 4 per cent of all homicides in England and Wales between April 1996 and November 1997 were committed by people who had suffered from schizophrenia. The more extreme forms of violence are usually aimed at themselves through self-mutilation. Attacks requiring any advanced degree of planning are rare and harm to others usually occurs during delusions, often of infidelity or extreme jealousy.

Schizophrenia manifesting itself exclusively in delusions is considered more likely to be associated with violence than other forms of the illness (Robertson and Taylor 1993). Nevertheless, the danger posed by schizophrenics has to be kept in proportion: as a group they form about 1 per cent of the general population, and it has been estimated that only 0.05 per cent of them engage in serious violence. Moreover, many schizophrenics will respond to drug treatment. In an Australian study, it was found that increased rates of offending by schizophrenics were consistent with changes in criminal patterns in the general community (Mullen *et al.* 2000). It seems, however, that the public still remains to be convinced, and mentally disordered offenders are still widely considered to be dangerously violent (Hurley 1994). Selective reporting can certainly play a part in this. Research in Germany by Angermeyer and Matschinger (1996) showed how there was a marked increase in desired social distance from mentally ill people following the publicity given to violent attacks by two schizophrenics against prominent politicians.

Psychopathy

Although schizophrenia may, in practice, be the form of mental disorder most frequently connected with violence, the sensationalized media portrayals are usually reserved for psychopathy. The term has always been a troublesome one and American psychiatrists tend to avoid using it: indeed, the highly authoritative American Psychiatric Association's *Diagnostic and Statistical Manual* does not include the word at all, preferring the expression 'antisocial personality disorder'.

Much of the problem arises from the lurid and often inaccurate usage of the term by the media and in films. Further difficulty is created by the legal definition of psychopathic disorder in s. 1(2) of the Mental Health Act as 'a persistent disorder or disability of mind (whether or not including significant impairment of intelligence) which results in abnormally aggressive or seriously irresponsible conduct'. The definition is circular, in that the disorder is assumed from the behaviour, which is then in turn used to explain the disorder (Ashworth and Gostin 1985). This is a particularly important point, as it is unusual to find civil commitments to hospital for psychopaths under the Act, which one would expect if the condition caused problems for the individuals themselves (Peay 1997). In effect, psychopathic behaviour is criminal behaviour.

The word 'psychopath' has therefore become a label attached to a person suffering from a particular form of personality disorder rather than a diagnostic expression. The public also relates psychopathy to violence, but individuals whom psychiatrists would describe as psychopaths commit a range of offences.

The Revised Psychopathy Checklist (PCL-R) suggests that lack of empathy, callousness and – crucially – lack of remorse or guilt are key predictors of psychopathy (Rice and Harris 1992). Hare (1986) has provided his own checklist, which includes indicators such as superficial charm, grandiose sense of self-worth, proneness to boredom, pathological lying, lack of realistic long-term plans, and impulsivity. Psychopaths are said to have an inability to trust anyone, which makes them difficult, if not impossible, to treat in conventional therapeutic and hospital settings. Howells (1983) has argued that psychopaths assume that anyone they deal with has negative views towards them and, instead of waiting to appraise a situation, they have a tendency to resort to violence first.

The causes of psychopathy remain elusive. There is some evidence from adoption and twin studies that it can be genetically transmitted (Cadoret 1986). Researchers have found an association between brain damage and antisocial personality or psychopathic disorder (Raine *et al.* 2000). Claims have also been made that early childhood problems and family influences are relevant.

With the increasing focus on dangerous offenders, which is discussed in Chapter 9, politicians have turned their attention to the possibility of locking up people who are *predicted* to be dangerous. The Government has proposed the introduction of a 'reviewable detention order' for untreatable but dangerous individuals with a personality disorder. It is stated that 'admission to the new regime *will not be dependent on the person having committed an offence*, nor whether they are treatable under the terms of the current Mental Health Act' (Department of Health 1998a, para. 4.33; emphasis added).

This proposal is objectionable on several grounds. There are clear ethical problems about incarcerating innocent people. There would also be concern about the possibility of using such a measure for social control purposes: totalitarian regimes have frequently attached the label of 'mentally ill' to people whose opinions they do not approve of. The term 'personality disorder' could come to perform that role: as Rafter (1997: 250) has stated, '"psychopaths" is a metaphor for "those who are not like us"'. Prediction techniques are notoriously unreliable (although see Walker 1996). However, the biggest threat to such a provision may be a legal one. It has been claimed that its introduction could amount to an infringement of the protection against unlawful detention provided by Article 5 of the European Convention on Human Rights, which has been incorporated into the domestic law of England and Wales in the Human Rights Act 1998 (Bartlett and Sandland 2000).

Post-traumatic stress disorder

In recent years, there has been a growing awareness of post-traumatic stress disorder (PTSD), and some research suggests that it can be related to violence. Individuals suffering from PTSD can experience a range of symptoms, including problems of concentration and memory, a constant alertness to danger and, in extreme cases, a need to re-enact the traumatic situation that underlies their condition. In a prison sample of 1140 males, Collins and Bailey (1990) found a relationship between PTSD and violent crime which was apparently unrelated to any interest in armed combat. The 2.3 per cent of the group who met the strict testing criteria for PTSD were significantly more likely to have been arrested or imprisoned for a violent crime, and generally the symptoms had preceded the offence.

In conclusion, it is not clear that any association between mental disorder and violent crime means that the offending occurred as a result of the disorder. The mental disorder may have been related to wider social problems which themselves precipitated the offending. Moreover, even where an association is apparent, it does not provide an explanation for the vast majority of violent crimes. Evidence from the USA suggests that major mental disorder accounts, at most, for 3 per cent of the violence in American society (Monahan 1992). However, a note of caution must be added: the link between mental disorder and violent crime is considerably strengthened when the additional factor of 'substance disorder' is added (Monahan 1997).

Drugs and alcohol

For the purposes of this discussion (and in keeping with the organization of most research and the creation of criminal offences), drugs and alcohol will be considered separately, although it is clear that alcohol is a drug for the purpose of considering its psychopharmacological effects.

Drugs

It has been suggested that there is a relationship between drugs and violence at three different levels: the psychopharmacological; the economic compulsive; and the systemic (Goldstein 1985).

The psychopharmacological connection considers whether some individuals will behave violently following the ingestion of certain substances. The evidence is equivocal. More recent studies suggest that, whereas the use of cannabis, amphetamines or hallucinogens (such as LSD) is not related to physical aggression, cocaine or opiates may lead to violence in certain situations (Taylor and Hulsizer 1998). On the other hand, a study of 427 New York City male adolescents found that, although cocaine usage and crime rates were similarly high, the ingestion of cocaine was unrelated to any particular type of crime, including violent crime (Kang *et al.* 1994). It has been observed that withdrawal symptoms from severely habit-forming drugs can involve an irritability which sometimes results in attacks on treatment programme workers (Mednick *et al.* 1982).

It is of little value to consider even psychopharmacological effects without taking any account of environmental factors. Different drugs gain reputations for having a particular type of impact, and the expectation accompanying the use may, in many cases, serve to enhance the perceived effect. For example, some people may act violently after taking certain drugs because 'that is what you do'. A particular drug may be taken with the intention of giving the user courage to commit a crime, or even to provide an excuse in the case of apprehension.

The 'economic compulsive' level of relationship states that some drug users commit violent crimes such as robbery in order to obtain the funds to support their drug use. The significance of this is that the violence is not a direct consequence of ingesting the drug – although a recourse to robbery in the case of a severe craving might seem to come quite close to it. The use of violence is here purely instrumental to a particular purpose. Heroin and cocaine users have traditionally been regarded as the main culprits, as their drugs have been the most expensive. However, research by Johnson *et al.* (1985) into heroin addiction and violence in Harlem found that such people usually avoid the use of violence where other means are available, such as drug-selling, prostitution or theft. The researchers also discovered that many of the victims were drug users themselves or involved in other illegal activities in the area. A study of crack cocaine and heroin users by Parker and Bottomley (1996) revealed that most individuals gained their income from acquisitive crime and their state benefits.

Even where an apparent connection is indicated between robbery (or any other crime) and drug use, it does not follow that the two are causally related. In research for the Home Office, Mott and Taylor (1974) found that a high percentage of heroin users were already involved in criminal activities before they started taking drugs. It is also possible that individuals who are prone to violence are more likely to assume violent roles in the drug business. Adler (1985) discovered evidence of this in her research among Californian drug traffickers.

The third type of relationship is the 'systemic'. On this analysis, violence is an inevitable part of the pattern of distribution and use of illegal drugs. It will arise out of territorial disputes; the operations of rivals; the supply of adulterated or imitation drugs; the failure to pay debts; and the entrepreneurial activities of street dealers lower down the supply chain. This phenomenon is hardly new – it can be traced at least as far back as the liquor rackets of Al Capone. However, the large increase in illicit drugs circulating in many major cities nowadays has caused a considerable escalation in this type of violence.

Alcohol

In historical terms, it is only fairly recently that the behavioural effects of alcohol have been considered in anything other than a moral context. It was widely assumed that drinking loosens moral restraints and that people who drink lose personal control and are consequently liable to behave in an antisocial way, including acting violently. Therefore, when researchers first began to consider the relationship between alcohol and violence, it was natural that they should start from the widely held premise that the pharmacological effects of alcohol directly affect the brain in such a way as to loosen inhibitions, and that one of the consequences is an enhanced tendency to behave violently. It now appears, however, that the situation is not so straightforward.

There is certainly a large body of empirical evidence suggesting that violent offenders have often been drinking at the time of the offence. From an analysis of several studies, Collins (1986) concluded that prisoners with drinking problems had committed more assaults than prisoners without such problems. Rada (1975) discovered that half his sample of convicted rapists had been drinking at the time of the offence. In a study of homicides in Sweden, Lindqvist (1986) found that two-thirds of the offenders were intoxicated when they killed. A US Department of Justice survey revealed that 64 per cent of state prisoners convicted of violent offences claimed that either they, their victims, or both, were under the influence of drugs or alcohol at the time of the offence. The strongest link appeared for manslaughter and the weakest was for sexual offences (US Department of Justice 1990). The National Bureau of Economic Research has found a relationship between the price of alcohol and level of spousal assault in several American states (Markowitz 1999).

An analysis of data from the 1989 British Crime Survey by Mott (1990) showed that young men who had been drinking heavily were more likely than moderate drinkers to be involved in offences of minor violence. Even allowing for the possibility that some of these respondents were lying or exaggerating the effects of alcohol to try to excuse their conduct, the evidence still indicates that many violent offenders were intoxicated at the time of their offence.

However, it is by no means clear that these findings show a causal relationship between alcohol and violent crime. The fact that men who are continuously drunk are less likely to assault their partners than men who are very often drunk could be interpreted as suggesting that men find it excusable to assault their partner while drunk, rather than that the attacks are caused by the disinhibiting effects of alcohol (Coleman and Straus 1983). Not only do large numbers of non-violent offenders claim to have been drinking prior to offending, but vast amounts of alcohol are consumed by people (particularly in their own homes) who do not proceed to break the law at all.

Many studies suggest that victims are also likely to have been drinking. In Britain, Gottfredson (1984) discovered that the chances of being victimized increased from 5 per cent among non-drinkers to 15 per cent among heavy drinkers. This was still the case when controls were introduced for age and area of residence, although the connection was strongest for the young. A similar finding was also made in the 1989 British Crime Survey (Mott 1990). In research by Hodge (1993), two-thirds of a sample of assailants and 50 per cent of their victims said they had been drinking immediately before the offence. The 1996 British Crime Survey found that victims of domestic violence had far higher levels of alcohol consumption than non-victims (Mirrlees-Black 1999). It is possible that offenders realize that people who have been drinking are easy targets. It may also be that drinkers are less careful about protecting themselves from attack or are more likely to promote arguments.

In Australia, researchers have studied public drinking places where violence is a recurring problem, and have concluded that there are 'violent drinking situations' (Tomsen et al. 1991). They found that several factors precipitate violence: the type of customer; the atmosphere in the pub or club; the amount of alcohol consumed; and the behaviour of the security staff. Large gatherings of males can lead to sexual competitiveness so that, if the men are in identifiable groups and the groups are strangers to each other, violence is likely to ensue. 'Atmosphere' is reflected by excessive noise, lack of space and resultant discomfort; this can result in faster drinking. Aggressive security staff can lead to a troubled, edgy atmosphere, and they themselves can precipitate violence. The Bristol research into assault victims discovered several cases which fitted this model (see Chapter 2).

Different drinking patterns can also affect the way individuals respond to alcohol. For example, America not only has a high level of alcohol consumption, but its citizens tend to drink heavily during short periods of time, whereas inhabitants of other countries (such as France) spread their alcohol intake more evenly throughout the course of a day (Bartol 1991).

There are, therefore, difficulties in assuming a direct causal relationship between the use of alcohol and violence. Alcohol does not have the same pharmacological effect on everyone; factors such as body weight, build and even race can be significant. For example, Eskimos and Native Americans metabolize alcohol more slowly than whites. Research has suggested that proneness to alcoholism can be genetically transmitted (Goodwin *et al.* 1973). Any drug – including alcohol – can worsen psychological symptoms in individuals who are already mentally disturbed. People who are slightly paranoid could become extremely paranoid after consuming alcohol, and may resort to violence in the belief that they are defending themselves against some imagined evil.

The clearest physiological effect of alcohol consumption is that it slows a person's reaction time. It has been claimed that this contributes to drinkers' experiencing difficulty in noticing inhibitory cues, thus increasing the likelihood of conflict (Pernanen 1991). Evidence suggests that alcohol users are more likely than other offenders to be arrested (Petersilia *et al.* 1978). This seems hardly surprising – inebriation is unlikely to assist a swift escape – but it should be remembered when research based on samples of convicted offenders is considered. Some offenders take alcohol before committing their crime to calm their nerves. A causal link between alcohol and violence is thus established but, being of an entirely voluntary nature, it is wholly different from that which is usually assumed. Coid (1982) has suggested that, rather than alcoholism being related to violence, some alcoholics suffer from a personality disorder which increases the likelihood of their acting aggressively.

There has been a growing realization that factors other than the purely physiological effects of alcohol are important in influencing the behaviour of an individual who has been drinking. Laboratory experiments have shown that people act more aggressively when they think they have consumed alcohol even though they have been given a placebo (Lang *et al.* 1975). Research also indicates that people's expectations greatly influence the effects of alcohol on aggressive behaviour (Koss and Gaines 1993). Social conventions can affect the way people act after drinking and this can vary among different societies (MacAndrew and Edgerton 1969): there are particular periods, such as festivals, when drinking is considered far more acceptable (and even encouraged) than others. There is also a widespread belief, especially among people working in the criminal justice system, that some offenders use the fact they have been drinking as an excuse for their crimes, or as a demonstration of male machismo.

Conclusion

Whereas in many situations individuals might resort to violence through anger, or make a calculated decision to use it for a particular purpose, on other occasions people find they are unable to resist, or experience considerable difficulty in resisting, an urge to act violently on account of some physical or mental factor.

There is a growing interest in the study of genetic influences on human behaviour, and this has been heightened by scientists' increased ability to analyse DNA structure. This has led to claims that there is an 'aggressiveness gene'. Although it seems clear that certain genetic mutations could prove so overwhelming as to render any other influence – such as the environment – largely irrelevant, these will affect such a small number of people (many of whom will probably be in hospitals) as to be of no real value in a broader consideration of violence. Otherwise, as Rutter (1997: 390) indicated, environmental factors cannot be ignored:

> Nature and nurture do not operate independently of each other, and, to an important degree, genetic effects on behavior come about because they either influence the extent to which the individual is likely to be exposed to individual differences in environmental risk or they affect how susceptible the individual is to environmental adversities.

Although many forms of mental disorder, including some which cause people to act violently, can have their etiology traced to environmental factors, mental disorder with a proneness to violence only applies to a very small percentage of the population. The ingestion of alcohol and (to a lesser extent) some other forms of drug appears to be associated with aggression, but, once again, it seems that environmental factors play a significant part in determining whether violent behaviour results. In the case of illicit drugs, far more violence results from their sale and acquisition than from their use.

Further reading

The issues arising from mental disorder are fully discussed by Jill Peay's (1997) chapter, 'Mentally disordered offenders', in *The Oxford Handbook of Criminology*. In America, the National Research Council's Panel on the Understanding and Control of Violent Behavior has published a three-volume report. Volume 2 (Reiss *et al.* 1994) deals with biological influences on crime. The Department of Health report *Psychiatric Morbidity among Prisoners in England and Wales* (Singleton *et al.* 1998) provides a very detailed description of the mental problems suffered by a representative sample of prison inmates. The association between alcohol and violent crime is considered in *Alcohol and Crime: Taking Stock* (Deehan 1999).

chapter four

Theories of socialization

In the previous chapter, various accounts were discussed which suggest that a person's recourse to violence may be significantly affected by constitutional or mental factors. In this chapter, consideration will be given to an alternative explanation: that violent behaviour is largely related to an individual's socialization. This approach can broadly be divided into two strands: one based on learning theories, and the other on a psychoanalytic model.

Learning theories

It is possible that the expression of some violent behaviour is causally connected to either the experience or observation of aggression. Writers since Aristotle have argued that most human behaviour is based on learned experiences rather than instinct or some other innate characteristic. Both sociologists and psychologists have shown an interest in the significance of learning in criminal and antisocial behaviour.

Differential association

One of the best-known sociological explanations is Edwin Sutherland's (1947) theory of differential association. The theory is set out in a series of propositions. Criminal behaviour is learned in interaction with others, mainly in small, intimate groups. Most people come into contact with both individuals who think that laws should be obeyed and individuals who think that laws can be broken. The principle of differential association states that a person becomes delinquent because of a stronger exposure to law-breakers than to the law-abiding. This is likely to be qualitative rather than quantitative: Sutherland (1947: 7) stated that 'differential associations may vary in frequency, duration, priority, and intensity'. Hence, prison officers may spend much of the day in the company of criminals, but will not learn to copy their behaviour because of the greater intensity of their other, law-abiding associations.

The theory of differential association is based on two key notions: learning takes place within 'intimate personal groups'; and the content of what is learned includes not only techniques for committing crimes, but also motives, attitudes and rationalizations. Both of these derive from George Herbert Mead's (1934) theory of 'symbolic interactionism'. Mead argued that the cognitive notion of 'meaning' is more important in the learning process than the simple copying of behaviour. Meanings are attributed to particular experiences, and these then become 'definitions' which are taken forward into the future. Several people could experience the same situation and give it entirely different meanings or definitions. Sutherland argued that the meaning of a particular criminal act (such as violence) for an individual will be largely influenced by the meaning given to the act by other people with whom the individual associates in intimate personal groups. The extent of the influence will depend on such factors as 'frequency, duration, priority, and intensity'.

One difficulty with Sutherland's theory is that it is difficult to evaluate empirically. Juvenile delinquents in particular tend to associate with other delinquents, but this is not necessarily because they have learned criminal values from one another: they may simply choose friends who share the same values. Moreover, Sutherland's view of the learning process is not in accord with that of other cognitive theorists, who have generally rejected the importance he gave to learning in intimate social groups. However, Matsueda (1988), having analysed the empirical research conducted on the theory, concluded that it was generally supportive.

Social learning theory

The main division among psychologists who adhere to learning theories has traditionally been between behaviourists, who claim that individuals learn by trial and error through associating stimuli and responses, and cognitive theorists, who maintain that people learn to solve problems through the association of ideas and memories.

One of the most influential writers in this area is Albert Bandura, whose social learning theory combines aspects of behaviourism and cognitive psychology. Bandura argued that behaviour is reinforced not only by rewards and punishments, but also by observational learning of other people's actions (modelling). In this way, individuals can learn to anticipate the effectiveness of particular courses of action in achieving desired goals. Violence is one method of attaining these goals: others could include avoidance measures or resolution of the problem. Continual resort to violence may result from the reinforcement of such behaviour (for example, money obtained from robbery reinforces the use of violence), or the failure to learn alternative techniques of attaining desired aims or dealing with disturbing events. In so far as there is a cognitive analysis of a received stimulus, aggression can be seen as a rational response.

Perhaps Bandura's best-known experiment is the one involving the 'Bobo doll' (Bandura and Huston 1961). While a child played in a room, an adult would enter and start to hit and kick the doll. In order to frustrate the child, it would be told it could not play with some other toys that were present. The child would then be led into another room, where there would be several toys and another Bobo doll. Children who had seen the adult attack the Bobo doll would be more likely to attack the doll than those who had also been frustrated, but had not witnessed the adult's attack.

Bandura considered that individuals learn from one another both the attitudes necessary to commit a crime (for example, whether it is morally correct to attack a particular victim) and the necessary physical skills. People's attitudes do not need to remain fixed; they can be altered by normal cognitive processes, perhaps resulting from a greater exposure to different and stronger influences. Bandura (1976) stated that learning occurs mainly in three different settings: in the family; in a subculture; and through cultural forms such as cinema, television and books.

Child physical abuse and corporal punishment

Although there are explanations for the use of physical violence against children which are not based on learning theories, it is convenient to consider the whole question here, as there is a strong finding in the research that people who inflict such violence have often themselves been the victim of it.

Bandura and other learning theorists have generally attributed violent crime to the failure of socialization in childhood. Although many people would equate this with a lack of discipline, Bandura (1973) himself realized that violent crime can be learned from excessive or inappropriate use of physical punishment. A child who has been beaten will discover that the use of force, especially by a stronger person against a weaker one, can be an effective means to get one's own way. Moreover, the fact that this message comes from the parents can only serve to reinforce the learning. Such a child may develop antisocial behavioural patterns which lead to rejection by its peer group, and this could result in the child's either joining a deviant sub-culture (see Chapter 5) or living in social isolation. This rejection may lead to a deficiency in social skills, including the understanding of peer-group norms and how to respond to provocation.

There is a problem in determining the point where lawful corporal punishment becomes unlawful physical abuse. Criminal law provides little help: most societies accept the right of parents to inflict 'reasonable' physical punishment on their own children, although more severe forms of beating (particularly involving implements) are increasingly being considered un-reasonable (see Chapter 1). Wherever the legal line is drawn, there is no reason to believe that it will correspond to any change in the effect that the beating has on the child. For the purpose of this discussion, a distinction between abuse and punishment will be made, with the important proviso that, in terms of the psychological effects, it may be an arbitrary one.

Physical abuse   Traditionally, most people assumed that the justification for the use of physical force against children arose from a mixture of biblical dictate ('spare the rod and spoil the child') and an acceptance that it is understandable for overwrought parents to lose their temper with a difficult child. Whether the parent acted in hot or cold blood, the fault remained with the child. In more recent years, however, the growing realization that the physical abuse of children is a genuine problem has resulted in a closer look at the dynamics of the parent–child relationship where violence has occurred.

Some researchers have pointed to the frequency of child physical abuse at the hands of teenage mothers, and concluded that it is their inflexibility and lack of other parenting skills which underlie their recourse to violence (Haskett et al. 1994). However, other writers have claimed that it is not the age of the mothers, but their lack of financial resources and support mechanisms that places them under considerable stress (Buchholz and Korn-Bursztyn 1993). Abusive parents – and other violent individuals – may have a general perception of life which legitimizes the use of physical aggression. In one experiment, mothers who were considered at low risk for child abuse displayed considerable empathy when shown a picture of a distressed child, whereas mothers considered at high risk failed to show empathy on seeing the same picture (Milner et al. 1995).

There is also a substantial body of research linking alcohol and drug abuse to child physical abuse. However, just as with other areas of violent crime, it would be erroneous to conclude that there is necessarily a simple, direct causal relationship (see Chapter 3). In many cases, it is likely that other problems experienced by the family result in both substance and child abuse. This was found in research on a sample of prisoners by Sheridan (1995), which discovered that the level of family functioning and extent of offending were linked to both forms of abuse.

Research into delinquent and aggressive children has shown that their behaviour can be linked to the use of violence by their parents, both on each other and on their children. A survey of research findings by the Gulbenkian Foundation (1995: 134) discovered almost total unanimity that 'harsh and humiliating discipline are implicated in the development of anti-social and violent behaviour'. In a study of 900 abused children in Indianapolis, it emerged that children who had been physically abused up to the age of 11 were significantly likely to commit violent offences during the next 15 years (Maxfield and Widom 1996). In Canada, a report for the Ontario Ministry of Community and Social Services (1990) suggested that victims of child abuse are ten times more likely to commit criminal offences in adolescence than those who have not been abused.

Corporal punishment   A large amount of research has been conducted into the relationship between corporal punishment and violent behaviour. Some of the findings – particularly those trying to ascertain the frequency of corporal punishment – come from self-report studies or surveys based on distant recollections. In America, for example, it has been consistently shown that, whereas over 90 per cent of people claim to have received some form of corporal punishment, a far smaller proportion of adults admit to having administered it.

An alternative form of data-gathering involves contacting children directly in an attempt to find a connection between their current exposure to corporal punishment and levels of aggressive or violent behaviour. Straus, who is one of the leading researchers in this area, maintains that there is a causal connection between the use of physical punishment by parents and the commission of violent crime by their children in later life. In a national study of several thousand American schoolchildren and their parents, Straus (1983) found that 15 per cent of those who did not receive corporal punishment repeatedly committed severe attacks against a sibling, compared to 40 per cent of those who were physically punished, and 76 per cent of those who were consistently abused. In addition, Straus showed that parents who professed a belief in physical punishment were also more likely to assault their children. The same children were likely to hit their siblings and were significantly more likely to commit street crime. The more one parent used physical punishment, the greater was the probability that the parent would also assault the other parent (Straus 1991). In a Canadian study, MacMillan *et al.* (1999) found an association between the frequency of corporal punishment during childhood and subsequent psychiatric disorder.

However, this type of research does not preclude the possible explanation that children who are violent for some other reason are more likely to receive corporal punishment. Nor is it able to ascertain whether childhood aggression develops into adult violence. For these reasons, some researchers prefer to use a prospective or longitudinal study, where a sample can be monitored over a period of many years. The Cambridge Study in Delinquent Development (Farrington 1978) found that harsh disciplining of boys (including severe physical punishment) at the age of 8 was a predictor of violence up to the age of 21. McCord (1979) observed 253 boys over a 20-year period. At the outset, parents were classified as 'aggressive' or 'nonaggressive' towards their sons. After 20 years, McCord obtained the men's conviction and prison records, and discovered that parental aggression 20 years earlier predicted the commission of violent crimes.

The visual portrayal of violence
An issue which has been particularly controversial in recent years is whether aggressive and violent behaviour portrayed on television and in films can provide a model which viewers, particularly younger ones, may try to copy. Bandura and other researchers claim the evidence shows that this happens: others deny that such a link exists.

With its tradition of film-making, and the fact that widespread usage of television first occurred there, it is not surprising that it was in America that researchers conducted the first major investigations into possible links between the visual depiction and subsequent commission of violence. Early studies mainly consisted of laboratory experiments – similar to the 'Bobo doll' experiment described above – where subjects were first exposed to media violence and then asked to punish another subject (in fact, one of the researchers) for the inadequate performance of some task by apparently inflicting pain or an electric shock (in reality, the device would not inflict pain). The findings generally suggested a greater willingness to 'punish' following exposure to portrayals of violence. In 1972, the US Surgeon General published a report which concluded that the evidence supported a correlation between television viewing and violence (Surgeon General's Scientific Advisory Committee on Television and Social Behavior 1972).

An alternative research device to the laboratory experiment is the longitudinal study. One such project, which was designed to consider aggression among family members in Columbia County, New York, started in 1960 and involved checking the level of aggressiveness of 875 eight-year-old children after watching television. The researchers noticed that the aggression of boys (as assessed by their peers) was significantly correlated to the level of violence in their favourite television programmes. However, no similar relationship was found for the girls. When the group was studied ten years later, there was no evidence of a relationship between television viewing habits and aggressive behaviour for either the girls or the boys; but the boys' preference for violent programmes of ten years earlier was predictive of how aggressively they were now behaving. A further 12 years later, the researchers also found no relationship between current television viewing habits and antisocial or aggressive behaviour, but the viewing of television violence at the age of 8 was correlated with current self-reported aggression and the seriousness of arrests accumulated by the age of 30. These results were not influenced by IQ, class or parenting factors. The researchers concluded that early exposure to television violence is particularly significant and relatively impervious to change. It encourages aggression for a number of years, and early aggression is linked to subsequent criminal behaviour (Huesmann and Eron 1986).

These findings have been criticized. As the research had not originally been intended to study this particular area, a great deal of the original data had not been preserved and the final sample was very small. The researchers themselves conceded that their findings probably only applied to a small number of particularly violent viewers. It is unclear why no correlation was found for females. Freedman (1992) argued that, under such a cumulative theory, one would expect the correlations between viewing violence and aggression to increase with age.

In Britain, Bailey (1993) interviewed 40 violent young offenders and 200 sex offenders. She found that a quarter had seen violent television programmes, films and videos, and concluded that this was a significant causal factor in their offending. In evidence to the House of Lords Broadcasting Group, Sims and Gray (1993) identified over 1000 studies which claimed to have discovered a connection between exposure to depictions of violence in the media and aggression. On the other hand, Hagell and Newburn (1994) found that young offenders are exposed to the same level of violence on video as non-offenders and, following a review of recent research studies, Livingstone (1996) felt unable to draw any firm conclusions about the possibility of harmful effects to viewers of violence.

Charlton and Gunter (1999) studied the behaviour of children prior to, and following, the introduction of television to the island of St Helena in 1995. The amount of violence contained in the programmes was discovered to be slightly higher than in the UK. However, the researchers found no increase in violent or antisocial behaviour on the part of the children.

Some researchers claim to have identified causal links between the reporting of particular violent incidents on television and subsequent violence in the community. Phillips and Hensley (1984) maintained that the number of homicides in the USA showed a significant increase for a number of days after a big boxing contest, and a decrease following publicity surrounding long prison sentences and executions. It is clearly very difficult to control for possible environmental influences, and such findings should be treated with considerable caution. The same can be said for research by Centerwall (1989), which suggested that the fact that South Africa did not have television until 1975 explains why the level of homicide by whites was so much lower during the previous 25 years than the corresponding levels in Canada and the USA, where television was available throughout this period.

Claims of 'copycat' killings were made in America following the release of the film *Natural Born Killers* in 1984. After the conviction for murder in 1993 of two 10-year-old Liverpool boys for the killing of the child James Bulger, several newspapers alleged that the boys had watched a violent video, *Child's Play 3*, prior to the event. Although there was no evidence of this, the *Sun* newspaper demanded that all copies of the video should be burned, even though it had earlier been shown on a TV station owned by the newspaper's proprietor, Rupert Murdoch (Schubart 1995). The controversy stirred up by the case led to the insertion of a new provision in the Video Recordings Act 1984. The effect of section 4A is that the British Board of Film Censors must, in classifying videos, consider the 'harm' (the word is not defined) that may be caused to viewers by exposure to crime, drug use, violence, horror or sex. In May 1999, the US Senate voted unanimously to set up an inquiry to be conducted by the Justice Department and the Federal Trade Commission into links between violent crime and films.

In some respects, it would be very convenient if responsibility for a significant amount of violence could be laid at the door of violent film or television programmes. However, no such easy conclusion is possible. Even researchers who are convinced that a relationship exists, such as Smith and Donnerstein (1998), have conceded that such exposure is only one factor among many others which underlie the commission of violence. Wilson and Herrnstein (1985) stated that the only firm conclusion permitted by the evidence is that some children, with an existing proneness to violence, may be encouraged in the short term to commit further aggressive acts.

Sexual offences
In general terms, learning theorists attribute sexual offences to the formation of attachments to inappropriate stimuli. In the case of sexual offences involving violence, these could include the association of pleasure with pain and degradation, and the sexual attractiveness of children. McGuire *et al.* (1965) claimed that an initial arousing experience could lead to masturbatory fantasies. Laws and Marshall (1990) thought that certain stimuli are more likely to serve as conditioning agents for sexual arousal through their evolutionary importance. The difficulty with the assertion that different forms of sexual deviance can be conditioned is that it does not adequately explain why a particular form of deviance was chosen in the first place. In this area, psychoanalytic theories may provide a better explanation.

Megargee's violent personality theory

Megargee (1966) argued that physical aggression occurs when the push towards violence (usually arising through anger) is stronger than a person's ability to control it. He was particularly concerned to explain why so many apparently mild-mannered people resort to violence. Megargee attributed this to a distinction between 'under-controlled' and 'over-controlled' individuals. The former possess very low inhibitors against aggressive impulses, and therefore frequently resort to acts of violence under perceived provocation. In contrast, over-controlled individuals show a rigid inhibition against the expression of aggression, and violence will only occur if the provocation is intense or has been endured for a very long time. Megargee (1966) therefore predicted that, paradoxically, extremely assaultative offenders would score lower on tests of hostility and aggression than moderately assaultative offenders.

Blackburn (1968) compared the personality profiles of a group of 'extreme' violent offenders with a group of 'moderate' violent offenders. The results were in line with Megargee's theory in that the members of the extreme group were significantly more introverted, conforming, over-controlled and less hostile than the people in the moderate group. However, several more recent studies have shown a somewhat more complex picture. McGurk and McGurk (1979) found that some individuals who had committed serious assaults and homicide were under-controlled, and others were 'more appropriately called controlled than over-controlled' (McGurk and McGurk 1979: 47). Further doubts about the validity of Megargee's claims have come from more recent evidence suggesting that under-controlled and over-controlled types are found in the non-violent population approximately as often as in violent populations (Henderson 1983).

There are certain problems common to this sort of personality assessment. One is the accuracy of the devices ('personality inventories') which are used for the purposes of measurement. Another is the question of whether a personality is an enduring trait or something which is liable to variation. However, perhaps the strongest objection is that the testing has to be conducted outside the social context within which the violence occurred. Nevertheless, the question of control remains important in the study of violence, and will be returned to in Chapter 7.

Subcultural theories

Another source of learning which has been identified by sociologists is the subculture: a group of (usually) young people who come together because of shared values or interests in order to obtain mutual reinforcement. However, because of the group nature of their activities, subcultures are considered in more detail in Chapter 5.

Interactionism and labelling

Interactionism provides another explanation of socialization with the emphasis more on sociological than psychological processes. The term refers to the various means by which people react to their own self image, their perception of how others see them, and the settings in which they interact with others, in an attempt to provide a meaning for their overall situation. This can be simply illustrated by the fact that, to a large extent, many people consider themselves to be attractive or unattractive as a result of responses from, and evaluations by, other people. Mead, the main proponent of the theory (see above), referred to it as 'symbolic interactionism', as an individual's assessment is often built up from recognizable symbols, such as a person's style of clothing.

The idea of 'self' is problematic. It is a process rather than a structure because it is fluid and subject to continuous reassessment. As people are generally aware of the likely effects of what they say and do, their words and deeds are fashioned to take account of the anticipated responses of others.

Lonnie Athens (1997), who interviewed 58 violent offenders in prison, provided an interactionist explanation of violence. Rejecting pathological accounts as ignoring situational factors, he argued that the key elements were the actors' self image and the process by which they came to define themselves. Athens considered that there are four interpretations of situations made by the 'self' that can lead to violence: 'physically defensive', where the victim is perceived as intending to attack; 'frustrative', where the victim resists an order or encourages the offender to carry out an unwanted act; 'malefic', where the victim belittles the actor; and 'frustrative-malefic', which is a combination of the previous two categories.

A consideration of offenders' self images resulted in three categories: 'violent' self images arise where the actors are judged by others and see themselves as having a violent disposition; 'incipient violence' refers to the actors' tendency to make serious threats of violence; and 'non-violent'. The type of self image will directly relate to the definition of a situation as warranting a violent intervention. For example, people with a violent self image could define almost any situation as requiring violence on their part while, at the other end of the scale, offenders with a non-violent self image would only use violence in physically defensive situations.

Using data from the American National Youth Survey, Heimer and Matsueda (1994) also found support for the significance of symbolic interactionism in the creation of the violent individual. Association with delinquent peers, exposure to delinquent attitudes and the appraisal by others as delinquent produced a greater self-reported involvement in delinquency than exposure to social disorganization or poor control.

Labelling

Interactionism considers that the evaluation of oneself is just as important as an evaluation by others. However, the public meaning and interpretation of behaviour – including criminal behaviour – has received more attention from writers than changes to self-evaluation. During the 1950s and 1960s, criminologists began to take greater notice of interactionism in an attempt to show that the official 'labelling' of an offender by a court could transform that person's self-identity from being, perhaps, an occasional rule-breaker into that of a 'real' criminal, who would then assume the role which had been duly allocated. Further encouragement would be given to this process by the negative reactions of society, including the likely inability to find employment.

Edwin Lemert (1967) made a distinction between 'primary deviation' and 'secondary deviation'. An act of primary deviation can occur in a variety of situations and, according to Lemert, the reasons why it occurs are not particularly important and will not result in a fundamental self-reappraisal by the deviant. However, what is important is the response that is made to the primary deviation. If it is labelled as criminal by a person or institution with the authority to make the label stick (such as a court), acts of secondary deviation may occur as a means of dealing with the problems caused by the reaction to the primary deviation. Had the primary deviation been ignored, it might have been merely transitory.

Deviance amplification

A development of the labelling approach can be seen in Leslie Wilkins's (1964) notion of 'deviance amplification'. Wilkins sought to explain how societal reaction can influence the amount of crime that occurs. He described a spiral effect: deviance is reported, stereotyped, and then reacted to. If the reaction is hostile or punitive, the deviants will feel alienated, consider themselves as even more deviant, join with others in a similar position, and commit further acts of deviance. The whole process may repeat itself and deviance amplification will have then occurred. A well-documented example of this in England was the series of confrontations between 'mods' (motor scooter riders) and 'rockers' (motor bike riders) which arose at various seaside resorts in 1964. In his book *Folk Devils and Moral Panics*, Stanley Cohen (1972) explained how initially minor skirmishes between the two groups resulted in greater police numbers and an increased number of arrests, which seemingly justified the enlargement of the police presence. This was in many respects a repetition of an incident in California in 1947, which had given American bikers the label of 'outlaw' (Harris 1985).

Problems

The apparent inevitability of the labelling process has been questioned by several writers. In particular, criticism has been levelled at Lemert's assertion that the reasons behind acts of primary deviation are largely irrelevant. Although undoubtedly true in some cases, it can hardly be of general application. In the case of organized or political crime, it seems highly unlikely. However, situations where an individual seeks out or welcomes a criminal status must remain in the minority. In the longitudinal Cambridge Study in Delinquent Development, West and Farrington (1977) discovered that boys who were apprehended and then convicted of crimes became more delinquent than boys with an equally delinquent background who had managed to avoid apprehension.

If the alleged consequences of the labelling process do in fact occur, there are two clear policy implications: the criminal law should be invoked as little as possible; and, where its use is unavoidable, every effort should be made to prevent offenders – particularly those making their first court appearance – from being so devalued that they feel like 'real criminals'. The first of these could be achieved by minimizing the use of prosecution. Many countries have adopted this policy towards juvenile offenders, choosing to administer a caution on the occasion of their first offences. The creation of special juvenile courts in an effort to create a less formal atmosphere is a clear indication that at least some of the arguments emphasizing the dangers of labelling have made an impact. In England, members of the public are not allowed to attend juvenile court (now youth court) proceedings without good reason, and no information can be published that might identify the juveniles.

Adults do not enjoy the same level of protection. Although larger numbers are cautioned nowadays, this probably has more to do with saving costs than avoiding stigma. A quarter of a century ago the prospects looked different. The Rehabilitation of Offenders Act 1974 was passed to enable job applicants to withhold information about previous convictions for a certain period of time, which depended on the nature of the punishment imposed. However, the Act never applied to certain occupations and its effect has been whittled away, in that an increasing number of people must now disclose their criminal past. The Sexual Offences Act 1997 established a police-run national register of convicted sex offenders. Its contents are made available to 'interested groups', a category which is likely to expand as governments continue to react to newspaper-inspired campaigns for 'greater protection'.

The large rise in the level of recorded crime in most Western societies during the past twenty years has, indeed, sharpened both the tone of tabloid newspaper headlines and the response of politicians. The catchphrase that has emerged is 'name and shame'. The Government is considering removing the anonymity that juvenile offenders have enjoyed for more than 60 years in an attempt to shame them in the eyes of their peers and embarrass their parents into taking better care of them. This would operate alongside a policy of 'zero tolerance' – an expression originating in New York policing and increasingly used in Britain – which would result in minor transgressions being prosecuted, and a reduced likelihood of informal cautioning. There has always been a judicial discretion to waive the anonymity extended to juveniles in courts and, in recent years, this appears to have been exercised more widely. A well-known instance was the 1993 trial of the two young boys for the murder of James Bulger.

The idea that stigmatizing or shaming offenders is necessary to deter them and others probably strikes a chord with the public, although there is no strong evidence to support its efficacy. Indeed, as recently as the early 1990s, the Government appeared to be of the opinion that deterrence is not an effective aim of punishment (Home Office 1990). Local newspapers publish lists of (often unnewsworthy) sentences imposed by the courts, together with the names and addresses of the defendants. Police forces write to men who are suspected of 'kerb-crawling' in the hope that their wives or partners will see the letters. Judges in America order convicted offenders to wear signs around their neck or put notices outside their home proclaiming their guilt. As Pratt (2000) has pointed out, such shaming punishments are a return to the penality of the eighteenth century.

Unfortunately, there can be unintended side-effects to a policy of 'naming and shaming'. The idea of the sex offenders register is that police will know the whereabouts of convicted offenders, keep a watch on their activities and, where appropriate, inform interested groups in the community. However, this process – together with stories in local newspapers – also enables the identity of such individuals to become widely known in the area. This can lead to vigilante attacks involving serious violence and criminal damage. There have been cases of mistaken identity where innocent people have been attacked. Several such incidents occurred during the summer of 2000 following a campaign by the *News of the World* to name convicted paedophiles. Of course, vigilante action is not new, but there is a certain irony where it results directly from measures that have been introduced to reduce crime. The labelling process is alleged to be responsible for further offending, but it is usually envisaged that this will be crime committed by offenders and not against them.

Psychoanalytic theories

Modern psychoanalysis stems from the writings of Sigmund Freud (1856–1939), although certain aspects of his theory have been developed and modified by later writers. Perhaps the central element of Freud's work is the emphasis given to the part played in a person's mental functioning by the unconscious mind. This originates from traumatic incidents in early childhood, only some of which were consciously experienced, and contains both instinctive urges and repressed memories. Hollitscher (1947) neatly likened the unconscious mind to the submerged part of an iceberg.

The Freudian personality

Freud considered that everyone is driven by instincts, such as the desire to eat, to be comfortable, and to obtain sexual pleasure. These derive from the unconscious mind and are a form of psychic energy which psychoanalysts refer to as the id. The most important instincts are those of sex and aggression. As an instinct arises internally, a person cannot escape from it, but it is obvious that the instincts must be appropriately channelled if people are to be able to live together in a society. This function is performed by both the ego and the superego. The purpose of the ego is to restrict the urges of the id by showing what will happen if it is left uncontrolled. For example, a child's id may want to hit a sibling but, if it is punished for so doing, the child will learn through the operation of the ego that it is not worth the trouble. The ego can also serve the id in a positive way: babies quickly learn that they are likely to be fed if they cry. The ego is itself guided by the superego, which reflects the internalization of parental and social standards. It both provides the ego with positive goals and acts as a conscience to send strong feelings of guilt to the ego. Thus, if a child wants to hit a sibling and there is no one else present, a well-developed superego will cause the child to censure itself if it tries to do so.

In summary, there are three basic psychological processes in operation, and the effect they have on each other is very important. The id creates energies which, if not channelled elsewhere or neutralized, will emerge into consciousness or action, possibly in the form of antisocial behaviour. The superego, reflecting parental standards, will direct the powerful energies of the id on to the ego and feelings of guilt will ensue. The ego will then control behaviour in such a way as to avoid the pain caused by the guilt. If the superego is weak and the id is strong, the ego cannot function properly (Redl and Toch 1979). A person may be aware of the consequences of punishment, but the pleasure obtained by the id through committing a criminal offence will overcome any restraint from the ego. This may explain why severe punishments deter most people – who are, in effect, ruled by their ego – from committing crime, but fail to deter other people who are ruled by their id (Kline 1987).

Development of the instincts

Freud identified five stages through which the instincts develop. The first, known as the oral phase, continues for about the first year of a baby's life. The mouth provides the central outlet for the child to obtain pleasure through sucking, convey its feelings by crying, and start to show aggression through biting. The second stage is the anal-sadistic, which lasts from the age of 1 to $3^1/_2$. Strongly aggressive instincts can develop here – small children may attack each other, or animals, without any feelings of remorse. The third is the phallic, which lasts from the age of 3 to $5^1/_2$. The child starts to be interested in its genitals and becomes possessive of its same-sex parent and jealous of siblings. During the fourth stage – the latency period – instinctive urges recede into the background, only to re-emerge in the final stage of puberty. Until Freud's writings, it was widely believed that this was when human sexuality was determined. The final direction of a particular instinct (for example, loving or sadistic) will generally depend on what has happened in the first four stages.

The task of the ego in serving both the id and the superego is not an easy one: it has to ensure that the desires of the id are acceptable to the superego. In terms of child-rearing practices, the instinctual urges of the id have to be directed into socially acceptable outlets. One method is by displacement: for example, breast-feeding can be displaced on to bottle-feeding. Sublimation involves the diversion of the instinct to a new, more acceptable aim: aggression towards siblings could be directed into sports and outdoor pursuits. A reaction formation occurs when the original instinct is inverted into the opposite direction: the drive behind a desire to play with dirt could be used to strengthen the opposing tendency to be clean. For any one of these processes to occur properly, the change should be slow and gentle. Otherwise, an instinct, such as aggression, may be repressed into the unconscious mind, possibly to recur at a time of personal crisis in later life.

Of course, not all such problems result in criminal behaviour. Most people could easily identify individuals who are over-inhibited (because their superego is too censorious): nervous and neurotic, they are highly unlikely to break any rules at all. However, some problems can manifest themselves in antisocial and criminal behaviour, and this can sometimes take the form of violence. Many psychoanalysts believe that the failure to develop a properly formed superego is attributable to unloving or absent parents. In extreme cases, a weak superego can be associated with the self-centred and guiltless individual who is labelled a psychopath (see Chapter 3).

As traditional psychoanalysis places particular importance on the sexual instinct, sexual offences have long been considered as being particularly suited to this sort of explanation. Rapists may regress to the anal-sadistic phase of development at times of stress and displace their hostility on to women. Anal fixation could explain why buggery occurs during some sadistic assaults. Paedophiles, who are often narcissistic, may look for immature sexual partners whom they see as being like they were at that age, and then treat their victims in the way that they themselves wanted to be treated by their mother.

Attachment and loss

In more recent years, many psychoanalysts have started to focus their attentions on the importance of the initial attachment made between a parent and its young child. This has involved moving away from the original position of Freud, who considered psychological problems to be a consequence of internal psychic conflicts rather than the result of traumatic incidents in a person's life. Difficulties arising from the failure of proper attachment bonds to develop were identified by John Bowlby in the 1940s and presented by him in a report to the World Health Organization in 1951. Bowlby had observed the responses of children who had been separated from their mothers, and noticed that they were similar to those observed in adults after the loss of someone close. He concluded from case studies in his own clinic that the consequences of maternal deprivation involving a lengthy period of separation could include delinquency. Bowlby emphasized the crucial importance of mother–child attachment and the trauma resulting from separation.

Bowlby's findings were later subject to severe criticisms, particularly as they were misinterpreted by some as suggesting that proper attachments required almost continual physical proximity between mother and child. Nor did the growing number of middle-class mothers who were employing nannies so they could go out to work take kindly to this analysis. Although, as Rutter (1981) later pointed out, Bowlby had never stated that constant caring by the same person was necessary, there is still a continuing debate as to whether a young child's development can be harmed by its mother going out to work. Belsky (1988) claimed that infants who were cared for by a child-minder for more than 20 hours a week were more disobedient and aggressive between the ages of 3 and 8. More recently, however, Harvey (1999) found that early parental employment had no significant effect on a child's behaviour or self-esteem. Rutter (1981) argued that it is important in this context to make a distinction between *deprivation*, which refers to physical absence, and *privation*, which relates to the lack of some crucial component of attachment, such as love or care.

Bowlby's ideas on attachment and loss have been developed by other writers. A study of monkeys by Harlow and Mears (1979) found that maternal deprivation produced severe behavioural abnormalities in the infants, the extent of which largely depended on their age at the time of separation and its duration. Most of the infants' unusual behaviour could be related to the absence of particular types of experience. Formerly isolated females who were artificially impregnated proved to be wholly inadequate mothers: as they had never experienced any love themselves, they were unable to love their infants. Their behaviour towards their offspring ranged from totally ignoring them to physical abuse and even killing. Harlow and Mears argued that the creation of strong, affectionate bonds is the key to controlling aggression in all primates.

Other writers have claimed that core neurobiological functioning can be affected by separation. Many researchers have found that young primates may refuse to eat, lose weight and even starve themselves to death as a result of separation. Their immune systems may become deficient (Kraemer 1985). This is strikingly similar to Bowlby's original observation of three-month-old babies, separated from their parents and institutionalized, who would often die from infections and, even if they survived, would grow up significantly underweight and sometimes even mentally handicapped. Research has also shown that adults who lost a parent in early childhood, and did not subsequently acquire another supportive relationship, may suffer biological and immunological changes as a result (Breier *et al.* 1988). All of this evidence suggests that attachment is a key component in early life, and a failure to establish or maintain a proper attachment can lead to both psychological and physical problems later which, according to research on monkeys, may include violent behaviour. Learning theorists, however, would argue that attachment is simply an individual trait – an aspect of a person's genetically determined temperament (Kagan 1984).

Problems resulting from poor, or non-existent, early parent–child attachment have been linked to several different forms of violence and abuse. There is now strong evidence that women who have been abused are likely to abuse their own children: in one study the figure was as high as 70 per cent (Egeland *et al.* 1987). Weissberg (1983) considered that impaired attachment of parents to their children is a key element in problems of child abuse and neglect. The parents of an abused child show little identification with the child's needs and feelings. The child itself may well develop a poor sense of self-esteem and become egocentric. Abused children are also more likely to interpret other children's behaviour as being hostile and react aggressively. Main and George (1985) found that abused infants reacted negatively, and sometimes aggressively, to indications of distress from their peers: in contrast, a control group of non-abused children showed concern and sadness.

Another form of link may be created through the dissociation which some psychiatrists consider can occur when an abused or traumatized individual creates a separate being to deal with the effects of some horrendous event, or ward off the threat of its return. It is claimed that this can account for the fact that many victims appear distant and compliant while they are suffering abuse – they have dissociated themselves by splitting their personality and assuming another form. However, this 'other personality' can provide an outlet for the hatred they feel about themselves and their abusers: as Alice Miller (1983) has pointed out, Hitler was a child victim of extreme physical abuse. Alternatively, violence resulting from this anger can be directed at the self. Individuals may become self-mutilators – many such people have been abused in their childhood. Evidence suggests that male and female victims of abuse cope with their anger differently. Brown and Anderson (1991) found that men were far more likely than women to express their anger in the form of aggression towards others: most women directed their anger inwardly, with a significant proportion causing physical harm to themselves.

Conclusion

Each of these explanations of the socialization process has its strengths and weaknesses. Learning theories emphasize the important processes by which certain environmental influences can be translated into violent behaviour, but they depend on the application of a few basic principles to the complex variety of human behaviour (Nietzel 1979). The experiments underlying social learning theory often relate to specific tasks which are unlikely to be replicated outside the laboratory. Differences between individuals and variables such as sex and age are largely overlooked. Although boys are hit more often than girls, both are equally likely to observe inter-parental violence. It seems that something further is required to explain the subsequent greater recourse to physical aggression by males.

Psychoanalytic theory was widely believed to provide an explanation for juvenile delinquency in particular for some 30–40 years after Freud's major writings. One of the reasons why the theory became unfashionable is that it is very difficult to subject to empirical testing. A person, who according to psychoanalytic theory should manifest a particular pattern of behaviour, may act in a completely different way. However, this does not necessarily present a challenge to the theory, as Freudians may claim that a reaction formation occurred (see above). Yet, if this problem is overlooked, psychoanalytic theory can make an important contribution to the debate about sexual offences and hostile (that is, non-instrumental) violence. The increasing concern over family abuse has led to a growing literature about the importance of early attachments and the problems that can result if they are inadequately formed.

Whereas learning and psychoanalytic theories do not really allow for individual development, interactionism accepts that a person's self-perception – and, in an indirect sense, socialization – is liable to change. In the case of violence, this can have a lot to do with portraying an image, but the portrayal can eventually become reality. This may ultimately prove to be more telling than the involvement of the state, as required for 'labelling' or 'deviancy amplification'. As for the current vogue of 'naming and shaming', there is a danger that this will result in violence of another kind.

Social learning and psychoanalytic theories are explanations of socialization which depend on psychological processes. Subcultural and interactionist theories are broadly sociological approaches, and further examples of these are considered in Chapter 7.

Further reading

Freud wrote extensively and has been extensively written about. His essay *Beyond the Pleasure Principle* (Freud 1955) deals with the significance of the instincts of sex and aggression. Bandura has also produced a large number of publications, and his views on the origins of aggressive behaviour can be found in *Aggression: A Social Learning Analysis* (Bandura 1973). The extent and consequences of physical abuse is considered in detail in *Physical Violence in American Families* (Straus and Gelles 1990).

chapter five

Group violence

Crimes committed by groups seem different from acts of solitary law-breaking, particularly where violence is involved. It is not just that several people can usually inflict more harm: there is almost an expectation that a group will be more likely to indulge in violence in the first place. A group can have a more threatening presence than the aggregate of its numbers. A single individual running along a pavement will not arouse much interest: a group of people will. In this chapter, consideration will be given to the significance of 'the group factor' in the occurrence of violent crime. Three different types of 'group' will be discussed: the crowd, the gang and the military. Crowds are groups that come together – usually spontaneously – for a particular purpose which leads to violence. Such groups have often been referred to as 'mobs'. Gangs are violent groups of a more permanent nature, perhaps with a hierarchical structure, which usually concentrate on one particular type of activity. This classification is by no means a rigid one – in practice it may not always be simple to distinguish between a crowd and a gang. The chapter concludes with a look at violence committed in a military setting.

The crowd

In the late nineteenth and early twentieth centuries, the first real efforts were made to provide a detailed analysis of crowd psychology. The fact that the major contribution came from a Frenchman, Gustave Le Bon, is hardly surprising, given the crucial involvement of crowds in the turmoil that his country had experienced since the French Revolution. In his book *The Crowd*, written in 1895, Le Bon (1952) stated that the main characteristic of crowds is the union of individuals in a common feeling which masks differences in personality and intellect. Whatever the cultural background and level of education of the individual members, these will disappear into the collective spirit. Although scathing of the lower classes and considering them more likely to be participants in mob activity, Le Bon did not view the middle or upper classes as better able to resist this pervasive influence. Crowds may often precipitate criminal or violent acts, but this was not an inevitable consequence of their structure and behaviour.

What occurs, according to Le Bon, is a sort of mass hypnosis. The individual will be acting consciously but, as an entity, the crowd will be acting unconsciously under the direction of a leader. This person will be charismatic without necessarily being a great orator, and will make prominent use of suggestion, imagery and allegory. Reason and argument will be avoided: crowds are unable to follow abstract reasoning and are far more likely to respond to clichés and associations. Crowds are highly suggestible and prone to extreme attitudes. They can be carried from one extreme to another with little difficulty – a point well illustrated in Shakespeare's play, *Julius Caesar*. Le Bon considered that crowds are unable to distinguish between reality and what they would like reality to be. He himself provided the example of an actor playing the role of a villain who had to be protected from the audience when leaving the theatre after the play. Another illustration can be seen in the stories disseminated by the Nazis concerning the alleged wrongdoing of the Jews, which inspired mobs to participate in attacks against them.

Le Bon's views were expanded by Gabriel Tarde (1910), who showed how the growth in newspaper reporting had created a new mechanism for opinion formation. A large-scale type of hypnosis had been created: a process formerly confined to street gatherings could now occur in each home in the country, and every individual could thereby become part of a 'crowd'.

The fact that famous leaders such as Hitler and Mussolini are known to have read Le Bon's work with approval suggests that his writings may have had some practical impact. However, it is not so clear that his analysis of crowd psychology is wholly accurate. Le Bon all too readily dismissed the purposive aspects of group activity. A picture emerged of one crowd being pretty much like any other, which history shows to be inaccurate. In particular, Le Bon paid no regard to the genuine grievances arising from social and economic factors which provide a completely rational explanation for crowd behaviour (Rudé 1964). Historians have pointed out that many riots were not mindless, indiscriminate, or copycat incidents, but the purposive actions of impoverished labourers or minority groups seeking to better their lot. This has been illustrated by later writers in analyses ranging from American race riots in the 1960s (Kerner 1968) to the 1984 British miners' strike (Waddington *et al.* 1989). Nor, it seems, does a crowd necessarily need a charismatic leader. In a study of the 1980 St Paul's riot in Bristol, Reicher (1984) found that the crowd was just as likely to be aroused by ordinary individuals.

Another explanation of crowd behaviour is based on the idea of relative deprivation (Gurr 1970). According to this, riots and civil commotion result from feelings of discontent, frustration or despair. A psychological element was thus added to the prevailing sociological account which was largely based on economic factors. Individuals assess their objective circumstances in relation to a particular reference group, and a judgement is made as to the acceptability of the gap between what they want and what they have. Such factors as an increase in relative deprivation between whites and minority ethnic groups or simply between the rich and the poor (both of which have occurred in many societies in recent years) could be particularly significant. One of the weaknesses of the approach, however, is that it undervalues the role played by politicians in both creating the gap and manipulating expectations. Other accounts include the sociobiological explanation that aggressive crowds are expressing universal instincts such as protection of territory (Tiger and Fox 1974), and the psychological explanation that individual behaviour is facilitated by the existence of an audience (Geen and Gange 1977).

Waddington *et al.* (1989) viewed existing explanations of crowd disorder as sharing the common deficiency of being unable to account for the uniqueness of each event. For instance, many people have suffered from disadvantage and deprivation – relative or absolute – but have not taken to the streets with other similarly affected individuals in violent protest. Waddington *et al.* developed a model based on six different levels of analysis, which they considered sufficiently flexible to cover all eventualities. The 'structural' level refers to the distribution of resources and power between groups. This includes ethnic and gender as well as economic factors. The second level is the 'political/ideological': political groups (typically the government) and ideological agencies, such as the mass media, can create a setting which makes conflict more likely. The analysis of Tarde (above) may be relevant here. The 'cultural' level involves taking account of the diverse ways in which groups, subcultures and inhabitants of particular localities expect their rights to be upheld and rules to be enforced. The 'contextual' level relates to the time and set of circumstances in which the disorder takes place.

There may be a history of confrontation involving a certain group which makes trouble more predictable. The spread of information through rumour or media reporting could be important. The 'situational' level refers to the physical setting of the incident. Some locations have a particular significance for the groups involved, rendering them 'sacred turf'. The final level of analysis is the 'interactional'. This considers actions which the participants in the disorder consider break the 'unwritten rules' governing behaviour between the two sides. The mistreatment of a vulnerable person, such as a woman or child, by the police or the rough treatment of a politician by the crowd are given as possible examples. Waddington *et al.* emphasized that these six levels provide an aid to interpretation rather than a predictive theory.

A good example of the more recent approach used to analyse crowd disturbances is the examination in Baldassare (1994) of the 1992 Los Angeles riots which followed the acquittal of four white police officers who had been filmed in the act of beating a black motorist, Rodney King. In addition to this precipitating act, three distinct factors were identified as underlying the event. The conditions of life for impoverished urban blacks had, in relative terms, scarcely improved since the 1965 riots in the same city. Despite the presence of a black mayor, tensions between blacks and whites remained high because of endemic racism, especially in the police department. Finally, a new source of racial tension had developed – between blacks, Hispanics (who were favoured by white employers), and Asian (usually Korean) shopkeepers and small business proprietors (Baldassare 1994).

The approach taken by writers to crowd or group violence over the past hundred years has, therefore, undergone a change. Whereas the earlier explanations of people like Le Bon and Tarde assumed that a crowd was generally a rabble in the thrall of a dynamic leader, more recent accounts have emphasized the purposive actions of groups with genuine grievances which respond collectively to a particular set of circumstances, sometimes with recourse to violence. A common theme appears to be a challenge by the oppressed to the exercise of state authority. However, crowds or groups do not always resort to violence for such high-principled motives. Ordinary people can find themselves swept into collective violent activities against individuals or sections of society for reasons which most of their fellow citizens would strongly disapprove of. Consideration will now be given to three of these situations: racial violence, violence against gays and lesbians, and football violence.

Although any one of these forms of violence could be committed by an individual, it is common to find group involvement. Whether it is simply a case of 'strength in numbers', the desire for a joint celebration (akin to a party) to mark a mutually desired event, or some other reason, the preference for joint action against particular types of target is a striking feature.

Racial violence

Historically, the USA is a country which has been strongly associated with racial violence. An exhaustive record and account of lynching in southern American states is provided in Arthur Raper's classic study *The Tragedy of Lynching*, written in 1933. Raper (1970) found that lynchings were more common in sparse communities with a relatively small black population. Lynchings were also prone to spread contagiously from one community to another. The areas concerned would typically be poor, with a high rate of tenant farmers. Lynching was almost exclusively a racial act: Raper reported that 90 per cent of known cases involved black victims. At least half of the lynchings were carried out with police officers present, and in the vast majority of the remaining cases the police condoned the action. The involvement and connivance of local businessmen and community leaders in lynching was seen as the main reason why the activity was allowed to continue for so long.

Various explanations have been put forward to explain the phenomenon of lynching. The fact that its rate appears to have varied in proportion to the price of cotton has encouraged some writers to suggest that frustrated poor white farmers used blacks as a scapegoat for economic fluctuations (Hovland and Sears 1969). Inadequate legal institutions are also blamed, although this seems to be another way of saying that people in positions of power connived at the practice. Some social psychologists consider that lynch mobs were made up of frustrated poor whites using blacks for their displaced aggression, and others – perhaps mindful of Le Bon and Tarde – have highlighted the 'authoritarian personality' of the mob leader (Allport 1954). The main difficulty with such explanations, however, is that the attacks took place in settings where violence against blacks was the norm, and thus pathological accounts contain little, if any, predictive value. A different type of explanation has been offered by Messerschmidt (1997). He pointed out that, before the abolition of slavery, black lynchings were uncommon in the American South and that the victims of most such incidents were white abolitionists. It was only after emancipation that the new rights given to African-Americans were seen as a challenge to white male supremacy, a fact reinforced by the frequency with which the black victims were castrated.

Although the term has not been so widely used, lynching has occurred in Britain since at least the end of the First World War. Riots against blacks occurred in several British ports, and in 1919 a West Indian merchant seaman drowned in the River Mersey having been chased there by a crowd of over 200 people. Although there were no further known lynchings until a murder in 1959 in Notting Hill, London, it has been estimated that there were 74 occurrences between 1970 and 1990, and a further 18 between

1991 and 1997 (Sherwood 1999). The most notorious was the killing of a black teenager, Stephen Lawrence, where the police's initial reluctance to treat the case seriously resulted in a failure to obtain convictions in the face of apparently strong evidence. An official inquiry held that the Metropolitan Police was riddled with institutionalized racism (Macpherson 1999).

A growing concern is now being shown by government bodies and researchers about all aspects of racial violence, a phenomenon which is still predominantly associated with attacks by groups. One reason for the earlier lack of interest may have been an unwillingness to consider as violent and dangerous the man or woman who lived next door (Sibbitt 1997). A similar point has been made about Germans and the Holocaust (Goldhagen 1996).

In research for the Home Office, Rae Sibbitt (1997) used existing literature and case studies in two London boroughs to consider the factors underlying racial harassment and violence. The perpetrators were found to comprise individuals of both sexes and all ages, often acting in groups of friends or families. They saw their actions as legitimized by the fact that the wider community shares their racist views and, consequently, fails to condemn them. The expression of such opinions by the perpetrators often serves to divert attention from underlying concerns that they feel powerless to deal with. These include insecurity about the future, a lack of identity and health problems, both physical and mental. The climate of opinion is worsened by press reporting and the remarks of politicians on topics such as illegal immigration. The activities of far right political groups have relatively little direct effect.

Sibbitt therefore considered that there are two main elements behind racial harassment and violence: elements promoting stress and delinquency, and elements promoting racial prejudice. Each is a necessary condition, but neither alone is sufficient. To some extent, the same factors underlying crime in general are relevant for racial crime. This overlap was noted in the British Crime Survey (Aye Maung and Mirrlees-Black 1994), although the researchers also found that females, people outside the 16–25 age group, and white people are more likely to be involved in racial violence. Racial prejudice is widespread in society at large, but more common among certain groups for the reasons discussed above.

Sibbitt referred to German research by Willems (1995) into 'violence against aliens'. The study created a typology of offenders based on four groupings. 'Sympathisers' have a fairly normal background, but become involved in violence as a result of peer pressure. 'Criminal adolescents (thugs)' are low achievers from a poor family background, for whom violence is the normal way of dealing with disputes. They have many previous convictions for violent offences, although their early offending will not have involved racial violence. Unemployment is seen as their greatest problem. 'Xenophobics/ethnocentrics' come from very poor backgrounds and blame others for their lack of opportunity. Rather than being politically motivated, their xenophobia arises from feeling unequally treated compared to immigrants and asylum seekers. Finally, 'politically motivated extreme right-wingers' are a well-educated group who indulge in violence as a direct result of their beliefs.

Violence against gays and lesbians

The level of violence against gays and lesbians is very difficult to quantify. In societies where male homosexual practices were illegal, victims were reluctant to report violent incidents to the police. The growth of victim surveys has shed some light on the extent of the problem (see Chapter 2). In 1996, a survey by the London-based campaign group Stonewall found that 18 per cent of male and 10 per cent of female respondents claimed to have been 'hit, punched or kicked', and 10 per cent of male and 4 per cent of female respondents to have been 'beaten up' (Stonewall 1996). A review of Australian research by van Reyk (1996) discovered that between 8 and 30 per cent of gays and lesbians reported having been the victims of physical violence based on their sexuality.

Various explanations of violence against gays and lesbians have been put forward. Herek (1992) argued that such incidents cannot be understood except in the context of 'cultural heterosexism', which creates a climate that stigmatizes homosexuality. However, this does not explain why only a relatively small proportion of prejudiced individuals resort to physical violence. People who are prejudiced against one minority group are often prejudiced against others as well, and the explanations of racial violence considered above may also apply here. Groups of individuals, who believe that their attitudes are widely shared (a view reinforced by the lack of clear societal condemnation), gain mutual support by taking out the collective frustrations that have arisen from daily life (such as powerlessness arising from poverty or unemployment) on people who are 'different' and can therefore be identified as a 'common enemy'.

On the assumption that violence against minority groups is linked to efforts to gain power and control, Ehrlich (1992) suggested that three types of threat can result in a violent response: violations of territory or property; violations of the sacred; and violations of status. 'Territory' suggests that gays and lesbians should not flaunt their sexual orientation in public. 'Sacred' refers to their perceived challenge to traditional Christian values. 'Status' means that they are seeking the same rights as 'normal' people, such as to marry and adopt children.

Harry (1992) pointed out that, for gangs of young males who are seeking a fight, 'gay-bashing' has several advantages. It offers little risk of injury, as the target is unlikely to put up strong resistance. The prospect of arrest is small, because the victim is unlikely either to know the identities of the assailants or report the incident to the police. Finally, the assertion of male sexuality means that the virility of the attackers can be demonstrated to friends, rather than just being boasted about. Indeed, such violence can in general be a means of asserting masculinity (see Chapter 6).

Football violence

Violent incidents have accompanied football (soccer, not rugby) matches since the game has been played (Pearson 1983). However, unlike other areas of public disorder which have experienced a decline over the past 50 years, football violence does appear genuinely to have increased during this period. This has been accompanied by a vast growth in the amount of publicity given to such occurrences, and it is likely that the process of deviance amplification has occurred (see Chapter 4). Dunning et al. (1988) considered football hooliganism to be mainly a working-class phenomenon which reflects a decline in the use of the street for entertainment in the period since the Second World War, and a consequential shift of violent activities to organized sports and leisure activities. This would explain why violence rarely accompanies rugby matches, as in England they have traditionally been a middle-class pursuit. Dunning also thought that key aspects of soccer, such as strength, courage, group loyalty and confrontation, are appealing to the aggressive masculine culture of a patriarchal society, which can be particularly identified among lower working-class males, who have restricted opportunities for excitement in their dull urban lives.

The approach of Dunning and other writers from the so-called 'Leicester School' of research into football hooliganism is influenced by the 'civilizing process' theory of the sociologist Norbert Elias. This claims that there has been a gradual spread of the process throughout the major societies of Western Europe between the eleventh and eighteenth centuries, starting with the ruling groups and then spreading down through the rest of society (Fletcher 1997). Elias's writings originally concentrated on the development of manners, but spread to other socially required behavioural standards including the engagement in, and witnessing of, violence. Increasingly, social space – such as the street – came to be perceived as off-limits for violent activity. This served the purpose of strengthening the power of bourgeois groups (the safety of monetary transactions enhanced the volume of trade) while at the same time making it important for them to avoid public displays of aggression. Individuals may defend themselves if attacked, but should not initiate violence.

Dunning et al. (1988) sought to use this 'civilizing process' theory to explain the fluctuations in football violence during the twentieth century. They claimed that hooliganism before the First World War, which usually comprised attacks on players and officials, arose because the 'civilizing process' had yet to reach the rougher sections of the lower working class.

The reduction in football violence that continued to the 1950s was due to the growing impact of the process. The authors attributed the re-emergence of hooliganism around the mid-1960s to its attraction to young males from sections of society still not subjected to the process. Their aggressive masculinity results from two main factors: the frequent use of violence in their socialization at home, and their need to obtain approval and prestige from their peer group.

In recent years, there has been growing evidence of racial abuse and violence at football matches, and the increase in black players has not been matched by a growth in black supporters. Their absence may also reflect the fact that many working-class people have been 'priced out' of watching the top games. The concerns of commercial sponsorship and the move to all-seater stadia have pushed football violence into the surrounding streets, where the police now have well-organized systems to keep rival supporters apart. This, coupled with a growing interest in international fixtures, has resulted in violence following both club and national teams abroad. Both nationalist and racist sentiments are nowadays expressed by football supporters from all European countries, and the offenders share many of the characteristics that have already been identified in perpetrators of racial violence.

Gang violence

For the purpose of this discussion, a gang is distinguished from a crowd or mob on the basis that it is a group having some degree of permanence and internal cohesion. In practice, the distinction is not always clear-cut, but it is worth considering as several writers have claimed that there are features underlying the formation of gangs which differ from those which precipitate crowd violence.

Spergel's (1995) study of the literature found references to 'organized gangs' in seventeenth-century London. However, the most extensive studies have been found in American research since the early years of the twentieth century. At first, this concentrated on the activities of lower-class juveniles in deprived areas. Perhaps the best-known is Frederick Thrasher's (1927) study of 1313 juvenile gangs in Chicago. He described delinquent gang activity as essentially the over-exuberant action of youth living in deprived areas with few official recreational outlets. Their behaviour could include fighting to protect what they considered to be theirs, such as girls or territory. Thrasher considered that, for many of the boys (the members were nearly all boys), this was merely a stage between a childhood search for excitement and accepting the responsibilities of adulthood. This approach was expanded by Miller (1958), who claimed that juvenile gangs resulted from the need of lower-class boys to escape to the streets from the female-dominated households in which they grew up, and assert their masculinity in a 'one sex peer group' with other like-minded boys. This would involve an exaggeration of perceived masculine values, such as toughness, excitement and autonomy. Miller borrows the terminology of psychoanalytic theory in asserting that the 'obsessive' lower-class concern with masculinity is like a type of compulsive reaction-formation (see Chapter 4).

Cohen (1955) saw many working-class boys as being propelled into a delinquent gang to retrieve their self-esteem which had been destroyed by middle-class institutions, especially the school. He considered that most boys who have been socialized in lower-class families are inadequately prepared to perform successfully in a middle-class school setting. The school rewards and punishes acceptable and unacceptable performance in accordance with middle-class values such as ambition, constructive use of leisure time, cultivation of skills, individual responsibility (as compared with the lower-class notion of shared family obligations) and postponement of immediate gratification for long-term gain. Although all the pupils are measured against this standard, working-class children in particular are inadequately equipped to attain it, as they are less likely to have grown up in an educationally stimulating environment and are more likely to have restricted aspirations.

When such children encounter what Cohen referred to as the 'middle-class measuring rod', they are likely to react in one of three ways. The clever ones may seek the 'college solution'. The less able may become what Cohen called 'stable corner boys', who will try to conform to middle-class values and accept their lower status. Others will seek the 'delinquent solution' and come together to gain support and reinforcement in groups or gangs. New members will be socialized in the ways of the others (see Chapter 4). The gang's activities, described by Cohen as 'non-utilitarian, malicious and negativistic', will reflect their opposition to the despised school values and encompass all types of delinquency, including violence.

In his study of New York gangs, Yablonsky (1962) rejected the idea of the gang as a structured entity, and claimed that many violent delinquent groups were somewhere between a mob and a closely structured gang with deliberate aims. More recent research on American juvenile gangs has identified race as a significant feature, although the predominant background is still that of the urban underclass (Wilson 1987). Adult gangs become somewhat less concerned in defending territory for its own sake, and more interested in drug-dealing.

Another interesting explanation of American juvenile gang activity can be found in *Delinquency and Opportunity* (Cloward and Ohlin 1960). However, as this particularly relates to strain theory, it is discussed in Chapter 7.

These writers are sometimes referred to as 'subcultural theorists' because the gangs they described were created through individuals coming together to form a subculture based on adherence to values in opposition to those of the dominant culture. However, Wolfgang and Ferracuti (1981) argued that subcultural values can lead to violence without the requirement of an organized gang. They considered that such behaviour can arise from what they termed 'the subculture of violence'. Wolfgang and Ferracuti had observed that many of the homicides among lower-class people arose from trivial incidents which were given a disproportionate significance because of mutually held beliefs about how people were supposed to react in certain situations. Cultural norms could require that minor insults, perceived challenges to honour or masculinity, and aspersions cast on race or family members should all be met with a violent response. These views would be reinforced by other members of the group: a failure to respond in an appropriate manner would be ridiculed, whereas a suitably violent reaction would merit respect. Wolfgang and Ferracuti agreed with Sutherland that such beliefs are transferred in the form of ideas concerning what is considered appropriate behaviour (see Chapter 4). It is the ideas themselves that are the immediate cause of the violence, as the reasons they had developed in the first place have probably become lost in the past.

British violent gangs

British writers have discovered little evidence of violent gang activity: the 'West Side Story' scenario of gangs fighting over territory and girls has been far less apparent. One notable exception is James Patrick's (1973) book *A Glasgow Gang Observed*. Patrick found violent activity of a territorial nature conducted by gangs with a recognizable leadership and specific roles for the participants, although with a fluidity of membership more similar to the analysis of Yablonsky than of Thrasher. There was a strong tradition in Glasgow of gangs centred in run-down areas which did not exist anywhere else in Britain and, to that extent, they could be considered unique. Otherwise – with the main exception of 'football hooliganism' – British research on juvenile gangs has shown that considerations such as social class and style have proved far more important than the use of violence either to protect territory or as part of a wider criminal enterprise (P. Cohen 1972).

Female violent gangs

Writing on violent gangs traditionally gave the impression that this was an exclusively male activity, and that women played only the minor supporting role of the tomboy or hanger-on. Yet female gangs have probably always existed, albeit in far smaller numbers (Thrasher managed to identify six), and Anne Campbell (1984) discovered a willingness among American female gangs to use violence for the defence of territory. Campbell considered that many women were attracted to gang membership for the same reasons as the men: the activities seemed more exciting than the alternative of welfare dependency and single-parenthood that would otherwise form their future.

Two basic types of female gang organization have been identified. The more common type, sometimes called an 'auxiliary' gang, is based on an affiliation to a male group. The men make the important decisions and try to control the women. The other type is the truly independent female gang, which is not subordinate to the males and establishes its own rules. Laidler and Hunt (1997) interviewed 65 women from seven San Francisco female gangs. All the women, who were from poor families often with absent parents, claimed that the main benefit from gang membership was the sense of kinship.

The researchers found that patterns of violence varied according to the organization of the gang. Women in the auxiliary gangs were subject to more 'violence-prone situations', largely because of their association with male gangs. The women in the independent gangs would generally only encounter violence in confrontations with members of other female gangs. However, women in both types of gang were far more likely to encounter violence from their boyfriends, who themselves were often gang members.

American violent gangs

Following the strong focus on American gangs in the 1950s and 1960s, academic interest waned for some time, even though the number of gangs began to escalate considerably after that period (Klein 1995). The renewed attention that arose in the 1990s was in the context of alleged 'drug wars' and the belief that gang activity had become significantly more violent. In September 1994, President Clinton declared a 'National Gang Violence Prevention Week' to highlight the increasing concern. In the following year, the Office of Juvenile Justice and Delinquency Protection published some data about juvenile gangs. The fact that only 6 per cent of serious violent crime was committed by juvenile groups put the issue into some perspective. The report also revealed that 92 per cent of group offenders were male and that about half were African-American (Snyder and Sickmund 1995).

Most American law enforcement officials and some researchers (for example, Skolnick *et al.* 1993) assume that violent juvenile gang activity is nowadays inevitably connected to the increasingly profitable illegal drugs trade. This could be seen as an extension of adult activity and thus provide support for Cloward and Ohlin's account of gang formation. However, this is unlikely to provide the whole explanation (Waldorf and Lauderback 1993). It may be that many gangs are formed as protection against the few violent gangs that try to dominate the area. One study found that the more hierarchical the structure of a gang, the less likely it is to be involved in drugs. Even gangs that do operate in the drugs trade do so only sporadically, often combining their illegal activities with lawful employment (Hagedorn

1994). There is widespread agreement that the creation of gangs to protect local territory for its own sake (rather than from the incursions of other gang enterprises) is far less common nowadays, perhaps reflecting the wholesale breakdown of local inner-city communities.

Alternative explanations of juvenile gang formation contain similarities to some of the classic gang theories of the previous generation. The need for status features prominently in the literature, as does the requirement of self-esteem, which played such a central part in Cohen's theory. On the other hand, there is nowadays little support for Cohen's idea that gang members are seeking upward social mobility (Hagedorn 1988). The run-down nature of the neighbourhood and lack of amenities are redolent of Thrasher's account, although some would argue that this could at least in part be the result of gang activity rather than the cause. Poverty inevitably features prominently: the prospect of immediate financial gain is bound to be appealing to youths with little likelihood of obtaining gainful employment in anything other than low-wage service industries. This may explain the disproportionate number of African-Americans and Hispanics in gang activities.

Although gang violence has traditionally been considered a street activity, it has in recent years been growing in schools. Groups of schoolchildren who bully others have probably always existed, but organized gang activity, accompanied (particularly in America) by the use of lethal weapons, has spread to the playground and the classroom. Many American schools experience considerable problems with children carrying knives and guns (Elliott *et al.* 1998). Some have installed metal detectors and others employ security guards. The fact that this phenomenon is not confined to disputes over drugs in run-down inner city schools was illustrated in April 1999, when two boys walked though their school in an affluent suburb of Denver, Colorado, shooting at their fellow pupils and killing several of them (*Newsweek*, 3 May 1999).

War and genocide

The purpose of this section is to consider group violence committed in a military or quasi-military structure where the group claims to act in the pursuit of some ultimate political objective, such as the overthrow or influencing of an existing political authority, or in the defence of the existing authority or predominant culture from a perceived challenge, be it military or otherwise. This definition also encompasses so-called terrorist acts when they are committed for one of these purposes.

In certain respects, the manifestations of genocide and war are similar. In the former, a society moves against a group (usually an ethnic minority) considered to be an internal enemy: in the latter a society attacks a group considered to be an external enemy. Violence is utilized, and death and injury will ensue.

Article 6 of the Charter for the International Military Tribunal at Nuremberg in 1945 specified three types of crime that would fall within its jurisdiction: 'crimes against peace', including the 'planning, preparation, initiation or waging of a war of aggression'; 'war crimes', including murder or ill-treatment of the civilian population (including deportation to slave labour), prisoners of war, the killing of hostages, and the destruction of communities otherwise than for military necessity; and 'crimes against humanity', including murder, enslavement, deportation and other inhumane acts committed against the civilian population, and persecution on political, racial or religious grounds.

Genocide would fall within the second and third of these overlapping categories, but it received its own definition in the UN Convention on Genocide in 1948 as any one of several acts perpetrated with intent to destroy 'a national, ethnical, racial or religious group'. The acts are killing; causing serious bodily or mental harm; deliberately inflicting conditions of life calculated to destroy the group; imposing measures to prevent birth; or forcibly transferring children to another group. Many countries had argued that the definition should include political groups, but this was opposed on the basis that interference by outsiders in a country's internal affairs would thereby be facilitated.

War

Hinde (1991) has argued that a significant difference between a group conflict and a war is that war is an institution. The behaviour of the many groups and subgroups involved – from generals and politicians to doctors and nurses – is determined not only by the interaction between them, but also by their prescribed roles within the institution. According to Hinde, the actions of the soldier in combat are therefore more likely to be governed by a sense of duty than by aggressive tendencies. Karsten (1978) identified several factors behind atrocities in Vietnam, including individual personality traits, ethnocentric views and poor leadership. Support for the institution of war can also depend on cultural factors. Some countries have a long historical record of warfare, whereas others, such as Switzerland, have preferred neutrality.

Archer and Gartner (1984) claimed that countries may come to be characterized by different levels of aggressiveness according to the extent to which they take part in collective violence through war. Such participation can result in at least partial legitimation of violence. Archer and Gartner found that the countries involved in the two world wars were more likely to have experienced a post-war increase in homicide rates than countries which had remained neutral. The same effect – although to a lesser extent – could be observed from smaller wars, such as the Vietnam war. The authors considered that the apparent rewarding of violent activity by victory over opponents can provide a strong message about its instrumental value.

Despite the obvious horrors of warfare, it is arguable that certain benefits may ensue, both within and without the countries directly involved. Throughout history, wars have led to the spread of ideas and the acceleration of social change. The resultant disruption can assist the breaking down of rigid cultures and the dissemination of genes over a wide territory. This may result in a greater understanding – and tolerance – of other societies. Within the participating countries, war can deflect unpopularity from governments (as Margaret Thatcher found during the Falklands war). Even the losers may gain some benefit by receiving wide publicity for their views (Gunn 1993).

Genocide

Given the relatively broad definition of genocide, it is probably the case that it has featured to some extent in most wars, particularly in the past two hundred years. In comparison to war, genocide has attracted more interest from writers trying to account for the capacity of individuals, even when acting under military direction, to indulge in or condone the mass slaughter of their fellow humans, often in the absence of any direct threat from their victims. This may also be attributable to the fact that genocidal events such as the Holocaust and the tribal massacres in Africa involved violence which seems incomprehensible to most people, whereas wars are assumed generally to arise from political or territorial disputes.

Sociobiologists, such as Lorenz (1966), have argued that this sort of mass killing is a consequence of the instinctual aggression that has evolved in humans, and that sudden explosions of wholesale violence can arise from the fact that its use is generally prohibited. Lorenz also claimed that there is a separate instinct to establish a communal defence, which has evolved from our distant ancestors. There are, however, problems with the biological approach. Genocide is a peculiarly human response which can only occur in a social setting. In any case, genocide is comparatively rare in the overall picture of human interaction – which is not what one would expect in an explanation based on natural aggression.

One interesting point raised by Lorenz is that the invention of the weapons of modern warfare has destroyed the fine balance between the human aggressive instinct and the inhibitions against killing members of one's own species. The twentieth century in particular saw a massive increase in types of weaponry able to kill vast numbers of people from a considerable distance, with the added advantage of rendering the process that much more impersonal. The Germans took full advantage of this for the purpose of genocide in the Second World War, although the mass bombing of German cities by the Allies and the use of atomic bombs in Japan – if not genocide – at least demonstrated a willingness to engage in mass slaughter for the purpose of 'good' against 'evil'.

Although it has been customary for writers to offer explanations of particular instances of genocide, it is still possible to identify some general themes running though these accounts. A common argument is that 'outsider' or 'stranger' groups, who have never fully assimilated into a society, are made scapegoats by governments seeking to deal with social problems. Scapegoating requires a distinct, identifiable group within a society. Its members are stereotyped in negative terms and efforts are made to dehumanize them through propaganda. The group must be physically vulnerable: if it is able to defend itself and retaliate, it is less likely to be subjected to this process. For centuries, there was the myth of a Jewish conspiracy to take over the world, which was handed down from generation to generation, and used as justification for pogroms and, ultimately, the Holocaust.

The existence of social problems is often a necessary condition for successful scapegoating. Germany suffered from rampant inflation before the rise of Hitler, with unemployment, homelessness and widespread unease about the future. An authoritarian government is usually found, emphasizing a particular set of values and beliefs, and discouraging cultural pluralism, as this would enable the general population to develop and express views in sympathy with those of minority groups. Leaders will emerge and attract support for a variety of reasons, perhaps including some of those outlined by Le Bon (above). Joining a movement and embracing an ideology can provide powerless individuals with imaginary or real authority which, in a military context, is likely to include the power to inflict violence on others. Many emotions, including fear and anger, which might otherwise have no obvious target, can be channelled against the perceived enemy. When a group of like-minded individuals assembles, the members are able to change their shared problems into the shared solution offered by the governing ideology. The group members come to develop a shared perception of reality.

Genocide can also be explained as having a functional value in particular circumstances. Hunter-gatherer tribes were considered to stand in the way of progress, particularly in South America, and were effectively eliminated in the name of economic advancement. Hitler admitted that he would use anti-Semitism to rally support not only in Germany, but also in other countries where he wished to expand German influence.

Kuper (1981) cited Jean-Paul Sartre as having argued that much genocide could be related to colonial expansion. According to Sartre, it is often necessary for the invaders to slaughter the local civilians both to enforce their authority and to remove a potential source of opposition to the main aim of plundering the country for raw materials. However, genocide can never be total in these situations, as it is still necessary to harness a local workforce to this end. Indeed, the greater the workforce that is necessary, the more protection against genocide is provided. Kuper observed another link between colonization and genocide: that boundaries created by colonizers – particularly in Africa – arbitrarily forced different groups to live together in the same society, with the resultant problems on the granting of independence. The atrocities committed in fighting between the Hutu and Tutsi tribes during the past 30 years provide a good illustration of this.

Psychologists have also sought to explain the origins of genocide and mass killing. From an experimental perspective, Milgram (1974) has shown that people are willing to administer what they believe to be life-threatening electric shocks to someone else, simply because they were instructed to do so by the person in charge of the experiment. Over 60 per cent of the subjects were prepared to administer the highest level of shock, even when they could hear the victim's (apparent) distress and complaints. In a variation of the experiment, Milgram demonstrated how the influence of a group can either help or hinder those in authority. A person was asked to administer the shocks with two other people. Each of the two 'volunteers' (in reality, part of the experiment team) in turn stopped, despite the urgings of the person in authority. Eventually, the subject did so as well. Where group pressure was exerted by the two 'plants', 90 per cent of the subjects desisted. Where there was no such pressure, the figure was only 35 per cent.

Conclusion

Earlier writers, such as Le Bon, portrayed crowd violence as typically the activity of a mindless rabble. Although crowds can be influenced by oratory or charismatic leadership, Le Bon's view has rightly been criticized as ignoring the genuine motivations that underlie most forms of crowd protest. It does not matter whether the grievance is considered justifiable by others (often with the benefit of hindsight): from the point of view of the participants, demanding the right to vote is just as meaningful as attacking a police station which contains a suspected paedophile (see Chapter 4).

Far more has been written about violent gang activity, which was considered one of the major social problems in America during the 1950s, and has remained a feature embedded in the culture of that country. If there is a common theme in these accounts, it is that of alienation: young people in particular feel excluded from what is going on around them. They come together in some sort of grouping to find friendship, support and status. Violence may be involved in the obtaining or maintaining of position; indeed, most of the violence is intra-gang rather than inter-gang. It may also be used in the pursuit of money-making criminal activities.

The waging of war involves a different set of motivational factors than is found in crowd or gang violence. Service in a national army may result from

legal compulsion, a sense of duty or societal pressure. It may not be attributable to a strong belief in a cause. In the 1999 war in Kosovo, there were
reports that large numbers of disillusioned Serbian soldiers deserted. On the
other hand, service in a militia is more likely to arise from a genuine desire
to fight for a cause. However, once the fighting starts, there is little difference
in the extent and nature of atrocities that can result. This was illustrated in
1999 in East Timor, where the militia and the Indonesian army became
indistinguishable in their genocidal activities. There is the same need to
dehumanize the enemy in order to facilitate the mutilation and killing.

Further reading

Street Crime (Maguire 1996) contains a collection of classic essays on gangs.
There is also an interesting chapter by Dick Hobbs (1997) in *The Oxford
Handbook of Criminology*. *The Los Angeles Riots: Lessons for the Urban
Future* (Baldassare 1994) explains the various factors underlying those particular disturbances. *Law, Soldiers, and Combat* (Karsten 1978) includes
accounts of the participants in various group atrocities in Vietnam. Stanley
Milgram's (1974) laboratory experiments with the use of electric shocks
provide a powerful illustration of our willingness to impose pain when
encouraged by others.

Gender and violence

Although the word 'gender' is often used interchangeably with 'sex', it is becoming increasingly common to make a distinction between the biological given of 'sex' (male/female) and the social construction of 'gender' (male role/female role). According to Collier (1998), the sex–gender distinction as currently used in sociology can be traced to the work of Stoller (1968), who argued that a person's gender identity arises from post-natal psychological differences which totally transcend the person's genital, chromosomal or hormonal sex.

In recent years, there has been a growing interest in the significance of gender in the commission of crime and, in particular, in violent crime. This has largely arisen from the concern of feminist writers since the 1970s with female involvement in crime. Previously, the phenomenon of the female offender had usually been explained in terms of sex differences and the question of gender had been ignored (Smart 1976). Likewise, little, if any, attention had been given to the question of why women are so often the victims of male violence. Once the issue of gender in criminality had been raised by feminist criminologists with regard to women as victims, the focus turned increasingly on to men as aggressors, and studies of 'masculinities' began to appear.

In this chapter, consideration will first be focused on women – as offenders and then as victims. It will become apparent that women are frequently the victims of male violence, especially in the home. Attention will then be given to the notion of masculinities, and the idea that men form hierarchies, with both 'inferior' men and women lower down in the order.

Women as offenders

In spite of the problems surrounding the collection of data on crime that were identified in Chapter 2, it is widely accepted that in most societies men commit more criminal offences than women. In 1997, women comprised 17 per cent of known offenders. Eight per cent of women have a conviction by the age of 40, compared with 34 per cent of men. Serious violence against the person accounted for 10 per cent of women's offending (Home Office 1999b). An analysis by Tarling (1993) revealed that the ratio of male to female crime fell from 7.1 : 1 in 1955 to 5.2 : 1 in 1975 and remained fairly steady thereafter. The pattern appears to be similar in other countries. Heidensohn (1991) found that, in 1986, 81 per cent of those convicted of criminal offences in France and 80 per cent in Germany were male. American figures show that, in 1997, women formed 16 per cent of those arrested for crimes of violence (US Department of Justice 1998). Why does this discrepancy occur?

Historically, criminologists were interested neither in this question nor in any kind of female crime. Early explanations were grounded in biology. In *The Female Offender* (1895), Lombroso and Ferrero considered that females represented a lower form of evolution than males. Faced with the problem of explaining why such inferior creatures committed fewer crimes than the allegedly superior men, Lombroso and Ferrero argued that, as a lower life form, women were better equipped to adapt to an unappealing environment, and could always turn to prostitution as an alternative to crime.

This approach was continued in a slightly more sophisticated form by Thomas (1923). He blamed female crime on sexual promiscuity and a loosening of the social constraints on their behaviour. Pollak (1950) thought that the real level of female crime was similar to that of males, but was less likely to be detected because of feminine cunning and deceit, or prosecuted because of male chivalry. He considered that women perfect the art of deceit through having learned to fake an orgasm and conceal their monthly menstruation. The most common forms of female crime would result from a psychological disorder (such as kleptomania – an urge to steal) or involve sexual offences surrounding prostitution. A couple of decades later, Cowie *et al.* (1968) argued that, where girls commit crimes, it is often because they were born with masculine characteristics.

None of these explanations gave any serious consideration to gender issues such as female socialization. Indeed, they would probably have merited little attention had not the mainstream criminological theorists chosen largely to ignore female crime. There were some exceptions. In his theory of differential association (see Chapter 4), Sutherland attributed the relative lack of female criminality to two factors. One was that their socialization into a feminine role and the greater supervision that is consequently exercised over them result in far less chance of their being exposed to 'criminal definitions'. The other was that girls are not taught to be tough, aggressive risk-takers – attributes which Sutherland considered necessary for a successful criminal.

Subcultural and gang theorists did not discuss female criminality in any detail, partly because they considered that women would not encounter the financial strains which confront men. On the other hand, Campbell (1984) discovered that girls are prepared to form delinquent gangs, and in Carlen's (1988) research half of a sample of imprisoned women claimed to have been members of such gangs. Although leading sociologists such as Becker (1963) sought to emphasize the normality of male deviance, no such claims were made for women, who were expected to behave in a feminine way.

Several writers have suggested that control theory may explain the lower level of female criminality. In essence, control theory shifts the focus from asking why people commit crimes to asking why people conform. The Canadian researcher John Hagan and his colleagues found that the strongest forms of control are the informal ones used at home, and that this could explain women's lesser involvement in crime. In a study based on a sample of high school children in Toronto, Hagan et al. (1979) considered whether self-reported delinquency rates could be linked to differences in socialization. They concluded that the home had increasingly become the domain of women, and that girls were therefore more likely to be the objects of informal social controls than boys.

In a later study based on a similar sample, Hagan et al. (1985) discovered that the relationship between a particular sex and common forms of crime weakened with movement down the social scale. Nor does the pressure to conform reduce when women move away from home. Carlen (1988) thought that most working women are subject to dual controls: at work, where the need for employment will discourage temptation to crime; and at home, where they will be under the influence of their parents or partner.

Radical feminist criminologists have concentrated more on the position of women as victims in a patriarchal society and the anti-female bias of the criminal justice system, rather than on theorizing about the causes of women's crime. Several writers, such as Carlen (1985; 1988), have also provided an outlet for the views of convicted female offenders.

Women as victims

Even if there were any real scope for arguing that actual (as opposed to recorded) female crime rates are not greatly different from those of males, it could not seriously be doubted that men are more likely to commit violent crimes than women. Official statistics show that women are convicted of about 11 per cent of violent crimes. Victim and self-report studies indicate a narrower gap: in a survey of 14- and 15-year-olds, Bowling *et al.* (1994) discovered that four times the number of boys admitted to wounding someone with a weapon. A similar situation was found in the British Crime Survey (Mayhew and Elliott 1990).

A review of victim surveys and other literature reveals that women's involvement with violence is far more likely to be as a victim than a perpetrator. When women do hit, it is generally in self-defence. They also use less severe forms of violence, such as slapping or throwing objects (Straus and Gelles 1990).

One of the main achievements of feminist writers has been to highlight the extent of physical and sexual violence committed against women in the home by their partners. Previously, both criminologists and politicians appeared to be preoccupied with more visible forms of violence on the street. In Britain, violence in the home is usually referred to as domestic violence, although some feminists claim that the term 'domestic' is misleading, as it emphasizes the private nature of the abuse rather than the more significant gendered nature. Little of this behaviour had ever been reported in official crime statistics for reasons which are explained in Chapter 2. The development of sensitive victim surveys and left realist research (see Chapter 8) has resulted in a fuller picture of the extent of this abuse, and both psychologists and sociologists have offered explanations of the factors which may underlie such attacks.

Domestic violence

Estimates of the extent of domestic violence vary, depending on the definition used. In a North London survey, Mooney (1993) found that one in three women reported having experienced domestic violence (ranging from mental cruelty to assault, or rape, or both) at some time in their life, and one in ten claimed to have experienced it during the previous 12 months. Using data from the National Survey of Wives in Great Britain, Painter and Farrington (1998) discovered that 28 per cent of wives alleged they had been 'hit' by their husbands. (Other examples of research findings are given in Chapter 8.)

Psychological explanations
Relatively few psychological studies have been conducted in this area, and most of the contributions have come from sociologists. Some of these are

dismissive of psychological input, arguing that such approaches are trying to absolve violent men of blame and shift the focus away from the patriarchal nature of society. Yet, although cultural factors are undoubtedly very important in explaining domestic violence, reliance on patriarchy as the sole explanation of this type of abuse would considerably over-predict its occurrence.

One of the strongest findings to emerge from both controlled studies and clinical surveys is that many abusers have either experienced violence in childhood or witnessed violence between their parents. This supports the view that violent behaviour patterns are passed on through social learning mechanisms (see Chapter 4). Violent men are also likely to experience problems with alcohol and have a criminal record. Some may have learned a 'traditional' attitude of the subservient role of women from their fathers. There is evidence that abusers suffer from low self-esteem, perhaps as a result of having been abused as a child (Johnston 1988).

Some writers have even suggested that female victims of physical abuse from their husband or partner may themselves have been abused in childhood. The connection, if any, is not completely clear, but it has been argued that such women may have carried an expectancy of a violent and dependent relationship into adulthood, with their compliant response only reinforcing the abuser's physical aggression (Walker 1988). It has also been claimed that some abused women may look for relationships similar to those of their mothers (Hanks and Rosenbaum 1977). However, most feminists would reject these arguments and ask why there are not large numbers of cases where women abused in childhood assault their male partners. This illustrates the difficulties in seeking to rely on one 'cause' when explaining violence.

Sociological explanations

The key term in sociologists' explanations of domestic violence is patriarchy. Feminists would describe most societies (and certainly all 'Western' ones) as patriarchal, in that they are designed to create and maintain the power of men over women. In the traditional perspective, societies are based around the family. This is considered an essential (and non-problematic) institution for the smooth operation of everyday life. It is viewed as a functional unit, where the husband and wife, although having different roles, are broadly equal in status and have the joint responsibility of bringing up their children. Any violence would be far more likely to occur in poor or 'problem' families, and either the husband or wife could be responsible. If the violence came to be a particular problem, the parties could separate.

Feminists have pointed out that this view of family life simply does not accord with reality. For a start, all the evidence shows that the vast majority of violent acts are committed by men against their female partners, as opposed to vice versa. This immediately places a question mark over the idea of equality. Closer inspection reveals that the traditional perspective breaks down in most other respects as well. Women in relationships are generally dependent on men for their financial support. This provides a major explanation as to why they do not readily leave their violent partners. In addition, they would usually want to (or have to) take the children with them, and there may be nowhere to go. Some women may believe the derogatory remarks that their partner makes about them. Others may feel that they will 'give him one more chance' – that they can do something to make him stop hitting them.

Nor is domestic violence confined to poor or lower-class households: in the research by Painter and Farrington (1998), mentioned above, about 16 per cent of middle- and upper middle-class wives claimed to have been hit by their husbands.

Information provided by battered women suggests that abuse generally occurs in the home between 10 p.m. and 2 a.m. at weekends, and often in the presence of children or relatives (Dobash and Dobash 1984). Violence is most likely to take place in homes where the traditional male–female role division is particularly rigid. Most such events begin with arguments based on four general themes: men's jealousy and possessiveness; disagreements about domestic work and resources; men thinking they have the right to punish 'their' women for perceived wrongdoing; and the importance to men of retaining or exercising their power and authority. Men usually consider that their partners were responsible for the arguments and the resulting violence (Dobash and Dobash 1998). It also appears that the majority of battered women have been raped by their husbands or partners (Walker 1988).

Domestic and other forms of abuse have a particularly damaging effect on women (see Chapter 8). One of the consequences is that they themselves may be propelled into violence and other forms of crime. Research on women in prison shows that up to three-quarters of them have been abused by their husband or partner.

Sexual violence

It is now widely accepted that official crime statistics considerably under-record the amount of sexual violence that occurs (see Chapter 2). The 1988 British Crime Survey estimated that the police recorded less than one-fifth of indecent assaults and rapes (Mayhew *et al.* 1989). Victim surveys will probably uncover more incidents, but they are unlikely to result in anything approaching complete disclosure unless conducted with extreme sensitivity. These surveys show considerable differences in the percentage of women claiming to have been the victims of rape or attempted rape. In America, findings range from 9 per cent (Kilpatrick *et al.* 1985) to 44 per cent (Russell 1984). Such discrepancies may in part arise from the definitions adopted by researchers (particularly with regard to attempted rape) and the way in which the respondents interpret them.

It was pointed out in Chapter 1 that in some countries (including Britain) non-consensual male buggery has now been legally defined as rape. There is relatively little information available on this – men would find it as least as embarrassing as women to report to the authorities – but it appears to be far less common than male–female attacks. Male rape probably occurs more often in institutions, such as prisons, where heterosexual intercourse is unavailable.

Self-report studies also show a higher level of victimization than revealed in official statistics. A sample of imprisoned rapists and child molesters admitted to between two and five times more crimes than those for which they had been convicted (Groth *et al.* 1982). In another study, 8 per cent of male students said they had committed rape or attempted rape (Koss *et al.* 1987), but the methodology has been criticized (Sommers 1994) and the whole question of 'date rape' on American college campuses has proved to be controversial (Muehlenhard and Hollabaugh 1988).

Early research suggested that a significant number of rapes were committed by two or more assailants, but more recent evidence indicates that this is now less common. In a study of all reported rapes in six English counties between 1972 and 1976, Wright and West (1981) found that only 13 per cent involved two or more attackers. Where multiple offenders were implicated, about two-thirds of them were under 21; they had fewer previous convictions for sexual offences; and they showed less psychological disturbance than solitary rapists. A more recent study of rape convictions in England discovered even more solitary rapists, but fewer offenders and victims under 21 (Lloyd and Walmsley 1989). Rapes are rarely accompanied by serious physical injury – only 6 per cent of the cases in Wright and West's research – but severe psychological consequences may result. Kilpatrick *et al.* (1985) found that 19 per cent of rape victims reported attempting suicide, compared with just 2 per cent of non-victimized women.

Psychological explanations
A major issue emerging from research into rape is whether the crime is based on a desire for forcible sex, or is essentially motivated by the need for control and power. Groth (1979) classified rapes as either 'anger rapes', which are an expression of hatred and contempt for women, or 'power rapes', where the offender is seeking either to express his virility or overcome doubts about his masculinity.

Anger rapists do not usually confine their violence to sexual assault, and beat their victims severely, often causing serious injuries. The offender, who is usually aware that he is attacking through anger, wishes to displace his feelings on to anyone who is available. He combines the sexual assault with his physical attack because he believes this will be particularly hurtful to his victim. To illustrate their argument that such an attack is not primarily a means of fulfilling sexual desire, Groth and Burgess (1977) pointed out that

75 per cent of an imprisoned sample related sexual failure during rape. A strong relationship between rape and anger was also found in a study of adolescent rapists by van Ness (1984), in which 86 per cent of the boys reported having an argument with someone between two and six hours before the offence. As extreme anger heightens autonomic arousal, it is likely to interfere with sexual arousal. This could explain the finding of Groth and Burgess.

Such violent rapes can also occur between spouses or partners. Finkelhor and Yllö (1985) discovered that, where violent rape occurs between spouses, it is because the husband wants to dominate, punish and humiliate his wife, rather than as a result of any sexual difficulties within the marriage. Groth (1979) estimated that about 40 per cent of his sample were anger rapists.

Power rapes, on the other hand, do not involve any more force than is necessary to carry out the offence. The research of Finkelhor and Yllö (1985) showed that these were generally committed by educated middle-class men, whose problems with their wives centred around sexual dysfunction. A power rape would be designed to demonstrate to both the man himself and his wife that he was in control. Outside the context of a relationship, power rapes may be committed on strangers to establish (or reinforce) the man's sense of dominance.

This analysis has been criticized. Felson (1993) thought that most rapists have a strong desire for sexual intercourse and consider themselves to be sexually deprived. Most feminist writers deny that rape is a result of individual pathology, and argue that it is an inevitable consequence of the power differentials between men and women that are institutionalized in most societies. On the other hand, even people who consider that psychological explanations downplay the significance of the social context of sexual violence between partners might be prepared to accept that they provide a plausible explanation of 'blitz rapes' on strangers (Levi 1997).

Anthropologists have discovered that rape is not an inevitable feature of organized society. Sanday (1981) considered information on 156 tribal groups studied by anthropologists and divided them into rape-free societies, rape-prone societies, and those for which there was insufficient information. The 47 per cent classified as rape-free societies were characterized by a high degree of sexual equality and low levels of violence. In the 18 per cent which were rape-prone societies, women had little status or power, male toughness was encouraged and physical violence tolerated.

Research suggests that rapists have similar family backgrounds to other aggressive offenders, with parental cruelty a common feature. Christie *et al.* (1979) discovered that half of his sample of rapists had previous convictions for non-sexual assault, and that many of these were serious enough to attract long prison sentences. There is evidence of sexual abuse, although with less frequency than for paedophiles (Carter *et al.* 1987).

The fact that rapists often claim that they were intoxicated at the time of their attack is usually dismissed as an attempt to deny culpability for the crime. Yet there is some research indicating high levels of drinking prior to the rape. Rada (1978) found that half the rapists he questioned had been drinking at the time of the attack and that a third had an alcohol problem. Amir (1971) reported that both victim and offender had been drinking in over 60 per cent of the cases he studied. Koss and Gaines (1993) claimed that, in their research, alcohol was a strong predictor of sexual aggression. An intoxicated person can also misread cues from another individual, which itself can result in violence (see Chapter 3). Lipton *et al.* (1987) discovered that rapists were less adept than other offenders in detecting cues of affection in simulations of a first date.

Gove and Wilmoth (1990: 286) have argued that many rapists (and other offenders) experience an 'intense neurological high' which, together with a need for dominance and control, reinforces the risky and sometimes difficult nature of the crime.

The question of whether rapists are encouraged to commit their crimes by exposure to pornography has been increasingly discussed in recent years, especially with the growing availability of 'hard-core' sexual images on the Internet. The popular press encourages the view that such a connection exists, and some feminist writers assume a relationship from their view that pornography dehumanizes women (Brownmiller 1975).

However, the evidence is far from conclusive. Two national commissions in America reached opposite conclusions. Although the liberalization of the pornography laws in Denmark was not accompanied by any increase in recorded sexual offences, Court (1984) suggested that the greater availability of aggressive pornography since the 1970s renders this finding of little significance. Sex offenders are known to make extensive use of pornography, but non-offenders do as well. Carter *et al.* (1987) found that child sexual abusers were more likely than rapists to have had recourse to pornography, both before and during their offences. On the other hand, Quinsey (1984) discovered that sex offenders had received less exposure to pornography than non-offenders during their adolescence.

Another important factor is that rapists are particularly likely to accept 'rape myths'. Examples of these are that the women were 'asking for it'; that all women want to be raped; that rape only occurs between strangers; and that no one can be made to have intercourse against their will (Lonsway and Fitzgerald 1994). Perse (1994) claimed that, although there was a link between sexist behaviour and the acceptance of such views among people who used pornography for sexual *enhancement*, no such connection existed for people who used pornography for sexual *release*.

Efforts have been made to ascertain whether rapists are distinguishable on the basis of personal, social or sexual characteristics. Lack of empathy with the victim appears to be particularly common. In a study by Rice *et al.* (1994), 14 non-rapists, on being presented with an account of a rape where the victim was suffering, showed significantly more empathy for the victim than 14 rapists.

Sociological explanations
The rise of feminist criminology in the 1970s not only underlined the neglect of women's criminality by male criminologists (until then nearly all criminologists were male); the growing interest in women as victims emphasized the 'maleness' of much crime. The early focus of interest was on rape, and several writers have claimed that its frequency belies any notion of rape as being an activity committed only by abnormal males (see, for example, Russell 1982). It would be difficult, for example, to attribute the widespread use of rape in war to a small number of disturbed individuals. Instead, rape is viewed as learned behaviour in a patriarchal society. The idea of patriarchy became a major theme in women's writings: sexual harassment (MacKinnon 1979) and the effects of pornography (Russell 1993) are two of the other areas that have received detailed attention in the growing awareness of men's violence against women.

Another achievement of feminists has been to highlight the level of rape that occurs within marriage. As common law had traditionally considered the wife to be, in effect, the property of her husband, such conduct had not amounted to a crime. However, in many jurisdictions marital rape is now an offence (see Chapter 1). Painter and Farrington (1998) discovered that 13 per cent of wives claimed to have been coerced into having sexual intercourse with their husband against their will.

Contrary to widely held opinion, rapists are not necessarily strangers. Home Office research has shown that almost 40 per cent of rapes were committed by men who were described by their victims as 'intimate friends' (Barclay 1993). Out of 100 women who replied to a questionnaire, 20 had been raped by men with whom they had previously had consensual sexual intercourse; 46 had been raped by acquaintances; and 20 had been raped by men whom they had met within the previous 24 hours (Lees 1996).

Not all sociologists agree with the common view that rape is fundamentally a crime of violence. Researchers in Switzerland were able to compare the views of a small number of undetected rapists with those of an imprisoned sample (Godenzi 1994). The undetected group generally attributed their actions to sexual motives. In contrast, most of the convicted rapists said that their actions were an expression of violence. Godenzi thought that this was because the imprisoned men did not want to be thought of as sex offenders, or people who needed to resort to violence in order to have intercourse.

A distinction cannot always be made between physical and sexual abuse. Men's violence towards women can be seen as a form of control (Dobash and Dobash 1979). It results from the exercise of proprietorial 'rights' to both domestic and sexual services. Scully (1990), who spent many hours talking to convicted American rapists, concluded that they considered rape to be a low-risk, high-reward crime. In general, the rapists had been driven by a hatred of women, which was fostered by cultural values. Lees (1996) has suggested that rape may be used to increase a sense of 'manhood', which is under challenge from rising male unemployment and the greater number of women entering the workforce. Rape committed in war or by gangs may intensify feelings of solidarity.

More extreme statements of the inevitable consequences of patriarchy may not have helped the feminists' case. Some writers, such as Andrea Dworkin (1987), have argued that female subordination is an unavoidable result of heterosexual relationships. Brownmiller (1975: 15) considered that rape is the basis of a patriarchal society, claiming that it 'is nothing more or less than a conscious process by which *all* men keep *all* women in a state of fear' (emphasis in original). In some of the work, patriarchy is largely viewed as a single entity. Moreover, the idea of all men oppressing all women ignores differences between individuals, factors such as race or class, and social relationships in general (Messerschmidt 1993; Jefferson 1996). There is little explanation of the rape-free societies described by Sanday (see above). Other feminist writers (such as Tong 1989) have rejected this view of women as inevitable victims who are powerless to respond to the behaviour of men.

Men as attackers: masculinities and crime

Much of the main work on what has come to be termed 'masculinities' has so far come from men. In *Gender and Power*, Connell (1987) argued that societies contain a range of masculinities based on dominance. There is a hegemonic masculinity, reflecting a socially approved standard against which alternative, subordinated ('inferior') masculinities are measured. The use of the term 'hegemony' is taken from the writings of Gramsci (1971) and refers to the assumption of power within a society without the use of force. As this masculinity is inevitably heterosexual, the masculinities of gays provide a good illustration of the subordinated forms which constantly come up against this prevailing benchmark. Connell considered that there are three particular advantages in adopting a sex-role approach in the study of gender differences. It replaces the traditional biological explanation with one based on learned expectations. A way is also provided to integrate the effects of social structures into an understanding of personality. Finally, role theory offers a means of change: if people have suffered through the impact of socialization, the process can – at least, in principle – be changed for the better.

A more specific application and development of this approach to criminal behaviour can be found in Messerschmidt's book *Masculinities and Crime*

(1993). Messerschmidt was critical of some radical feminist writers for their essentialism – the assertion that all men are violent and all women are victims. He attempted to construct a sociology of masculinity which is able to explain crime and delinquency. Using Connell's analysis of hegemonic and subordinated masculinities, Messerschmidt argued that there are three distinct social elements underlying gender relations: the gender division of labour; the gender relations of power; and sexuality. These elements, considered together at any particular time, show the conditions within which gender identities are created.

Messerschmidt (1993: 82) defined hegemonic masculinity as 'emphasiz[ing] . . . authority, control, competitive individualism, independence, aggressiveness, and the capacity for violence'. Men use resources available to them to assert their gender – to show they are 'manly'. Subordinated masculinities are discredited or oppressed. If other masculine outlets are unavailable, crime may be an appropriate means of 'doing gender'. This is especially likely where circumstances demand an extra show of masculinity. Gender thus becomes a 'situated accomplishment', a status that is achieved as a result of others' attitudes and expectations, together with the subject's own actions.

Messerschmidt considered that different masculinities can result in different patterns of crime. The variation in men's positions in the hierarchies of race, class and gender will determine the means used to accomplish masculinity. White middle-class boys usually conform at school, which accommodates the hegemonic masculinity, but outside school may take part in different masculinities which, if they involve crime, are likely to be non-violent. White working-class boys will participate in opposing masculinities, both in and out of school. Members of poor and minority ethnic groups, who can see no connection between school and obtaining a job, seek different ways of accomplishing gender. In their case, 'doing masculinity necessitates extra effort' because they have fewer resources, and they are therefore more likely to create 'a physically violent opposition masculinity'. All of this can be contrasted with a sex-role explanation of crime, which maintains that boys behave in this manner because 'that's the way they are'.

To illustrate his theory, Messerschmidt considered a range of crimes. One of these was a notorious attack in New York's Central Park, where four teenage African-American youths violently and repeatedly beat and raped a female jogger, who nearly died as a result of her injuries. What appeared particularly unusual about the attack was the participants' excessive show of jubilation throughout the incident – so-called 'wilding' behaviour involving jumping around, laughing and throwing the victim's clothes in the air. Messerschmidt argued that the horrific behaviour was one resource that the group had at its disposal to 'do masculinity' in the context of both racial and social disadvantage. The youths had no investment in society's traditional gender divisions of power and labour, so they acted out their own version of 'male conquest' in which each member of the gang could vie with the others for supremacy.

In *Crime as Structured Action* (1997), Messerschmidt incorporated considerations of race and class into his discussion of gender. None of these three elements should be viewed in absolute terms – the significance of each will vary according to the context of the situation. Messerschmidt (1997: 5) asserted the interdependence of structure and action within society: 'structure is realized only through social action and social action requires structure as its condition'. He argued that less common forms of research, such as the study of ethnographies, life histories, and historical documents, are particularly useful in understanding the interplay of gender, race and class in a 'structured action' theory of criminal behaviour.

One of the ways Messerschmidt illustrated this was by looking at violent female gangs. Most writers have traditionally considered the violent gang to be an almost exclusively male preserve (see Chapter 5). Messerschmidt, however, claimed that some young, poor women – particularly from ethnic minorities – use the gang to challenge conventional notions of femininity and create their own versions in ways peculiar to their race and social status. Although men and women are likely to commit 'gender-appropriate' crimes, there may be an overlap in the types of offence involved. In terms of Messerschmidt's structured action analysis, the social structure of the gang is constituted by social action which itself furnishes the resources for 'doing' race, class and femininity in special ways.

Bourgois (1996) spent almost five years studying a group of Puerto Rican crack dealers in New York. The parents and grandparents of these young men had wielded traditional patriarchal power over their families in the rural settings of their homeland. Having been attracted to America by the prospect of plentiful (if low-paid) employment, they had arrived just in time to find the work disappear – ironically as a result in part of the transfer of production to cheap labour economies similar to their own. Although their wives and daughters had been prepared to adapt to the new circumstances by taking the more readily available employment in the service and retail sectors, this was considered 'women's work' by the men and their sons. Unable to support economically or exercise control over their women and children, who had gained their own measure of independence, a growing number of the men reacted to this crisis of masculinity by taking refuge in a drug economy whose subcultural norms include gang rape, sexual conquest and the abandonment of their families. According to Bourgois, such actions enable the men – mindful of the former power of their fathers and grandfathers – to attain a level of masculine dignity.

There is an increasing amount of literature suggesting that a consideration of competing masculinities can provide a better explanation of violence than the more common accounts, including those based purely on the sex of the offender. Kersten (1996) studied the frequency and nature of sexual assault in Australia, Germany and Japan. Both official and self-report data show Australia as having a far higher level of such incidents than the other two countries: by a factor of more than 20 over Japan, and three times the number recorded in Germany. Sexual assaults are rapidly increasing in Australia, are growing since unification in Germany, but are declining in Japan. It is unlikely that these disparities have been greatly influenced by differences in the levels of reporting, although it seems that sexual offences have a higher media profile and are generally more visible in Australia.

Kersten considered the common explanations for the relatively low crime rate in Japan to be inadequate. Rigid control of crime is not the answer: although the Japanese police have greater powers than their Australian or German counterparts, formal crime control is less efficient than in those countries. The existence of the much vaunted 'shaming' culture (Braithwaite 1989) has been challenged by some writers (for example, Buruma 1994). Japan has a lower level of job equality and a higher level of pornography readership than the other two countries. Japanese men have frequent recourse to prostitution.

Messerschmidt (1993) referred to public displays of toughness as a particular form of masculinity associated with violence. According to Kersten, such activities in Japan would only be performed by members of the underworld: street fights among other men are very rare. The expression of caring values and displays of emotion among groups of men are routine. 'Real manhood' is also expressed in devotion to group membership and, in particular, the workplace, which remains largely male-controlled and perhaps offers less of a challenge to masculinity. At the other extreme, Kersten viewed the Australian hegemonic masculinity as the celebration of physical prowess which can both perpetrate sexual assaults on women (and other 'inferior' individuals) and provide protection against such assaults by others, perhaps to compensate for the decline in other traditional forms of showing masculinity, such as manual farm labour.

Masculinities and crime: problems

Several difficulties have been identified in the analysis of masculinities and crime as developed by Connell and Messerschmidt. Their accounts arguably lack a subjective or motivational element. In his enthusiasm to highlight the important role of gender, Messerschmidt has failed to consider fully why some men assert their masculinity in the form of violent criminal behaviour, whereas others choose different means of offending or even non-criminal activities such as sport (Jefferson 1994). The assertion that there is a variety of possible masculinities that can be adopted does not completely deal with this problem. Although it is now clear that the victims of male crimes are female to a far greater extent than was once thought, it is still the case that the majority of men do not physically or sexually abuse women. As it stands, an explanation based on masculinity is open to the same charge as more traditional criminological writing: that it over-predicts the amount of crime that is committed.

Another problem is that hegemonic masculinity is portrayed as both the underlying cause of crime as well as something which is 'accomplished' as a result of it. Walklate (1995: 181) has highlighted the danger of tautology: 'the maleness of crime . . . becomes the source of the explanation'.

Hearn (1996) argued that there has been a failure throughout this debate to explain adequately what is meant by the term 'masculinity'. It is an imprecise notion which is used in different ways depending on the context. Sometimes it is used to describe a general form of culture (an ideal to which all 'real' men should aspire), but on other occasions it is portrayed as something that can vary both within and between cultures. Furthermore, it is unclear at what point of a male's life masculinity can be related to crime. Is it at birth (a biological given) or at some later point? This question is relevant to the widely held belief (supported by official statistics) that men eventually 'grow out of' crime. On this basis, the meanings of masculinity can vary throughout a male's life. This has hitherto remained a largely unexplained area, as the masculinities and crime debate has concentrated on the dangerous aspects of young men's behaviour.

Collier (1998) considered that the sex–gender distinction and the notion of hegemonic masculinity are both problematic. The latter is trying to answer the question of how one can recognize both a culturally dominant form of masculinity (hegemonic) and a range of diverse masculinities (subordinated). Connell's own conception was that hegemonic masculinity is always contested and never finally resolved. However, subsequent writings have generally associated hegemonic masculinity with negative characteristics such as lack of care, lack of emotion, and violence. This seems particularly ethnocentric: anthropological and cross-cultural studies have shown that the concept of masculinity is either unknown in other societies or is associated with positive qualities such as nurture and concern. The assumption that 'real' men are oppressive takes no account of what determines whether a particular attribute is 'masculine' or 'feminine' in any particular setting. Moreover, from a woman's point of view, there may even be ambivalence as to the characteristics she wants to see in a man. As Walklate (1995: 181) put it, 'do women really want their men to be "wimps"'?

The sex–gender (or body–mind) distinction is also seen by Collier as invalid. For him, it is misleading to speak of the 'body' in the traditional biological sense. Collier preferred the notion of the 'sexed body': for instance, a male 'body' may have incorporated characteristics which, under hegemonic masculinity, would be considered as 'female'. The need to make assumptions as to what constitutes any particular form of masculinity would disappear, and a subjective approach would allow for the study of individual differences without the need for classification. Gender would now be 'performative' – a series of subjectivities repeated over a period of time.

Conclusion

The fact that female victims of violence usually suffer at the hands of males, rather than vice versa, cannot readily be explained on the grounds of physical constitution. Although it is true that women are generally smaller than men, they still have the capacity – especially with the use of weapons – to inflict considerable harm. There is no valid evidence of innate female docility. If it is accepted that women are usually assigned an inferior status to men, it becomes more apparent that society provides men with structural approval (formerly explicit, but now implicit) to assert themselves physically at women's expense. No such approval is given to women, who have traditionally been socialized into a passive role. In addition, the fact that women are more likely to suffer in a practical sense from the breakdown of a relationship provides a disincentive to their acting aggressively towards their male partners.

Writers such as Messerschmidt and Connell have gone further and argued that, among men, there are 'subordinated masculinities', typically delineated on the basis of ethnicity or sexual orientation, which are also likely to be the targets of violence and other expressions of the exercise of 'hegemonic' power on the part of the 'dominant' masculinity.

However, although analyses based on either feminist or masculinities theories have provided important insights into the study of violence, they are open to the objection that they are essentialist. Masculinities theories are perhaps better equipped to withstand this, although even they do not explain adequately why only some dominant males resort to violence. Other cultural factors must, therefore, be considered. These could include historical or religious influences. It is suggested elsewhere in this book that early childhood experiences may be significant. In the next chapter, the relevance to violence of traditional sociological notions of poverty, strain and power will be assessed.

Further reading

The shortcomings in the traditional explanations of women's crime are discussed in *Women, Crime and Criminology* (Smart 1976). Domestic violence is well covered by Dobash and Dobash in *Violence against Wives* (1979) and *Women, Violence and Social Change* (1992). Sue Lees considers sexual violence in *Carnal Knowledge: Rape on Trial* (1996) and *Ruling Passions: Sexual Violence, Reputation and the Law* (1997).

Anne Campbell has studied violence committed by women in groups (1984). Connell's *Gender and Power* (1997) and the work of Messerschmidt (1993; 1997) provide an extensive discussion of masculinities and crime. This topic also forms the content of a special issue of the *British Journal of Criminology*, vol. 36, no. 3 (1996). An interesting collection of essays on the issues discussed in this chapter is contained in *Just Boys Doing Business? Men, Masculinities and Crime* (Newburn and Stanko 1994).

chapter seven

Sociological theories: poverty, strain and power

Most of the crimes recorded in official statistics were committed by people who could not be described as rich or powerful. This does not mean that wealthier individuals do not break the law; it is just that the criminal justice process in most countries has been prone to downplay or ignore their offences. Moreover, domestic violence, which involves people from all social backgrounds, has often remained behind closed doors or been ignored by the authorities.

Nevertheless, it is not surprising that a belief has developed that the consequences of poverty can be related to violent offending. The majority of recorded crimes involve the acquisition of other people's property by (relatively) impoverished individuals. Yet even these offences can involve violence. It can be used for instrumental purposes such as a means of acquiring property, as in robbery, or as a way of obtaining or maintaining status in an increasingly competitive and hierarchical world. The poor may also be prone to non-instrumental or hostile aggression on account of the frustration that results from their powerless or degraded position. In this chapter, consideration will be given to arguments that these sort of factors can be relevant to the commission of violence.

Poverty and violence

The link between crime and poverty has been explored at least since the publication of the first national crime statistics in France in the early nineteenth century. The researchers Guerry and Quetelet each tried to show that such a relationship existed. They both found that the wealthier areas of France had more property crime, but less violent crime. Quetelet also highlighted a greater inequality between rich and poor in the wealthiest districts, and suggested that this might cause particular resentment among the poor. However, these findings pointed to a possible link with acquisitive rather than violent offending (Beirne 1993).

By the middle of the nineteenth century, several writers were beginning to make a connection between crime and the appalling conditions found in many major cities, as large numbers of people left the countryside in search of work. In 1840, Frégier, a former policeman in Paris who was already well acquainted with the slums in the city, published a study of the situation he found in such areas. He estimated that robbery was the only means of support for at least 30,000 Parisians (Beirne 1993).

In *The Conditions of the Working Class in England*, written in 1845, Friedrich Engels (1993) used pamphlets, newspapers and individual accounts to supplement his own observations of working-class life in the major cities, particularly Manchester. He concluded that the deprivation and crime could be blamed on the middle and upper classes, who ruthlessly exploited the workers within capitalism. Violence or 'conflictual' crime could be seen as a form of retaliation against 'the bourgeoisie and their henchmen'. However, violent crimes could also be committed against other members of the working class. Engels (1993: 143) saw the irony of this within a capitalist system: 'This war of each against all . . . it is only the logical sequel of the principle involved in free competition'.

Since these early writings, there has been a vast amount of empirical research into the connection between poverty and violent crime. The findings have been inconclusive and sometimes contradictory. There is, for instance, no clear evidence linking crime rates with national economic downturn or depression. Some research has suggested that levels of violence can be correlated with the number of people in the area living below a defined 'poverty line'. Loftin and Hill (1974) discovered a strong relationship between state homicide rates and a poverty index based on measures such as income, infant mortality, education level and prevalence of one-parent families. Messner (1983), using the same index, came to a similar conclusion, but only where the homicide victims were family or friends.

Earlier studies have been criticized for failing to differentiate adequately between the various forms of violent offending (Braithwaite 1981). Research by Kandel-Englander (1992) suggested that street-violent men were more likely to come from a lower social class (defined in terms of income and prestige of occupation) than family-violent men.

Unemployment is sometimes considered to be a gauge of economic conditions, and there is a common belief that it too may be related to the incidence of offending. In a 1994 MORI/Reader's Digest opinion poll, 71 per cent of those surveyed thought that unemployment is a major cause of crime. However, a note of caution is necessary. The recorded unemployment rate shares many of the drawbacks of official crime figures: both reflect counting practices which are arbitrary and liable to change (see Chapter 2). Both provide considerable underestimates of the true position. Moreover, the fact that both levels are high does not prove that the two are linked. Unemployment is often associated with other factors frequently related to offending such as age, class and educational attainment.

Despite the problems, research on a possible link between crime and unemployment continues to be conducted, with conflicting results. There is little indication of a positive correlation between unemployment and violent crime, with the exception of robbery (which is classified as a property offence, but requires the use or threat of force). In a review of 63 studies of unemployment and crime, Chiricos (1987) found a positive relationship, particularly for property offences and where small regional areas (as opposed to countries) were studied. Yet Land et al. (1995) discovered negative relationships between unemployment and either homicide or robbery (that is to say, if one went up the other would go down) and only a statistically insignificant relationship between unemployment and rape or assault.

Poverty and family violence can be related. Couples experiencing economic difficulties may become frustrated, and disputes over the allocation of their resources can result. Poor accommodation could lead to more arguments about use of space or noise than occur in families who have a greater amount of room. In addition to loss of income and status, and related arguments concerning blame, unemployment can force couples into closer contact than usual for long periods, resulting in a high level of irritation (Frude 1994).

Factors such as family size also appear to have a connection with certain forms of violence. Densely populated households are more likely to produce violent criminals (Mueller 1983). In the Newcastle Thousand Family Study, Kolvin et al. (1988) found an association between multiple deprivation in childhood and subsequent violent behaviour. The researchers defined 'multiple deprivation' as a group of factors, including overcrowding and economic dependency. Cicchetti (1990) discovered that, although the stress of financial difficulties can increase the probability of family abuse in general, the provision of support can result in a decrease of, at least, child abuse.

Economic inequality and violence

One of the problems in relating rising crime to poverty is that in most societies there has been an overall improvement in the level of national wealth over the past 50 years. However, it does not follow that this improvement has been spread equally throughout the population. In many countries, there has been a widening of the gap between the rich and the poor. An analysis by the Institute of Fiscal Studies (Goodman *et al.* 1997) found that the United Kingdom had become 'massively' more unequal than just 20 years earlier. The income of the lowest 5 per cent of earners hardly changed between 1983 and 1993, whereas that of the top 5 per cent increased by nearly a half. The combined income of the top 10 per cent of earners was equal to that of the lower half of all earners. In America, income inequality has increased rapidly since the early 1970s, reversing a long-established downward trend (Unnithan *et al.* 1994).

Hsieh and Pugh (1983) evaluated 34 studies which considered the relationship between poverty, economic inequality and violent crime. Most of them dealt with homicide or violent crime in general, and some were specifically concerned with assault, rape or robbery. Some were based on national data, others on small areas. The authors found a strong overall indication that both poverty and economic inequality were linked with increased levels of violent crime, particularly involving homicide or assault. In an analysis of each of the 50 American states, Stack (1983) discovered that income inequality was significantly related to the rate of homicide.

Box (1987) also thought that a person's relative economic position to others could account for increasing crime rates during times of economic recession, especially among the young, women and members of minority ethnic groups, who realize that their chances of closing the wealth gap are particularly poor at such a time. He assessed 16 studies on crime and economic inequality that had been conducted between 1974 and 1985. Eleven of them (most of which involved a consideration of some violent offences) showed a positive correlation. However, in an analysis of US National Crime Survey data, Sampson and Lauritsen (1994) found that poverty and income inequality were related less to violent crime in a particular area than factors such as family structure, density of housing and residential mobility.

Hagan (1994) provided an account of the impact of inequality on crime in America in what he called 'a new sociology of crime and disrepute'. Since the late 1970s, funds have been diverted from socially and economically deprived communities. Previously, the members of such communities had been able to attain a measure of upward social mobility. If this failed, they were able to fall back on the underground economy, involving such activities as vice and racketeering. However, the run-down state of America's inner cities and the general economic climate now made this very difficult. The underground economy was far more competitive, and serious violence had become part of the world of drugs and vice. Meanwhile, at the opposite end of the social and economic scale, the widespread diversion of investment to the business world and the better-off had enabled such people to take advantage of the poor by both disreputable and illegal means.

Conflict and Marxist explanations of violence

These two approaches share the assumption that violence can result from inequality of power within a society. Where they fundamentally differ is in their accounts of the source of that power.

Conflict explanations challenge the prevalent view that democratic societies are based on a general consensus of values, where the state (typically through the courts) will arbitrate in such a way as to represent the general interest. Conflict theorists can point to history to illustrate how societies usually comprise groups with opposing interests and values, and the state represents the interests of whichever group has sufficient power to control it. This will result in the use of violence: by agents of the state to try to maintain power on its behalf, and by members of the powerless groups to try to gain it. Vold (1958) offered disputes between employers and trades unions, and black civil rights activists and white supremacists, as examples of such conflicts.

To support their arguments, conflict theorists point to the rigorous enforcement of the criminal law against groups lacking power, and contrast it with the 'hands-off' approach which is the more likely reaction to the white-collar offending (and domestic violence) of the powerful. Having analysed police practices in Washington, DC, Chambliss (1995) claimed that the same unlawful acts would evoke a completely different response from the police depending on whether they were committed in the slums or on the university campuses.

Marxist criminology is essentially a more specific form of conflict theory: the conflict arises from challenges to the power resulting from the exercise of capitalism. Marx predicted that the material forces of production would continue to develop, and both property and goods would be concentrated in the hands of fewer people as they took over the operations of their competitors. At the same time, the growth of mechanization would result in a surplus population of workers, greater unemployment and lower wages. Society would polarize into two groups, with a diminishing number of individuals becoming increasingly rich and a growing number increasingly poor. This would eventually become intolerable to the masses and there would be a revolution to take over the means of production.

Marx himself wrote very little about crime, and it has fallen to later authors to offer a Marxist analysis of offences involving violence. In *Criminality and Economic Conditions*, the Dutch criminologist Willem Bonger

(1916) concluded that capitalism encourages egoism and greed rather than altruism. The lower levels of the working class in particular have no reason to experience altruistic feelings towards those in power. Capitalism encourages the poor to compete against each other for material gain. The poor in general, and certain sections of society in particular, have been dehumanized by capitalism. Bonger attributed a range of crimes to capitalism in an appraisal that was far ahead of its time. Domestic violence and rape occur because of the low economic status of women. Violence in general results from the degradation of the individual and the military ethos of capitalist societies.

After the work of Bonger, there was no significant Marxist criminology until the 1970s. Quinney (1977) argued that crimes committed by the working class should be considered within the context of capitalist oppression. Criminals reproduce in their own law-breaking activities the exploitation they have suffered under capitalism. Crimes can be divided into 'predatory', such as burglary, robbery and drug-dealing, which arise from a need to survive; 'personal', such as murder and rape, which are committed by people who have been brutalized by capitalism; and 'defensive actions', such as industrial sabotage, which are committed by alienated workers.

Much of the writing during this period concentrated on what was portrayed as a major social problem – street robbery or 'mugging'. Platt (1978) claimed that the high level of such incidents in America is an inevitable consequence of capitalism. Most of these attacks are committed by the poor and the unemployed. Although the working-class movement has become, to a large extent, organized and politicized, there remains a residual layer of the poor who still resort to this form of crime.

Schwendinger and Schwendinger (1985) argued that the breakdown of family and community life caused by capitalism creates and maintains adolescent street-corner subcultures, whose members commit serious property and violent offences (see Chapter 5). Middle-class youths, who have different outlets for their activities, are more prone to commit vandalism, vehicle violations and crimes related to drunkenness.

White and van der Velden (1995) provided a similar analysis. They contended that patterns of crime are related to particular social classes, as people's class and their relationship to the means of production affect their ability to organize economic and political resources. The criminal behaviour of the poor, who have been alienated by capitalism, may well take the form of brawling, mugging, gang violence and other offences against the person. The rich, on the other hand, are in a far better position to engage in large-scale fraud.

There are clearly problems with Marxist explanations of violent crime. It is necessary to distinguish them from the relatively simple theories based on poverty or economic inequality. Marxist accounts are not grounded purely in lack of resources; they involve either a challenge to the capitalist system, or the actions of people who have been so 'brutalized' (a term often used by Marxists) by capitalism that they are unable to appreciate the harm caused by their actions. This latter point could be used to meet the objection to Marxist criminology that most of the victims of crime are themselves from the working class. The implication is that, were capitalism to be replaced by some other form of economic and political system, violent offences would either considerably reduce or even disappear. This seems highly unlikely. Many critics would point to the history of the Soviet Union and its satellite states, which were hardly crime-free societies. However, it can be argued that these were not truly Marxist states, and it is interesting that many of the emergent nations from the former Soviet bloc have experienced increases in violent crime.

Although crime, including violence, is viewed as proto-revolutionary in its origins, this belief would hardly survive a close examination of working-class street subculture in many large cities, where the ideology of far right groups has had more impact than that of the left (Robins and Cohen 1978).

Moreover, even if Marxists and conflict theorists are correct in suggesting that governments focus their attention on street crime and the crimes of the poor to divert attention from the widespread offending of the rich and powerful, this does not diminish the impact of violence on society as a whole. Indeed, it was this perceived lack of concern for victims that led to a split among Marxists in the 1980s and the development of left realist criminology (see Chapter 8).

Anomie, strain and violence

The idea that crime may result from strain has engaged sociologists for over a century. Interest was first shown in the strain that can result from economic inequality, and came to be associated with the work of Emile Durkheim (1858–1917). One of the leading figures in sociology, Durkheim wrote during a time of considerable social change. The Industrial Revolution had led to a breakdown of the old established order, and vast sections of the population had exchanged the relative tranquillity of the countryside for the stress and insecurity of making a living in the city. Darwin's books on evolution had weakened the foundations of religion. The old certainties were increasingly being challenged.

For Durkheim, all of this had reduced the individual's attachment to society and the development of social solidarity. The collective sentiment of society was becoming individualistic and secular, and the values that were necessary for stability – such as individual dignity and social justice – were at odds with the values of obedience and discipline that were required by capitalist enterprise.

In his writings, Durkheim used the word 'anomie', which is derived from the Greek *anomos* and means 'lawless'. One of the contexts in which he used the term was in his book *Suicide*, written in 1897. Durkheim (1951) distinguished different types of suicide, one of which he termed 'anomic'. These occur when the disturbances caused by major changes in economic conditions result in a weakening of the forces of regulation in everyday life. A rapid enhancement of economic prospects is just as likely to increase the suicide rate as their rapid diminution. Sudden economic upheaval can reduce the effectiveness of societal regulation, which normally settles the limits of individual aspiration. For individuals lacking adequate internal self-restraint mechanisms, a state of anomie or normlessness will result, whereby nothing will be considered impossible.

The term 'anomie' was taken up some 20 years after Durkheim's death by the American sociologist, Robert Merton (1938). Whereas Durkheim considered that the condition of anomie would only arise exceptionally when weak social regulation was unable to restrain people's aspirations during economic turmoil, Merton felt that it was an ever-present feature in American society. For Durkheim, anomie could be attributed to poor social regulation: for Merton, it arose from 'the American Dream', where material wealth is indiscriminately held out to all as the ultimate goal. Not everyone will be able to attain such wealth, but everyone is expected to try, or risk being called 'lazy' or 'unambitious'. Unlike Durkheim, who thought that the appetites of members of society were 'natural', Merton declared that they are 'culturally induced', in particular by advertising, which had already become a significant factor in American life by the 1930s.

Merton assumed that in America there is an overriding cultural goal of material success; an unequal availability of legitimate means to attain this goal; and a consequent resort to alternative deviant means. There are five different ways in which people can react to the challenge. The particular form of response will depend on the strength of the individual's commitment to the goal and the availability of institutionalized means to pursue it. The prescribed means – which Merton terms 'conformity' – are based on the 'Protestant ethic' of hard work, education, honesty and deferred gratification. The antithesis to this involves 'get rich quick' schemes involving fraud or force. This forms the first of the four deviant means, which Merton calls 'innovation'. Here, the ultimate goal of material wealth is accepted, but the institutionally available means are rejected as being inadequate. Various alternative means can be adopted, including robbery. 'Ritualism' is perhaps too common to be referred to as deviant, as it refers to the typically mindless pursuit of routine employment without the willingness to take the risks required for advancement.

The two remaining deviant means are 'retreatism' and 'rebellion'. The former refers to the drop-out, such as the tramp or addict. The latter is adopted by the revolutionary, who both rejects the system and challenges it. These 'adaptations' (as Merton called them) were not meant to reflect personality types, but accounts of how people may react under the strain of anomie.

Anomie is not restricted to an explanation of seemingly rational economic crime. Merton (1968) emphasized that deviant and criminal behaviour in response to anomie may be rational, non-rational or irrational, and that anomie theory can explain vandalism or assaults as well as apparently rational crimes such as theft.

Although some early studies were critical of the theory, Menard (1995) has claimed their methodologies were inadequate and that, with the use of proper techniques, there is much stronger backing for anomie as a causal factor in crime, including violent offences.

The best-known development of Merton's theory is its application to delinquent gangs by Cloward and Ohlin (1960). The authors considered that juvenile delinquents who suffer from the strain of being ill equipped to obtain the ultimate goal of wealth may seek reinforcement in a delinquent gang. (Factors underlying the formation and sustenance of such groups are considered in Chapters 4 and 5.) The type of gang that exists in a neigh- bourhood will depend on the local opportunities for crime. Cloward and Ohlin referred to one such type as the 'conflict' gang, which could be found where there was insufficient opportunity for the juveniles to progress to adult 'rackets'. The emphasis with the conflict gangs is in obtaining what one lacks by coercion.

Messner and Rosenfeld (1994) also modified Merton's theory. They accepted his analysis that, for many people, the American Dream creates strong pressure to achieve the impossible – material wealth – but they con- sidered that widening the legitimate opportunities for the attainment of such wealth would only increase this pressure. Whatever redistribution is made among the winners, there will still be losers and, with an apparently more egalitarian society, they will be even more likely to blame themselves for their failure. Nothing less than a fundamental questioning of the goal itself is required. The reason why America has higher levels of serious crimes, such as homicide and robbery, than many other countries is that the wielding of economic power is paramount over other important institutions of society, such as the political system, the family and the school. Messner and Rosen- feld argued that, whereas in America education is seen as a way of obtain- ing a better job, in other countries it is one of a range of influences which mould values and beliefs.

Agnew's general strain theory

Other writers have adapted Merton's theory in an attempt to focus more on the individual feelings and emotions that result from strain. A good example is Robert Agnew's (1992) general strain theory. Agnew considered that strain is more prevalent than simply a divergence between aspirations and expectations. He identified three particular types of strain: a failure to achieve desired goals or goods (this is similar to Merton's theory, but includes strain where personal – as opposed to economic – expectations do not materialize); the removal of positively valued stimuli (for example, the death of a friend) or the presentation of negatively valued stimuli (for example, an argument); and the existence of negative stimuli, such as physical pain, embarrassment or psychological trauma.

Critical variables in Agnew's general strain theory are the feelings of fear, disappointment and, in particular, anger. Strain can vary in its effect on delinquency according to its intensiveness, duration and proximity in time. Everyone feels disappointment and anger, but it is unusual to react to these emotions by committing crimes. Agnew considered that some people have higher levels of aggressiveness than others. Such individuals are irritable; impulsive; have a low tolerance of adversity; are prone to blame their problems on others; and are more likely to react to their difficulties by committing crimes. These can be instrumental (trying to regain what has been lost or what one is not allowed to have), retaliatory (striking back at the source of strain) or escapist (attempting to find relief from the disagreeable states of anger and strain). People can respond to strain with acts of theft, vandalism, drug or alcohol use, or violence.

The theory has been subject to empirical testing. Agnew and White (1992) found that four of the eight measures of strain they used were significantly related to delinquency. More extensive research was subsequently conducted by Paternoster and Mazerolle (1994). In a longitudinal study, the authors were able to assess variations in the intensity and duration of strain in a national American sample of youth aged 11–17. They discovered that four out of five measures of general strain (neighbourhood problems, negative life events, school or peer hassles, and negative relations with adults) had a significant effect on criminal behaviour, including violence. They also found that having 'conventional moral beliefs' and obtaining good results at school were effective inhibitors to involvement in delinquency. In addition, strain appeared to have an indirect effect on delinquency by weakening conventional social control and increasing ties to delinquent peers.

Control theory

One of the strongest criticisms of strain theories has come from Hirschi (1969). He claimed that criminologists had been asking the wrong question: the issue should not be why people commit crime, but what stops people from committing crime. For Hirschi, crime does not result from a pathological condition, but is a normal form of behaviour. He considered that people who are tightly bonded to social groups such as the family and the school are less likely to commit offences. Hirschi listed four interrelated elements in the creation and maintenance of the bond: 'attachment', usually to the family; 'commitment' to society; 'involvement' in conventional activities; and 'belief' in society's rules. He administered a questionnaire to high school boys aged 12–17, which enquired about their family, school and friends, and the type of delinquency they participated in. One of the questions asked if the boys had 'beaten up on anyone or hurt anyone on purpose' (not counting fights with a brother or sister).

Hirschi found that there was no significant relationship between reported crime and class, except a slightly higher tendency to delinquency among children from the poorest families. He claimed that these findings could not be reconciled with strain theories, which are largely reliant on class. Boys who had a closer attachment to their parents were less likely to report involvement in crime, regardless of the criminal activity of their friends. Ambitions for, and expectations of, educational success were lower for delinquents than non-delinquents, and Hirschi argued that this finding was also contrary to strain theories, which suggest that delinquents have high aspirations but find them structurally blocked. There was a strong correlation between self-reported delinquency and the statement 'It is alright to get around the law if you can get away with it'. The only finding that did not appear to fit Hirschi's explanation was that the boys who reported most involvement in crime also participated in conventional activities. The results of Hirschi's study are interesting, but are restricted to self-reported low-level offending among predominantly middle-class teenage boys.

Gottfredson and Hirschi (1990) have put forward a theory based on individual self-control, which identifies crime as resulting from deficient training in early childhood. They claimed that their explanation can account for all 'acts of force or fraud undertaken in pursuit of self-interest'. The authors criticized existing theories for paying too little attention to certain key facts that consistently emerge from empirical research into crime – particularly that offending typically involves the obtaining of short-term gratification, such as excitement. This is at the expense of long-term planning or consideration of negative consequences such as punishment. Crime is part of a wider personal irresponsibility, which includes behaviour such as speeding in cars, proneness to accidents, smoking and casual sexual relationships. Criminals have often failed at school, at work and in their marriages, all of which require planning and the delay of gratification.

The theory hinges on two basic features: lack of individual self-control, which is the main factor, and the opportunity to commit a crime. Gottfredson and Hirschi considered that social factors such as poverty and class have no significance in the aetiology of crime. Deficient child-rearing will have caused its damage by an early age and the emerging traits – including difficulty in withstanding temptation to commit crime – will never completely disappear. This is one of the key points that distinguishes their approach from social learning theory, which is discussed in Chapter 4. Low self-control does not primarily result from innate differences between individuals. In adulthood, when it is generally agreed that crime rates decline, the lack of self-control manifests itself in other activities, such as heavy drinking, a poor employment record, a failed marriage, or even an increased possibility of being involved in road traffic accidents. The overall lower levels of female crime result from their more intimate socialization in early childhood and the relative lack of criminal opportunities compared to men.

Gottfredson and Hirschi's general theory of crime has been criticized, not just by writers who consider they are wrong to ignore the effects of social variables, but also by those who claim that an early propensity to antisocial and delinquent behaviour can be overcome. For example, Sampson and Laub (1993) used a longitudinal study to show that bonds arising in adulthood from a stable job or a steady marriage can redirect offenders into a law-abiding way of life.

Tittle's control balance theory

Whereas Gottfredson and Hirschi attributed crime, including violence, to individuals' not learning how to apply self-control, Charles Tittle (1995) has argued that it is the amount of control that people can exercise over their own behavioural options that is relevant to offending behaviour. The imbalance in the 'control ratio' results when a person has either a 'control surplus' or a 'control deficit'. A control surplus exists when individuals, in accordance with their status or personal strengths, can exert more control over other people than other people can exert over them. In contrast, individuals of low status, with little opportunity to control others, but who themselves are subject to considerable control, have a control deficit.

For the motivation to commit a crime to exist, people with a control surplus must want to extend their control further, or people with a control deficit must want to eliminate it. According to Tittle, this will often be fired by provocation, in the form of a challenge, an insult, or perhaps some unwelcome observation about the control deficit (or surplus). If a crime is to result, there must also be a lack of constraint imposed by others, and the opportunity for it to occur.

Tittle claimed that different degrees of control imbalance will result in different forms of deviant or criminal behaviour. Individual violence is most likely to result from relatively mild forms of control deficit, which Tittle called 'predation'. People may be directly provoked, or they may feel the need to assert their autonomy in a world where they perceive that they have little influence over their own lives or, indeed, any other events.

Changes in the amount of control individuals can exercise will affect the nature of their deviant or criminal behaviour. Tittle used the example of

African-Americans to illustrate this. During the slavery period, they had practically no control and were largely submissive. Following abolition, acts of defiance became more common and, with increased emancipation, they turned to the same types of 'predatory' behaviour as disadvantaged whites.

The theory provides an explanation of the relatively low levels of criminal behaviour found among the very young and the very old: they do not expect to have any significant control over anything. On the other hand, people in their late teens and early twenties – the peak age of offending – are trying to establish their independence. Because the traditional male role has involved the exercise of control over their family and territory, men are more concerned about the loss of control than women are, and so are likely to have a greater involvement in crime.

Tittle was particularly influenced by Jack Katz's (1988) book, *Seductions of Crime*. Katz was scornful of traditional functionalist explanations of offending, such as anomie, as he considered that they fail to explain why the majority of people in the alleged causal category do not commit the crime. What is important is the meaning of the behaviour as perceived by the individuals themselves. The book consists of accounts given by six 'categories' of criminal: novice shoplifters; youthful 'badasses'; street elites (gangs); 'hardman' robbers 'doing stickup'; 'righteous' killers; and cold-blooded murderers. Each crime has its own special thrills. What the criminals have in common with other people is a need to be valued, to be considered of worth, and to avoid being humiliated. The difference is that they go further in their desire to make their feelings practically real.

'Doing evil', according to Katz, results from a search for moral transcendence – a feeling of righteousness in the face of bored and chaotic lives. For instance, the 'hardman' robber, in Katz's (1988: 169) words, 'discovers, fantasizes or manufactures an angle of moral superiority over the intended victim'. Tittle considered that Katz's criminals found crime attractive because it put them in control. Katz himself referred to the desire of violent offenders to humiliate their victims.

Conclusion

The explanations of violence discussed in this chapter are broadly concerned with the strain that can result when individuals feel they occupy an inferior or debased position in relation to other people in society. Conflict (including Marxist), anomie and control balance theories all deal with power differentials which can arise from economic, political or other forms of stratification. It is not simply a question of violence being a reaction to absolute poverty: some of the poorest areas of the world have the lowest crime rates. Perhaps the inhabitants, although poor, consider themselves as valued within their society – or perhaps it is simply a case of their being surrounded by so many of their fellow citizens in the same circumstances. It is unnecessary to subscribe to all the tenets of Marxism to recognize the 'brutalized' individuals for whom the chances of making something of their lives are rapidly receding. As the gap between rich and poor expands in most industrialized countries, it seems that a growing underclass is developing whose members, in their struggle to amount to something, are becoming increasingly deficient in human empathy.

Nor is the strain resulting from increasing social stratification the only problem. The squeeze on jobs which has arisen from the collapse of traditional industries has served to increase the likelihood that individuals will evaluate other people first and foremost as rivals to be regarded with suspicion, rather than fellow-humans to be treated with compassion.

Further reading

For those interested in the historical perspective, *The Condition of the Working Class in England* (Engels 1993) remains a fascinating read. *Advances in Criminological Theory: The Legacy of Anomie Theory* (Adler and Laufer 1995) contains a detailed account of Merton's anomie theory and some of the subsequent developments. *A General Theory of Crime* by Gottfredson and Hirschi (1990) emphasizes the significance for criminality of a failure to learn self-control in childhood. *Control Balance: Toward a General Theory of Deviance* (Tittle 1995) argues that control is important in a different way, in that crime can result from an individual's having either an excess or lack of it. *Seductions of Crime* by Jack Katz (1988) provides an interesting range of accounts of why violent crime can be appealing to the residents of deprived inner-city areas.

part three

The aftermath of violence

chapter eight

The consequences
of violent crime

Violence has far-reaching consequences and most areas of society are affected by its impact, ranging from those people who are directly on the 'receiving end' of physical violence to the direction and cost of government policies. This chapter will consider the implications of the status of victim and the notion of blame: why it is felt important to make a clear distinction between offender and victim; the extent and consequences of fear of violent crime; the impact of violence; and the problems that can arise in the criminal justice system through an increased focus on victimization.

Victims of violence

Although, in one sense, everyone is a victim of violence (see below), the term 'victim' in the present context is usually reserved for individuals who are the direct recipients of physical aggression. For many years, governments viewed crime primarily as an attack against society as a whole, and a major part of criminal justice policy was aimed at its reduction. Criminologists devoted little attention to victims, partly through a growing tendency to view offenders as victims, whether as a result of individual pathology or social forces. The direct victims of offenders were often only discussed in the context of their absence: should victimless crimes, such as drug-taking and homosexuality, be criminal offences at all?

The term 'victimology' was first used in the 1940s by American writers, who concentrated on aspects of the victim's lifestyle which might be said to encourage or facilitate crime. For example, von Hentig (1948), whose work had no empirical basis, thought the law posited an arbitrary division between offender and victim which was unjustified. He claimed that victims often make the first move in violent confrontations and that certain people are consequently victim-prone. This view was supported by Wolfgang (1958) who, in an examination of the police records on 588 homicides in Philadelphia, found that in 26 per cent of the cases the victim had made the first recourse to physical violence.

However, this approach began to change in the 1960s with the development of victim surveys in America (see Chapter 2) and the revelation of the impact that crime has on many individuals. As a result, when Amir (1971) suggested, also on the basis of police reports, that 19 per cent of rapes were victim-precipitated, in that the women had retracted an earlier agreement to have sex or had not resisted strongly enough, there was a strong adverse reaction from feminists. They were now able to point to the evidence that many rapes are unreported, and to claim that the level of emotional devastation resulting from such incidents made it inappropriate to suggest that they were self-induced (Morris 1987). Curtis (1974) identified victim precipitation in only 4 per cent of rapes, although for other offences against the person the corresponding figures were higher: 11 per cent for robbery, 14 per cent for aggravated assault and 22 per cent for homicide. Sparks *et al.* (1977) reported a significant association between self-reported violence and the likelihood of being an assault victim.

Fattah (1979) tried to rescue the idea of victim precipitation from the notion of blame that was increasingly accompanying it by claiming that it is perfectly legitimate to consider what may be a complex interactional process between offender and victim. However, such an argument was by then going against the tide of academic opinion.

The early writers have been accused of creating an impression that there are two types of victim – innocent and blameworthy. The innocent victim, who is fully deserving of sympathy, is typified by an elderly lady or child who has been mugged. Such people are considered 'helpless' and in need of society's protection. The blameworthy victim, who is less deserving of sympathy, includes the woman whose demeanour or dress suggests that she was 'asking for it', as well as the drunken victim of an assault sustained during a fight (Walklate 1989). There is also an expectation that women should try to fight back: this is reflected in the rape laws of some American states (see Chapter 1) and was highlighted in a notorious case in 1999 when an Italian court decided that a woman could not have been raped as her jeans were too tight to have been removed without her cooperation (*The Times*, 12 February 1999).

This view of victim culpability is reflected throughout society in a number of ways. The part played by the victim in the crime may affect the level of sentence passed on the offender. The Criminal Injuries Compensation Scheme, which was introduced in 1964, has always made a distinction between deserving and undeserving victims. People who were considered to have provoked offences, or had failed to report the crime to the police, or were even related to offenders, were originally excluded from the Scheme's ambit. Financial incentives are offered by insurance companies to policy holders who take certain precautions to reduce the risk of being victimized. Female students in universities and colleges are strenuously warned about the dangers of walking alone at night. Are these simply exhortations to take common-sense precautions, or a suggestion that people who fail to heed such advice will be partly to blame for any misfortune that befalls them?

The growth of feminist writing about the effects of violent crime on women has provided one of the main challenges to such approaches to victims. Feminists have been particularly critical of the neglect of violence in the home. Many of them would consider the estimate given to a House of Commons Select Committee that up to 25 per cent of women have been struck by their partner to be on the conservative side (House of Commons 1993). They have also argued that female victims are further victimized in the criminal justice system as the police show little interest in domestic incidents, and the police and judiciary do not take allegations of rape seriously. A rape victim can often appear to be the real defendant in the trial (Dobash and Dobash 1992). Moreover, little attention was given to the practical and emotional needs of victims. This problem has been addressed by the National Association of Victims Support Schemes (now known as Victim Support), an umbrella organization established in 1974 to co-ordinate the network of small schemes. Since the 1970s, refuges for battered women and rape crisis centres have also been established (Zedner 1997).

Other writers have highlighted additional areas of victimization which have traditionally been overlooked. In describing cases where death resulted from breaches of safety regulations, Box (1983) argued that corporate crime also has real victims. In recent years, there has been a growing awareness of this problem, largely as a result of publicity resulting from illness and death in high-profile cases ranging from pollution to train and ferry disasters.

In addition to the writings of feminists, interest in victims was encouraged by the emergence of left realism. This arose in part as a reaction to the radical criminology of the 1960s and 1970s, which appeared to some people to be obsessed with the agenda of an earlier age – such as the labelling of offenders by powerful elites and the romanticizing of crime as a political act

– and unconcerned with the daily plight of the poor as the victims of inner-city crime. Left realists argued that ordinary people do not share the Marxist preoccupation with the crimes of the rich; they are more concerned about what is happening in their own everyday lives. For left realists, victims should be considered at the forefront of criminal justice policy.

Although by the 1980s there was an appreciation that victimization was far more widespread than had previously been thought, there was still no reliable means of assessing the extent or impact of crime. The introduction of large-scale victim surveys in Britain was therefore timely. After a number of small surveys in England in the 1970s (see Sparks *et al.* 1977), the British Crime Survey was first published in 1982 (see Chapter 2). The various reports of the BCS have confirmed that more crime is committed than recorded in the *Criminal Statistics*. The findings have consistently shown that single young males (aged 16–29), who have been drinking and are either on the streets or using public transport in inner-city areas at night, are the most likely to be victims of assault. Female victims of mugging tend to be older and married.

The 1992 BCS revealed that assault victims and their assailants had at least a casual knowledge of each other in 57 per cent of the cases (Mayhew *et al.* 1993). A similar figure has emerged from surveys in other countries, including Australia (Australian Bureau of Statistics 1994). In the Bristol research (see Chapter 2), around 40 per cent of the victims said they knew their assailants well (Cretney and Davis 1995).

At first, left realist, feminist and other critics argued that the BCS continued the earlier concentration on street crimes, as its research methodology was insufficiently sophisticated or sensitive to highlight domestic crimes which were committed behind closed doors. As a result, left realist and feminist researchers conducted smaller, more intimate surveys, which they claimed were better equipped to reveal the extent of such crimes and – perhaps more importantly – the devastating consequences of these for victims (Jones *et al.* 1986). More recent reports of the BCS have adopted techniques intended to encourage the respondents to disclose incidents of physical and sexual abuse in the home. Questions relating to such incidents were printed on cards, which were given to the respondents to read and reply to. The 1992 survey included a card-based assessment of lifetime experience of domestic violence, but the researchers still considered that this approach had its limitations. Therefore, in the 1994 survey computer-assisted self-interviewing was introduced. The interviewers passed a laptop computer to the respondent, who read the questions on the screen and responded directly into the computer. This device was used to measure illegal drug use and sexual victimization.

In the 1996 BCS, computer interviewing was used to assess the extent of domestic violence between partners and ex-partners during the previous 12 months (Mirrlees-Black 1999). Violence was defined as encompassing physical attacks and violent threats. Just over 4 per cent of the sample claimed to have experienced domestic assault. Women were twice as likely to say they had been assaulted as men. More than three times as many women than men said they had received frightening threats from a partner. The researchers estimated that there were 6.6 million incidents of domestic assault in 1995.

In Australia, a national Women's Safety Survey found that about 7 per cent of women had been victims of physical or sexual violence during the previous 12 months, and that in four out of five cases the violence was perpetrated by men (Australian Bureau of Statistics 1996).

Respondents in the BCS were also asked if they had been the victim of domestic violence at any time in their life. Twenty-six per cent of women and 17 per cent of men claimed to have been victims of an assault or threat. In general, the women had been victimized more frequently. Women aged 20–24 were most likely to have been assaulted or threatened by a partner: for men, the corresponding age range was 30–34. The proportion of women assaulted by a partner was highest in households where the annual income was below £5000. Both sexes living in households which reported being in financial difficulty were at far greater risk of domestic violence. There was no significant difference in the ethnic grouping of women victims. The risk for white men was slightly greater than for black or Asian men.

The victims were asked to describe the most recent occurrence. Almost two-thirds of domestic assaults involved pushing, shoving and grabbing. Throwing objects at the victim occurred in about one-fifth of the cases. Injury was caused in 41 per cent of incidents, the commonest form being bruising. Female victims were far more likely to say they had been upset.

Repeat victimization

The 1998 BCS showed that almost one-third of the victims of violence in 1997 were attacked more than once. Just over 15 per cent were victims on two occasions, and almost 16 per cent reported being the victims of three or more incidents. This latter group experienced more than 42 per cent of all violent occurrences (Mirrlees-Black et al. 1998). In the Bristol study, 55 per cent of the sample claimed to have been assaulted previously as an adult (Cretney and Davis 1995).

In the 1993 Australian crime survey (Australian Bureau of Statistics 1994), more than four in ten victims of assault had been assaulted more than once during the previous 12 months.

Domestic violence and the sexual abuse of children are particularly likely to involve the same participants over long periods of time. The 1996 BCS classified people who reported three or more incidents of domestic violence as 'chronic victims', and around 12 per cent of women and 5 per cent of men fell into this category. Racially motivated harassment and violence also usually involve persistent repeated attacks on the same individuals (Fitzgerald and Hale 1996).

From the point of view of the offender, repeat victimization can make sense (Pease 1998). Reinforcement may be gained from discovering that the victim will not fight back or does not have a protector (Farrell *et al.* 1995).

Walklate (1998) has criticized the customary approach to repeat victimization as being 'event-orientated', in that it centres on counting the number of incidents that have occurred and thus suggests that repeat victimization is exceptional. On the contrary, Walklate argued that all victimization has the potential for repetition, and cited research by Genn (1988) which showed that it can be seen as a normal part of many women's daily existence. Rather than reflecting a 'split' between the offender and the 'unfortunate' (and perhaps, by implication, blameworthy) victim, Walklate claimed that victimization is often part of a continuing process.

Fear of violent crime

Victim surveys usually ask respondents about the extent to which they are worried about, or afraid of, crime. There is certainly evidence that such fear exists in most Western countries and is particularly high in Britain. The 1996 International Crime Victims Survey (Mayhew and van Dijk 1997) found that the citizens of England and Wales topped the list of 11 industrialized countries for the number of security devices installed, with three-quarters of their homes containing alarms, grilles or special locks.

The early BCS reports suggested that those people who are most afraid of crime, such as women and the elderly, are often those with the least cause, as they are victimized less than young men, who in turn are generally not so concerned. The later surveys gave a similar impression. In the 1996 BCS, one in six respondents felt that they were certain, very likely or fairly likely to be mugged, whereas the statistical risk was less than 1 per cent. The greatest worries among women were about mugging and rape.

The implication of such observations is that much fear of crime is irrational. However, left realist and feminist writers have questioned whether this is an appropriate conclusion to draw. They have pointed out that stark figures alone can hide a wide range of experiences. For instance, people living in urban areas are far more likely to be at risk than those residing in rural areas. The concern women have about rape certainly appears rational if the extent of unreported crime is taken into consideration. The greater worries of the elderly and the poor may reflect the stronger impact that crime has on such people. Men generally admit to less fear of crime than women do, but this is likely to be a result of their socialization (Stanko and Hobdell 1993). Fear can be aroused by such local factors as vandalism, poor street lighting and the presence of drunks (Crawford *et al*. 1990). Questions about 'fear' of crime may really be tapping into people's concerns about the 'state of society' rather than eliciting assessments of their own likelihood of being victimized. Indeed, the very act of enquiring about fear of crime may serve to increase its level.

Sparks (1992) argued that crime should not be considered purely in terms of rationality. The ability of survey respondents to estimate a risk accurately will be governed by their fear of crime, which itself will be indicative of a range of factors relating to their personality. Most people are unable to make a reliable judgement about the risk of crime in their neighbourhood. The information they receive is usually second-hand and probably based on sensationalized reporting in the local press (Williams and Dickinson 1993) or by crime-solving TV programmes such as the BBC's *Crimewatch UK*. Walklate (1995) has stated that rationality in this context is a male construction: women should be considered as having 'expert' knowledge on the subject. Even local victim surveys, which are still based on measuring discrete events, cannot assess the pervasive, underlying threat to security that characterizes the lives of many women (Stanko 1987).

It is not inevitable that fear of crime will increase with age; some reports from Japan show that levels of fear decline with the advancement of years (Ito 1993). This underlines the point that the portrayal of crime in the media may be a significant factor in determining people's assessment of the likelihood of being victimized. Yet Howitt (1998) has pointed out that research findings do not show a strong correlation between the amount of television watched and fear of crime. It may be that the type of programme watched is important. Alternatively, Howitt suggested that some people may feel more in control of their own destiny than others, and that this 'locus of control' could be an important intervening variable between television viewing and worrying about crime.

On the other hand, research by Ditton *et al*. (1999) found that, rather than a *fear* of violent crime, a much stronger emotion experienced by people was *anger* about it. In a survey of around 1600 people in the Strathclyde region of Scotland, 55 per cent of the respondents claimed to be angry about assault some or all of the time, compared to 27 per cent who reported being afraid. There was no significant difference in the responses of victims and non-victims.

The cost of violent crime

This could refer either to an estimation of the financial consequences of violent crime for the state and its citizens, or an assessment of the emotional or lifestyle impact of violence on individuals.

The former can only be calculated in a fairly crude form. The Home Office has developed a computer model of the criminal justice process, which is designed to estimate the cost of policy changes. The figures are based on the expenditure for all criminal justice agencies, such as the provision of legal aid and prosecution services. For cases involving violence, it has been calculated that the average cost of each hearing in a magistrates' court is £800 and in the Crown Court £10,800 (Harries 1999). In America, it has been calculated that rape, robbery and assault cost victims $1.5 billion in 1992 (Klaus 1994).

Moreover, the financial costs of violent crime extend beyond those incurred by the various branches of the criminal justice system. Insurance premiums are affected by crime, albeit mostly by claims made in relation to property offences. The National Health Service provides treatment for assault victims. It has been estimated that the annual cost to the NHS in the Glasgow area alone of treating health problems related to domestic violence is around £12.4 million (Young 1995). Victims may have to miss work as a result of injury, depressive illness or court appearances, all of which will impact on the productivity of their employer and may lead to the victim's losing pay. The Government also loses tax revenue. It would be difficult to assess the loss of economic output from individuals who had underachieved at school because of bullying. Some people may incur expense, or even lose their job, through having to move home to escape continual harassment or violence.

Yet, whatever the financial impact of violent crime on both the individual and the state, most people would consider that it is of far less significance than the emotional effects on the victims and their families. Although early victim surveys gave the impression that crime has relatively little lasting effect on victims, more recent evidence suggests that victims of physical and sexual violence are likely to suffer both short- and long-term psychological consequences. Post-traumatic stress disorder is very common in rape victims immediately following the assault, and may persist for some time (Rothbaum et al. 1992).

In a study of 300 victims of assault, robbery or rape, Shapland et al. (1985) discovered that three-quarters of the victims still reported some effects some two-and-a-half years after the incident. Shepherd et al. (1990) compared the emotional impact of assault with the distress experienced by accident victims. The levels of anxiety and depression were similar for the two groups when measured one week after the event. However, after three months the accident victims had generally made a more complete recovery. The researchers concluded that self-blame and loss of confidence were commonly found among the assault victims. People who have been attacked in the street may feel that their inadequacies have been confirmed by their inability to defend themselves.

Female victims of sexual attacks can take several years to overcome feelings such as revulsion, anxiety, shame and guilt, and in some cases never succeed in doing so (Maguire and Corbett 1987). Research into victims of male-on-male rape has revealed similar findings. Indeed, some researchers believe that such incidents, which comprise between 5 and 10 per cent of all reported rapes (and are less likely to be reported than heterosexual attacks), cause even more severe forms of both physical and psychological disorders (Scarce 1997).

Domestic violence may lead to the break-up of the family. In a study conducted for the charity Crisis, 63 per cent of homeless women cited this as the reason for their predicament (Jones 1999).

Children who have been physically abused typically suffer from low self-esteem, which is likely to continue into adulthood, and experience difficulties at school (Finkelhor 1984). They may have problems in forming relationships (Cicchetti and Olsen 1990) and often blame themselves for having been abused, not only because the parent tells them it was their fault, but also because children often consider that they are responsible for everything that happens to them (Sroufe *et al.* 1996). Children are unlikely to report abuse to people who would be able to help them because, if they have never known anything else, they may consider it a normal part of life. Moreover, as children are entirely dependent on their adult carers, they may not want to risk depriving themselves of (as they see it) their only source of protection – a point which may well be reinforced by the abusing adult.

Many people, whether existing victims of violence or not, feel the need to make changes to their lifestyle through fear of physical attack. One of the commonest of these is a reluctance to venture out by themselves, especially in the dark. People who are on the streets alone late at night – and particularly women – are likely to keep to certain well-lit areas known to be 'safe'. Shapland *et al.* (1985) found that many victims avoid the scene of the assault. Almost two-thirds of the respondents in the Second Islington Crime Survey said that fear of crime was a reason for not going out, and more than 40 per cent considered it to be a substantial reason (Crawford *et al.* 1990). The 1996 BCS found a difference between men and women in this respect: 11 per cent of women and 5 per cent of men said that they never went out alone after dark.

On the other hand, there are many reasons why people choose not to go out at night, including a shortage of money. In the 1996 BCS, only 31 per cent of the women and 15 per cent of the men who stayed in after dark reported that this was due to fear of crime (Mirrlees-Black *et al.* 1996). As usual, the poorest sections of urban communities are likely to be worst affected: not only do they live in areas which are particularly prone to violence, but they are also unable to afford the luxury of travelling in their own cars or using taxis.

Another consequence of the growing fear of violent crime is an increase in the level of parental restriction placed on children when they need to leave their home. Children are increasingly ferried both to and from school and to see their friends. Play in the street and other open spaces is declining. A report by the Mental Health Foundation (1999) claimed that such a reduction in 'risk-taking' activities by children could lead to a lack of self-confidence and an increase in psychological problems among the young.

Routine activities theory

The relationship between the level of crime and victims' lifestyles was examined by Cohen and Felson (1979) in what they termed 'routine activities theory'. People satisfy their basic needs through routine activities, such as shopping, work and leisure. Such activities determine where people can be found and what they are doing at any particular time. Crime is seen as resulting from the convergence of three factors: a motivated offender; an appropriate target; and the absence of a custodian and guardian. The second and third of these are especially dependent on patterns of routine activities. Emphasis is placed on the day-to-day activities of both potential victims and those who can offer surveillance. Changes in routine activities can affect the crime rates. For example, the decline in public transport has resulted in people being more likely to walk alone in dark streets at night, and therefore being at greater risk of attack. Cohen and Felson claimed they could show that changes in the patterns of crime in America during the 1960s were significantly predictable from changes in routine activities.

A similar account of the level of violent crime based on routine activities was given by Hindelang et al. (1978). Based on an analysis of data from surveys conducted by the Bureau of the Census in eight American cities in 1972, the authors set out a series of propositions, all of which could be tested empirically. They found that the probability of individuals' being victims of personal crime was related to how long they were in public places, particularly at night; the extent to which they shared demographic characteristics with the offender; and the amount of time they spent with non-family members.

Although routine activities theory does not attempt to explain what motivates people to commit crimes, it does point the way to practical methods of crime reduction. It is for this reason that it came to interest several governments during the 1980s.

The impact of violent crime on government policy

Several factors contributed to the situation where, by the mid-1980s, the governments of both America and Britain – in contrast to a decade earlier – were showing more interest in the offence than the offender. One was the election of the right-wing administrations led by Ronald Reagan and Margaret

Thatcher. In a situation of general rising crime, and particularly sharp increases in recorded rates of violent offending, it was easy for such politicians to refer to the statistics to support their belief that it was pointless to be 'soft' on crime. The long and frustrating search for the Holy Grail of 'the cause' of crime appeared to be over. It made better political sense to turn the spotlight on to the plight of victims, especially as a growing interest in this area was being fostered by feminists and left realists. At the same time, attention came increasingly to be focused on preventing crime.

The routine activities theory of Cohen and Felson seemed particularly useful in this respect, a point observed by Ronald Clarke, who was then research director at the Home Office. Clarke began to work on ideas to reduce the opportunity for committing crime or, as it came to be called, situational crime prevention. This approach sees crime as the outcome of instant decisions and choices, and concentrates on these proximate causes rather than more fundamental sociological or psychological explanations. Opportunity is a key factor: the level of offending can be reduced by taking practical steps to reduce the opportunity for criminal behaviour. Other important considerations include the means to commit an offence (for example, a gun) and the level of surveillance. Since the early 1980s, a great deal of research has been carried out into various aspects of situational crime prevention. Although much of this has been concerned with reducing vandalism and burglary, the improvement of street lighting and widespread introduction of closed-circuit television cameras in urban areas have provided a possible means of deterring violence.

Reliance on situational crime prevention has been criticized. Its proponents claim that it is only concerned with 'opportunist' crime. Although most people are presented with the opportunity to offend, relatively few take it. The costs of 'target hardening' can be considerable and do not always relate to the types of street crime that cause most public concern (Trasler 1986). Financial expenditure is not always sufficient. Power and Tunstall (1997) analysed 13 riots and violent disturbances which occurred on various housing estates in the early 1990s. The fact that 12 of the estates contained predominantly houses with gardens rather than flats emphasized that high-rise blocks are not a necessary requirement for the fermenting of social unrest. Power and Tunstall found that the main problems arose from an unstable family life and poor economic prospects. There was little feeling of community among the inhabitants of the estates. In the authors' opinion, resources had erroneously been concentrated on buildings rather than on creating training and work opportunities.

Although in 1999 the Government announced it was to spend £170 million on fitting surveillance cameras in urban centres over a three-year period, research has suggested that such devices do not necessarily reduce violent crime, and may instead drive incidents behind closed doors, particularly into pubs and clubs (Sivarajasingam and Shepherd 1999).

American moves towards situational crime prevention were largely inspired by the 'broken windows' theory of Wilson and Kelling (1982). The authors considered that any signs of disorder – such as broken windows, graffiti or litter – would weaken the informal processes of social control within a community. Residents would be more likely to remain indoors and show little interest in what was happening on the streets. Drug-dealers might move into the area, which would start to fall into even greater decay. On the other hand, the prosecution of 'quality of life' crimes would clear the area of such undesirables, and send a message that no type of crime would be tolerated. In a review of American research, Skogan (1986) found evidence to support this hypothesis.

Such claims made an impression on politicians, including the Mayor of New York City, Rudolph Giuliani. He introduced the policy of 'zero tolerance', which led to a 25 per cent increase in the levels of arrest (and, therefore, fingerprinting). Giuliani claimed that this was responsible for the dramatic reduction of 30 per cent in the city's murder rate between June 1996 and June 1997. Assaults, rapes and robberies, together with burglaries and car thefts, declined be 13 per cent during the same period. New York fell to 144th position on the list of America's 189 most dangerous cities.

However, critics have claimed that the fall in crime may have been caused by factors other than the 'zero tolerance' approach. Wars between rival drug gangs had been decreasing for some time, with many of the leaders having been imprisoned. It has been suggested that other changes in policing practice may have been responsible for much of the decline in recorded crime. For example, in New York local precinct commanders were required to explain the level of offending in their area, and the measures they were taking to combat it, at weekly strategy meeting with senior officers (Bratton with Knobler 1998).

Problems with victimization

In view of the considerable impact of violence described above, it may seem inappropriate even to suggest that problems can arise from the increasingly high profile that victimization has gained in recent years. It is important to emphasize, therefore, that the validity of any of the following points does not imply a devaluation of the plight of individual victims, who should be offered every type of assistance to deal with the problems that have resulted from their ordeal.

The growing prominence given to the victims of crime has to be viewed in the context of the re-emergence of right-wing politics during the 1980s. Fuelled by strident headlines and editorials in the popular press, which sought to typify the most extreme cases of violent assault in lurid terms, governments found little resistance to their policies of imposing increasingly severe punishments on offenders at the expense of any consideration as to why the offence had occurred.

It is ironic that, although initially championed by left-wing or liberal interest groups, the success of the victims' movement has resulted from the adoption of its position by conservative politicians. By highlighting the fate of the victim, it became easier for governments to 'sell' harsher punishments to doubting members of the public. The public relations advantages of providing support for crime victims are considerable, and the appearance of 'doing something' for them may help to counter the view that the crime should have been prevented in the first place (Rock 1990). As Newburn (1995) has pointed out, in Britain the real attitude of successive governments towards victims can be seen from the fact that the Criminal Injuries Compensation Scheme (see above) operates more from a sense of public sympathy than from any notion that the state is under a duty to compensate victims of crime. Compensation is used as yet another penal measure rather than a result of any real concern for the plight of victims.

Not all victims' movements have campaigned for tougher penalties. In America, the victims' organization, NOVA, has developed as a right-wing body which has become associated with a more punitive approach to offenders, including support for the death penalty. However, in Britain, with the exception of high-profile campaigners such as Joan Jonkers (1986), political lobbying has been largely avoided, and Victim Support has concentrated its efforts on securing practical help.

In many American states, Australia and Canada, victims can make a statement as part of the trial process, which may include telling sentencers the punishment they would like imposed on the offender. Such 'victim impact statements' are encouraged by Declaration 6 of the United Nations Charter of Victim Rights, which states that the relevant judicial and administrative processes should:

> (6b) [allow] the views and concerns of the victims to be presented and considered at appropriate stages of the proceedings where their personal interests are affected, without prejudice to the accused and consistent with the relevant criminal justice system.

The use of victim impact statements is controversial. It is claimed that one of their main aims is to increase victim satisfaction with the criminal justice system (Erez 1999). However, critics maintain that the process introduces an undesirable subjective element into the sentencing process and encourages vindictiveness, leading to more severe sentencing (Ashworth 1993). Furthermore, it can also be detrimental to some victims in encouraging them to relive experiences that they would prefer to forget.

The Conservative Government claimed throughout the 1980s that victims had been neglected at the expense of offenders. However, it is arguable that there is no good reason why an increased concern for the victims of crime has to be at the cost of imposing harsher punishments on offenders. If it were felt desirable to include the harm and distress caused to the victim in the punishment or rehabilitation of the offender, it would be more useful to consider various forms of mediation or reparation involving the victim and the offender (Davis 1992). On the other hand, as Zedner (1997) has pointed out, it is hard to imagine such an approach developing to any great extent in the current punitive climate.

The police also have their own agenda in dealing with crime victims. In 1982, the Thames Valley Police was strongly criticized for its treatment of rape victims as portrayed in a documentary television series. Since then there has been considerable public and political pressure for the police to be more sensitive and considerate in dealing with victims. Nowadays, the police increasingly have to respond to performance targets, which inevitably include a reduction in recorded crime. In order to secure convictions, the police generally need the cooperation of victims. It may be that the police's interest in looking after crime victims is strengthened by the need to improve their reliability as complainants and witnesses (Miers 1992).

There is also some concern that the growing interest in victimization has led to an unnecessary and intrusive proliferation of private security operations. In Britain (unlike most other European countries and America), such organizations have not been subject to any form of official regulation. However, in 1999 the government published its proposals to establish a licensing system to be operated by a Private Security Industry Authority (Home Office 1999a).

Although most of their activities relate to the protection of property, private security firms also have a role in the prevention of violence, in the form of bouncers (door security staff) in pubs and clubs. Estimates of the number of people employed in providing private security in Britain vary considerably, but the figure is probably in excess of 100,000 (Jones and Newburn 1998). In the Bristol research, Cretney and Davis (1995) found several cases where the security staff exacerbated or even instigated assaults on customers. The police have been ambivalent towards the spread of private security. At first, opposition seemed total and even now rank and file officers are still generally unhappy about the prospect. However, it appears that some chief constables, beset by a shortage of funds, have accepted the inevitability of private security and there has been talk of working 'in partnership' (Blair 1999).

Within the criminal justice system, the status of victim is one that is ascribed in relation to discrete criminal offences. An alternative perspective would be that, from the point of view of many victims, it is meaningless to highlight individual offences because victimization is an ongoing occurrence in their daily lives – especially for women, members of minority ethnic groups and the inhabitants of run-down inner-city areas (see above). If governments had to face up to this, it could necessitate major shifts in social policy. It is therefore not surprising that such problems are instead left to the criminal justice system, which deals with the issue at the level of particular breaches of the law caused by individual defendants.

It could be argued that even the statuses of 'offender' and 'victim' are not as clear-cut as the criminal justice system requires them to be. Despite the objections that have been raised to the notion of victim precipitation, it still appears that some people, who could quite reasonably be described as victims, were not wholly innocent bystanders when the assaults were committed on them. Also, the growing emphasis on victimization entitles many perpetrators of crimes to argue that, through abuse or other problems in their early lives, they themselves should be considered as victims (Lamb 1996).

Such is the eagerness of certain groups to impose the label of victim on particular individuals that the question arises whether someone can be a victim without being aware of it. Two issues which illustrate this problem are 'date rape' and recovered memory loss. Although there is no such legal category as date rape, it has been suggested that it should be considered in essentially different terms from the stereotypical attack perpetrated by a stranger. A Home Office report found that the percentage of rapes by offenders unknown to the victim decreased from 30 per cent in 1985 to 12 per cent in 1996. This has coincided with a decline in the conviction rate from 24 per cent to 9 per cent. The report stated that consideration should be given to 'grading' the offence of rape to allow for different levels of seriousness (Harris and Grace 1999). Most feminists, however, strongly oppose this view, and claim that serious victimization occurs in all types of rape. Indeed, some researchers into the frequency of rape have gone beyond the legal definition and, in consequence, found extraordinarily high levels of victimization (Muehlenhard *et al.* 1992).

Recovered memory loss involves the use of hypnosis and other techniques by therapists, who suspect that their clients have repressed memories of childhood abuse. Psychologists have long been sceptical about such claims (Loftus and Ketcham 1994) and the Royal College of Psychiatrists has declared that there is no reliable evidence of such a syndrome.

Best (1999) argued that interest groups seeking to extend the definition of victimization have strongly influenced the creation (or, at least, redefinition) of criminal offences. The American example he used was 'stalking', which he claimed has now come to be identified almost entirely with battered women being followed by their former partners.

Another issue is whether the victims of violent crime are necessarily different from victims of any other misfortune, such as people injured in road traffic accidents or those who have contracted a serious illness. Hulsman (1986) suggested that members of the working class suffer a wide range of hardships which are unrelated to crime, such as poverty, housing problems and matrimonial difficulties. In his view, the people who are affected do not distinguish between such misfortunes and the problems that result from crime, and it is unnecessary for criminologists to do so.

A problem may also arise concerning a victim's self-perception. It has been claimed that such people increasingly join groups and define themselves 'only in terms of their claims to special identity and suffering' (Cohen 1996: 15). From an interactionist perspective, this could have significant implications for people's sense of identity and value (see Chapter 4). It may also help to support what some see as the growing 'medicalization' of victimology (Best 1999). In the view of certain groups, even the adoption of the correct terminology is important. It is becoming increasingly common for writers and campaigners to replace the word 'victim' with 'survivor'. According to Best, this approach has been borrowed from discussions of the Holocaust, and some people may therefore consider it inappropriate to describe victimization resulting from more routine criminal offences.

Conclusion

There is no doubt that violence has a considerable impact on society, both in terms of financial cost and the harm caused to individuals. Steps must be taken both to assist the victims and to try to ensure that such occurrences are kept to a minimum. It makes practical sense for people to adopt reasonable measures to minimize the likelihood of being victimized: the question of 'blaming the victim' should not arise. It is what amounts to 'reasonable' that is the subject of so much debate. Situational crime prevention has its place, but it is very expensive and, in some cases, may only have a diversionary effect.

Nor does it address the fundamental issue of why violence occurs at all. The crucial question is whether governments will react by facing up to this, or by using the quick political fix of latching on to simplistic slogans. For the present, blame is still central to the discussion: the move away from considerations of victim precipitation has been accompanied by increased blame being placed on the criminal. In the next chapter, the central role this plays in the sentencing of violent offenders will be discussed.

Further reading

There is an extensive literature on the impact of violence against women. The work of Rebecca and Russell Dobash in this area is always interesting and informative, and reference should be made to *Women, Violence and Social Change* (Dobash and Dobash 1992). *Victims and the Criminal Justice System* (Shapland *et al.* 1985) remains a leading text on the problems experienced by victims in general. *Victimology* (Walklate 1989) and the collection of essays in *Victims of Crime: A New Deal* (Maguire and Pointing 1988) are also important contributions to the literature. The chapter by Lucia Zedner (1997) in *The Oxford Handbook of Criminology* is among the best of the more recent contributions.

Victims Still: The Political Manipulation of Crime Victims (Elias 1993) discusses political decision-making in the light of victimization levels. *Random Violence: How We Talk about New Crimes and New Victims* (Best 1999) suggests that the victims' movement in America has been expanded by the 'discovery' of new offences. DeKeseredy and Ellis (1995) give an account of the extent of domestic violence in Canada.

The punishment of violence

This chapter considers what happens to violent offenders when they come to be sentenced in a court. To illustrate possible different approaches, sentencing practice in England and Wales will be compared to the sentencing guidelines systems which are increasingly being adopted in the USA. The corresponding sentencing provisions for Australia, Canada and New Zealand are contained in the Appendix.

First, a brief outline is given of the different approaches to punishment. The appeals process in criminal cases in England and Wales is then considered, as it is at this stage that the sentencing levels to be adopted in different types of case are established. The sentencing of violent offenders in practice is discussed. The American Federal Sentencing Guidelines are contrasted with those in the state of North Carolina. Finally, consideration is given to the degree of public awareness of sentencing levels.

Approaches to punishment

How do sentencers know the type and severity of punishment to impose? Very few crimes have a fixed penalty. The sentencer will usually be confronted with a range of community penalties and imprisonment from which to choose.

The answer to this question in principle lies in a determination of the purposes of punishment. This is vast topic, which can only be considered in outline here. Traditionally, the two main approaches have been described as 'consequentialist', where the punishment is targeted at affecting the offender's (or other's) future conduct, and 'retributive', where the punishment is commensurate with the amount of harm the offender has caused. Consequentialist punishments, which are forward-looking, include deterrence (of the offender or others), rehabilitation and incapacitation (removal from society). The minimizing of the risk of further offending is also becoming increasingly important (see below). Retributive punishments relate to past behaviour: the offender has gained 'an advantage', either tangible, or simply through breaking the rules that others feel constrained to obey. This advantage must be removed by an appropriately weighted punishment – no more, no less.

Consequentialist punishments rely on accurate predictions of their effects. The level of reconviction rates has caused some people to argue that this approach is not very successful. (In Chapter 10, it is shown that this belief may have been erroneous.) Sentences are tailored to particular offenders and, in principle, a punishment that is disproportionately harsh to the gravity of the crime (such as a long term of imprisonment) can be imposed if it is felt that this will have the effect of preventing future offending. Moreover, offenders who commit the same type of crime in similar circumstances can receive punishments that differ in both their type and severity. This inconsistency in sentencing has troubled many governments in recent years.

Retributive, or – as they are often called – 'just deserts' sentences, are not concerned with future offending. This proved to be one of the main reasons for their increase in popularity after the 1970s, when doubts as to whether consequentionalist sentencing 'works' began to be raised. Consistency is also easier to achieve, as ignoring factors peculiar to the offender makes it easier to rank in order of seriousness the range of factual circumstances in which a particular crime occurred. Concentration on the offence rather than the offender was particularly in keeping with the growing hardline attitude towards crime and criminals that developed during the 1980s. Clearly, the notion of blame plays a central part in retribution.

On the other hand, a retributive approach to sentencing can be criticized for its quest to remove the offender's supposed 'advantage', and its failure to be concerned with dangerous offenders who, under this approach, can strictly only be dealt with for the specific incident which brought them before the court, and whose future propensity for crime must be ignored.

By the 1970s, some American states – in particular, California – had moved towards the consequentialist approach, with a strong reliance on 'indeterminate sentencing', where imprisoned offenders could only be released when 'experts' considered it appropriate. The view arose that this uncertainty was unjust for offenders, who could see people imprisoned for similar crimes being released before them (Frankel 1973). As a result, several American states and the federal courts introduced sentencing guidelines, where maximum and minimum sentences are stipulated for each offence, with some allowance made for aggravating or mitigating factors. The judge is left with very little discretion in passing sentence and consistency is promoted. Critics claim that this approach is too rigid and has, in practice, served to lengthen prison sentences, as state legislatures, wishing to be seen as strong on 'law and order', have increased sentencing levels (see below).

Appeals in criminal cases

All the countries considered in this book have at least two levels of trial court for criminal cases, with one or more appeal courts above them. In England and Wales, minor or 'summary' offences are tried by magistrates' courts. Assault and battery are examples of such offences. Serious or 'indictable' offences are tried by a judge and jury at the Crown Court. Two examples of these are rape, and wounding or causing grievous bodily harm with intent. Many other offences are triable by either court ('either way'), with the defendant having the right to insist on a jury trial. Appeals from magistrates' courts usually go no further than the Crown Court: appeals from Crown Court trials go to the Court of Appeal. (Cases can proceed further to the House of Lords on important points of law; this is rare on questions of sentencing.)

The discussion will centre on the levels of sentencing recommended by appeal courts, rather than the sentences actually imposed by trial courts. The two are not necessarily the same. As no defendant will appeal against a sentence on the grounds that it is too lenient, sentencing in practice tends to be at a lower level than stipulated by the higher courts. Unlike most of the other jurisdictions considered in this book, in England and Wales there is only limited power for the prosecution to appeal to the Court of Appeal against a lenient sentence passed by the trial judge. The chief government law officer, the Attorney-General, must ask the Court of Appeal to review the sentence. In addition, the power can only be used for indictable offences and a small number of triable either way offences, including indecent assault. The Court of Appeal in England and Wales does not have the power to increase a sentence on an appeal by the defendant.

Sentencing violent offenders in England and Wales

The Criminal Justice Act 1991 emphasized a bifurcatory or 'twin-track' approach to sentencing. The policy of the Government was that offenders considered to be non-threatening should be sentenced on a proportional or just deserts basis (section 1(2)(a)). In contrast, those thought to be dangerous could receive longer custodial sentences than would be justified under that approach (s. 2(2)(b)). To be classified as 'dangerous', an offender must have been convicted of a violent or sexual offence, and a longer sentence must be adjudged necessary to protect the public from death or serious harm (physical or psychological).

Although the emphasis on the 'just deserts' part of the package was reduced by the Criminal Justice Act 1993 (for example, previous convictions could once again be taken into account by sentencers), the separate approach towards dangerous offenders remained, and was extended in the Crime (Sentences) Act 1997 s. 2. If a person who has already been convicted of a 'serious offence' is convicted of another such offence, a sentence of life imprisonment must be imposed unless there are 'exceptional circumstances'. The definition of 'serious offence' includes wounding or causing grievous bodily harm with intent, and rape, but not any lesser form of assault or indecent assault.

Since the early 1990s, an approach to punishment based on 'popular punitiveness' (Bottoms 1995: 39) has developed. This has been combined with an increased concern with the management of 'risk'. According to Feeley and Simon (1992), government policy has become less concerned with intervening and dealing with individual offenders than with the classification and management of groups on the basis of their perceived dangerousness. The concern of governments to minimize the risk of crime has arguably been shown in the introduction of measures to maintain an element of control over the offender, whether in place of, or at the end of, imprisonment. For example, the Sex Offenders Act 1997 has established the compulsory registration of people convicted of such offences (Maguire *et al.* 2000). The Crime and Disorder Act 1998 introduced 'antisocial behaviour orders' to deal with badly behaved individuals without the requirement of a criminal conviction.

Early release

The Criminal Justice Act 1991 changed the rules for parole. For sentences of less than four years, release will be automatic after half the term has been served, unless additional days have been added as a result of breaches of prison discipline. If the sentence was over 12 months, the offender will be on licence until the three-quarter point of the sentence. For sentences of four years or over, release will be automatic after two-thirds has been served, but discretionary release is possible after half the sentence on the recommendation of the Parole Board. Again, the offender will be on licence until the three-quarter point of the sentence.

Sentencing practice

The definitions of the crimes considered below are outlined in Chapter 1.

Assault and battery

In England, these crimes are only triable in a magistrates' court, and the maximum penalty is six months' imprisonment, a fine not exceeding £1000, or both. The Magistrates' Association Guidelines advise consideration of a community penalty. Custodial sentences are imposed in about 8 per cent of cases.

Assault occasioning actual bodily harm (s. 47)

This offence is triable either way. The maximum penalty in the Crown Court is five years' imprisonment. In the magistrates' court, it is six months' imprisonment, a fine not exceeding £5000, or both. Magistrates are advised to consider elements such as racial motivation, extensive injuries, and the use of a weapon as aggravating factors.

Only a small proportion of sentences for this crime are custodial, and the majority of these are for three months or less. However, the Court of Appeal has upheld heavier sentences in a number of cases. Six months' detention was confirmed for a youth for an assault on a bus conductor, who was considered a public servant (*Foster* (1982) 4 Criminal Appeal Reports (Sentencing) 101) and where the defendant fractured an opponent's cheekbone in a football match (*Davies* (1990) 12 Cr App R (S) 308). Short custodial sentences have also been upheld in 'road rage' disputes and for violence against an innocent bystander at a football match. More severe sentences are considered appropriate where violence is committed against police officers. Two years' imprisonment was approved in *Moore* (1993) 14 Cr App R (S) 273, where the defendant attacked two police officers in a pub. In *Nicholas* (1994) 15 Cr App R (S) 381, the Court of Appeal emphasized that assaults between spouses or partners should not be treated more leniently than other assaults.

Wounding or inflicting grievous bodily harm (s. 20)

This is supposed to be more serious than the s. 47 offence, but carries the same maximum penalties. Yet again, custodial sentences are only found in a minority of cases and rarely exceed three years. In *Martin* (1981) 3 Cr App R (S) 39, a sentence of six months was upheld for an unprovoked attack by a man of previous good character on a victim who wore glasses and suffered severe cuts around the eye. In *Fox* (1980) 2 Cr App R (S) 188, a three-year sentence was reduced to 12 months for a bouncer who lost his temper with a customer who refused to leave, and struck him in the face causing extensive injury.

The use of a weapon is an aggravating factor. In *Jones* (1984) 6 Cr App R (S) 55, the defendant struck his victim in the face with a beer glass which, on breaking, caused serious injury and the possible loss of sight in one eye. In contrast to *Martin*, the Court of Appeal approved the two-year sentence imposed at the trial. A three-year sentence was upheld in *Moore* (1992) 13 Cr App R (S) 130 where, following an argument at a telephone kiosk, the defendant knocked down the victim and kicked him so severely that he had to spend two weeks in hospital.

Wounding or causing grievous bodily harm with intent to do grievous bodily harm (s. 18)

This offence, which is triable only in the Crown Court, is punishable with a maximum of life imprisonment. It is therefore a far more serious crime than sections 20 or 47, and this is reflected in the sentencing range, which is normally between three and eight years' imprisonment. Cases of stamping on the head of a person lying on the ground fall into this category, and in *Ivey* (1981) 3 Cr App R (S) 185 the Court of Appeal considered that four years was appropriate for a man who had caused severe harm in this manner following an argument at a club. Incidents of 'glassing' are also likely to incur a substantial sentence, and in *James* (1981) 3 Cr App R (S) 223 five years' imprisonment was upheld for the defendant, who had pushed two broken milk bottles into the face of a shopkeeper, causing grave injury.

The use of a weapon will lead to a heavier sentence. A seven-year prison term was approved in *Robinson* (1980) 2 Cr App R (S), where the defendant had stabbed – almost fatally – a man who had refused to hand over money. *Pollin* [1997] 2 Cr App R (S) 356 was sentenced to nine years after repeatedly stabbing his victim in the arm (and severing an artery) following an argument about rent. The Court of Appeal felt unable to interfere with the sentence. The use of firearms or causing of injury to a police officer will increase the sentence even further. Both these aggravating factors occurred in *Chesterman* (1984) 6 Cr App R (S) 151. The defendant fired a shotgun twice at an officer and blinded him. The Court of Appeal refused to reduce a 12-year sentence, commenting that it was at the top end of the scale for this offence.

Indecent assault

This offence is triable either in a magistrates' court, where the maximum penalty is six months' imprisonment, a fine not exceeding £5000, or both; or in the Crown Court, where the maximum penalty is ten years' imprisonment. It can be committed against either a man or a woman. The Magistrates' Association Guidelines include breach of trust and the age or vulnerability of the victim as aggravating factors. Magistrates imprison about 11 per cent of those who have assaulted women and 17 per cent of those who have assaulted men. The remainder receive community penalties, the commonest being a probation order. In contrast, the Crown Court imprisons around 70 per cent, whether the victim is male or female.

An example of a case which the Court of Appeal considered should be dealt with by a non-custodial penalty is *Neem* (1993) 14 Cr App R (S) 18. The offender had been sentenced to 28 days' imprisonment for pressing against a woman in an indecent manner on a London Underground train. The Court substituted a fine of £300, together with a compensation order for £250. In *Freeman* (1980) 2 Cr App R (S) 194, a sentence of four years for a man who pleaded guilty to five charges of indecently assaulting girls by kissing and cuddling them was reduced to 12 months.

Indecent assault committed against young or vulnerable women in the defendant's care is almost bound to attract a custodial sentence. In *Wellman* [1999] 2 Cr App R (S) 162, the Court of Appeal upheld a two-year sentence on a man who had placed his finger inside a 13-year-old girl's vagina while she was staying the night with his daughter. In *Taylor* [1997] 1 Cr App R (S) 36, the Court approved four years for a man who indecently assaulted four disabled women he was escorting from one railway station to another.

If such assaults continue over a long period of time, the sentence is likely to be far higher. In *Cook* (1988) 10 Cr App R (S) 42, sentences totalling 11 years were upheld on various charges of indecent assault and buggery against a stepfather who had a abused his stepchildren over a nine-year period.

Rape

Rape, which can only be tried at the Crown Court, is punishable with a maximum of life imprisonment. The vast majority of convicted offenders are given a custodial sentence. Around a third are under 21.

This is an area where the Court of Appeal has given a guideline judgement for the benefit of sentencers (see below). In *Billam* (1986) 8 Cr App R (S) 48, the Court stated that the starting point for an adult convicted of rape without any aggravating or mitigating circumstances should be five years' imprisonment in a contested case. For a rape committed by two or more men, or by a man who had broken into the victim's residence, or by a man who was in a position of responsibility towards his victim, the starting point should be eight years. At the other end of the scale, a sentence of at least 15 years may be appropriate for a defendant who has carried out a campaign of rape. Where the defendant's behaviour suggests that he suffers from severe psychological problems and that he might be a danger to women for a long time, a sentence of life imprisonment may be necessary.

Rape can be aggravated by several factors: the use of violence beyond that necessary to commit the crime; the use of a weapon to frighten or wound the victim; the repetition or careful planning of the rape; the existence of previous convictions for rape or other sexual or violent offences; the victim's being subjected to additional sexual indignities; or the victim's being either very old or very young. The physical or mental effect on the victim is considered to be particularly serious. If any of these factors are present, the sentence should be 'substantially higher' than the recommended starting points. A guilty plea may lead to a reduction of sentence, particularly as it will save the victim from the distress of having to testify in court. The fact that victims acted incautiously (such as accepting a lift with a stranger) is irrelevant, as is their previous sexual experience. However, some mitigation should be allowed if the victim had acted in a way which was calculated to make the defendant think that consent would be given to sexual intercourse.

Exceptional circumstances must exist for a custodial sentence to be avoided. In *Taylor* (1983) 5 Cr App R (S) 241, the Court of Appeal overturned a three-year sentence where the mentally retarded defendant pleaded guilty to raping a girl suffering from Down's syndrome. The attack involved a minimal amount of penetration and amounted to little more than sexual fumbling. In *D* [1996] 1 Cr App R (S) 196, the defendant pleaded guilty to a series of sexual attacks on his sister, which had started in 1985 when he was 12 and lasted for seven years. It was only later that the facts emerged and the defendant underwent counselling. When this broke down, the police were informed. The Court of Appeal took a 'merciful' view and replaced a four-year prison sentence with a two-year probation order.

In *Stephen W* (1993) 14 Cr App R (S) 256, the Court of Appeal considered the appropriate sentence for spousal rape. Following an argument, the defendant had forced his wife to have intercourse by threatening her with a knife. The Court, in upholding the sentence of five years, said that the normal *Billam* guidelines should apply. Any mitigation to reflect the existing relationship would be lost by the use of violence or threats. The fact that the victim was a prostitute is irrelevant if the defendant proceeds to have intercourse on terms that were not consented to – including the use or threat of force (*Attorney-General's Reference (No. 12 of 1992)* (1993) 14 Cr App R (S) 233).

At the top end of the scale is *Robinson* (1980) 2 Cr App R (S) 206. The Court upheld a 15-year sentence on a man for violently raping three different girls, who had replied to newspaper advertisements in Ireland to come to London and work as a nanny. In *Thomas* (1995) 16 Cr App R (S) 686, the defendant was also sentenced to 15 years for assaulting and then raping a 78-year-old woman, whose home he had broken into.

Sentencing violent offenders in the USA

The federal courts are responsible for enforcing federal laws, which are passed by Congress and, to paraphrase Article III of the US Constitution, generally relate to 'controversies' between states; between a state and a citizen of another state; or between citizens of different states. In practice, most federal criminal offences have some requirement of an interstate transaction; or a threat to commercial transactions between different states; or some form of attack on federal employees; or damage to federal property. Exceptions include bank robberies, certain 'controlled substance' offences, and some activities of 'criminal street gangs'.

The states have their own courts systems and no two are identical. There is generally a three-tier system: lower courts; courts of general jurisdiction; and state appellate or state supreme courts. The vast majority of criminal cases are dealt with under state law.

Dangerous offenders

Around three-quarters of the states have passed laws which render convicted offenders considered as dangerous liable to extended terms of imprisonment. The most draconian – and notorious – of these is California's 1994 'three strikes and you're out' law (California Penal Code s. 667). Using the baseball analogy, any person convicted of two previous 'violent' or 'serious' felonies, and then convicted of a third felony, may be sentenced from 25 years' to life imprisonment (Shichor and Sechrest 1996). What distinguishes this law from comparable provisions in the vast majority of the other states is that the third felony does not have to be 'serious' or violent.

Early release

Under sentencing guidelines systems, 'truth' in sentencing is considered very important, and automatic remission has been abolished. In practice, however, there is still some scope for early release (see below).

Sentencing guidelines systems

The basic idea of sentencing guidelines and their background is discussed above. There are two types of guidelines: presumptive and voluntary. The former are created by a sentencing commission, which usually includes representatives of most groups working in criminal justice and, in some states, members of the legislature. Ultimately, the guidelines will have to be approved by the state legislature. They contain enforcement mechanisms – judges who depart from the guidelines must provide written reasons and, in most cases, a prosecution appeal against the departure is possible. Voluntary guidelines, which are generally developed by local judges and based on past practice, have no such mechanism. By 1996, nine states and the Federal Government had presumptive guidelines, while eight other states were in the process of creating them. Four states were still using voluntary guidelines.

Federal guidelines

The first set of Federal Sentencing Guidelines was enacted in November 1997 as a result of the Sentencing Reform Act 1984. A Sentencing Commission was created, and it is allowed to amend the Guidelines annually. In addition to reducing disparity and promoting 'truth' in sentencing, it was clearly intended that more people should be imprisoned, and for longer periods, for certain types of offence (Doob 1995). In this respect the Guidelines have undoubtedly been successful, although in almost every other regard they have been subject to fierce criticism from all quarters (including federal judges) since their inception (Doob 1995). They have survived a challenge in the Supreme Court claiming that they are unconstitutional on the basis that they breach the principle of separation of powers between the executive and judiciary (*Mistretta v US* (1989) 488 US 361).

Two of the main criticisms of the Guidelines are that they are complicated, and that their rigidity can result in unjust sentences. The grid from which the sentence is calculated comprises 43 levels of offence and six different 'types' of offender, based on their criminal history. An example from the 1998 *Sentencing Guidelines Manual* will illustrate how the system works. 'Aggravated assault', which involves a weapon or causes serious injury, has a base offence level of 15. The starting point on the grid is 18–24 months. If the assault involved more than minimal planning, it is increased by two levels (21–27 months). If a weapon was brandished or its use threatened, there is a three-level increase and, if a firearm was discharged, the increase is five levels. There are further levels of increase depending on the degree of any injury caused. Additional aggravating factors are the assault having been committed for money or in breach of a court protection order. All these terms require definition, and this is provided at some length in the 'application instructions'. Extra levels are also imposed if the accused has previous convictions. The maximum period for a level 15 offence is 41–51 months (Benzvy Miller 1999).

There is no system of parole under the Federal Sentencing Guidelines, but a prisoner will be credited with 54 days at the end of each year of imprisonment for good behaviour.

State guidelines

The first state to adopt presumptive sentencing guidelines was Minnesota in 1980. Prior to this, only voluntary guidelines had been used. The Minnesota approach attracted a great deal of interest and has provided the basis for several of the presumptive schemes that have since followed (Frase 1995). One of these is the guidelines system established by the North Carolina Sentencing and Policy Advisory Commission, which took effect in 1995.

This system is simpler than the federal one, in that it adopts only ten levels of offence, together with six different categories of offender based on their 'prior record level'. In this respect, it resembles the other state schemes rather than the federal guidelines, which take account of 'relevant conduct' not necessarily forming part of the conviction offence. For each read-out on the grid, the sentencer first has to choose between three levels of disposition: the presumptive range; the aggravated range; and the mitigated range. Once the appropriate 'cell' on the grid has been isolated, the sentencer is still left with some slight discretion, typically of several months. For minor offences, the grid can direct a community penalty.

An example will illustrate how the system works. 'Assault inflicting serious bodily injury' where no weapon is used has a base offence level of F. The presumptive sentence for an offender with no previous convictions is 13–16 months. The aggravated range is 16–20 months and the mitigated range is 10–13 months. Whichever range is adopted by the sentencer can then be increased in proportion to the accused's criminal record. The highest sentence that can be given on this basis is 31–39 months on the presumptive range, 39–49 months on the aggravated range, and 23–31 months on the mitigated range. The judge selects a minimum sentence from the range. A corresponding maximum term is provided by statute (approximately 20 per cent more). An offender will never be released before the expiry of the minimum term, but can earn time off the maximum sentence for good behaviour, participation in training or rehabilitation programmes, or for work performed. Although this is presented in terms of the abolition of parole, in practice a reduced discretion still exists to allow early release.

England and Wales have not adopted this approach to sentencing. The Magistrates' Association issues guidelines, indicating appropriate aggravating and mitigating factors. Crown Court judges are supposed to follow guideline judgements (where available) or decisions in similar cases given by the Court of Appeal. The Court is encouraged to provide sentencing guidelines in its judgements by the Crime and Disorder Act 1998 s. 80. Section 81 provides for a Sentencing Advisory Panel, which can advise the Court on appropriate guidelines.

Public awareness of sentencing levels

The evidence suggests that people generally do not appreciate the severity of sentencing for violent offenders. Information from the 1996 British Crime Survey shows that, when asked how many people are imprisoned for mugging, only 12 per cent of respondents were accurate, and 75 per cent underestimated the level of imprisonment (Hough and Roberts 1998). In response to the same question in the 1998 BCS regarding rape, 25 per cent of the replies were classified as 'underestimates' and 56 per cent as 'large underestimates' (Mattinson and Mirrlees-Black 2000). Similar findings have emerged from other countries. Although most Canadians think that sentences for violent offenders are too lenient, almost three-quarters of survey respondents considerably overestimated the level of violent crime in that country (Doob and Roberts 1988).

It is also apparent that, when asked what the appropriate sentence should be on a particular set of facts (as opposed to the tabloid newspaper practice of asking wide questions about crime in general), many respondents suggest a punishment broadly in line with what courts would probably impose, or even less severe. This emerged from the 1996 BCS (Hough and Roberts 1998), and in Australia research by Walker *et al.* (1988) came to a similar finding for cases of armed robbery and domestic violence.

Conclusion

This chapter has shown two different approaches to sentencing violent offenders: the traditional method, as in England and Wales, where the sentencer has a reasonable amount of discretion; and the emerging sentencing guidelines systems in the USA, where the sentencer has very little discretion. Although the American approach is likely to favour consistency, it is widely believed to have contributed to the massive rise in the American prison population, as local politicians have succeeded in increasing the offence levels. However, although consistency in sentencing remains an issue, it has to some extent been superseded by the latest perceived problem – the risk of harm caused by the dangerous offender.

Perhaps the main development in the sentencing of violent offenders in the countries considered in this book is that, where they are suspected of being dangerous, their punishment is likely to be increased and, in some cases (such as sex offenders), the state may wish to maintain a level of post-release control. In practice, this usually means that violent and sexual crimes are treated more severely than property offences, although under the infamous Californian 'three strikes' law any felony (serious offence) conviction can activate the mandatory extended sentence requirement (Shichor and Sechrest 1996). Even if this approach were defensible in principle, it seems hardly satisfactory that, in practice, it is driven by 'populist punitiveness', where politicians endorse what they believe to be the punitive mood of the general public. Moreover, New Zealand research into a cohort of offenders found that those released from prison before the introduction of serious violent offender provisions, but who would nowadays be subject to them, were no more likely to receive a further conviction within two-and-a-half years of release than the others (Brown 1996).

The notion of blame is, therefore, still very much to the fore, and when it is accompanied by (arguably exaggerated) concerns over risk and dangerousness – which can be very difficult to predict accurately – the resulting punishment can involve a lengthy period of incarceration. In the final chapter, consideration will be given to whether there is any form of treatment available in prison which could help violent offenders, or whether a larger proportion of them could be dealt with safely in the community.

Further reading

The different principles underlying sentencing and some of the English practice are discussed in *Sentencing and Criminal Justice* (Ashworth 2000). Canadian sentencing case law is considered in Ruby's *Sentencing* (Ruby 1999) and wider issues in *Making Sense of Sentencing* (Roberts and Cole 1999). *Hall's Sentencing* (Hall 1999) deals with New Zealand law and practice. The background to one of the original American guidelines systems is discussed in *Structuring Criminal Sentences: The Evolution of Minnesota's Sentencing Guidelines* (Parent 1988). *Three Strikes and You're Out: Vengeance as Public Policy* (Shichor and Sechrest 1996) illustrates the injustices that can result from mandatory sentencing provisions. The extent of public ignorance about sentencing (and other aspects of the criminal justice system) is considered in *Public Opinion, Crime, and Criminal Justice* (Roberts and Stalans 1997).

chapter ten

The treatment of violent offenders

In this chapter, consideration will be given to ways in which individuals, usually in prison or under a community sentence, can be 'treated' in order to help them avoid recourse to physical aggression.

This is not the only way to deal with the problem. It has been suggested in earlier chapters that, if certain aspects of society were organized differently, a significant reduction in violent crime could result. British governments have preferred to tackle the question from the other end, in the form of situational crime prevention strategies (see Chapter 8). However, individual offenders are also being targeted, particularly those who have committed crimes causing 'public concern', such as violent and sexual offences. There is an additional advantage for the state in this approach. An acceptance that a person's thought patterns or behaviour needs to be changed places the responsibility firmly on the individual, and relieves society from any blame for their violent actions.

If psychologists agree on anything, it is that people cannot change their personality or conduct unless they are motivated to do so. In relation to criminal behaviour, some forms of motivation can appear to be more genuine than others. It is improbable that an offender who is offered the 'choice' between probation with psychological treatment and a term of imprisonment will opt for custody. Nor is an imprisoned rapist likely to forgo therapy if attendance will help to secure his parole. Under the Criminal Justice Act 1991, the early release of prisoners is in part conditional on the tackling of their 'offending behaviour'. Nevertheless, a desire to change can be genuine: a violent robber may decide that he needs help, or an abusive partner may not want to see the break-up of the family.

Current approaches to treating violence

In Chapter 9, an outline account was given of how the popularity of retributive or 'just deserts' sentencing developed, at least in part, from a perception that attempts to rehabilitate offenders were not only unjust, but also unsuccessful. This view was largely fuelled by a report for the US Government by Martinson (1974), which comprised a 'meta-analysis' of 231 studies published between 1945 and 1967 into the efficacy of the different ways used to deal with offenders. His report was generally portrayed at the time as concluding that 'nothing works'. In fact, a more accurate summary would be that Martinson accepted that some of the approaches *might* 'work', but that inadequate research design and evaluation made it impossible to provide a confident endorsement. Indeed, Martinson (1979) himself subsequently acknowledged errors in his earlier report, but by then the damage had been done. It is notable, however, that the 'nothing works' view never became widespread in Canada, where a belief in the treatability of offenders persisted (Gendreau and Ross 1979).

However, the persistence of researchers and the adoption of more sophisticated techniques have resulted in a retreat from the 'nothing works' position (McGuire 1995), which culminated in the British Government's allocating £21 million to the prison and probation services to develop programmes to challenge offending (Home Office 1999c). A process of accreditation is under way, which is intended to promote the spread of high-quality programmes of proven effectiveness.

In the first part of this chapter, consideration will be given to various approaches that have been used to treat violent offenders.

Psychoanalytical approaches

Until the 1970s, psychoanalysis-based counselling was a common form of intervention with aggressive individuals. The underlying problem is seen as one of defective personality development. Violence in later life is considered a displacement of anger and hostility which arose in early childhood. Therapy involves clients' having to focus on childhood loss and rejection, rather than on the immediate circumstances which led to the violent incident. Clients must lose their fear of trusting relationships and become more aware of their feelings. They also need to develop a basis of trust with the therapist – something which may not have come easily to them in the past. Clients will be expected to discuss their aggressive tendencies and must be prepared to experience the unpleasant feelings that will arise. Difficult situations, including strong expressions of anger and grief, may ensue, but it is envisaged that these will have a cathartic effect. Treatment can either be on an individual basis or in small groups: the latter are likely to prevail where funding is an important consideration, or where clients would benefit from the support of their peers.

Psychoanalytic therapies are rarely used nowadays with convicted rapists or violent offenders diagnosed as suffering from severe personality disorders. In the case of the former, this is largely because such approaches are no longer in vogue in institutional settings. For the latter, the view has long held sway that the lack of guilt or empathy commonly associated with psychopaths renders such individuals unsuitable for these types of therapy, which are generally believed to require some feeling of remorse on the part of the client. For less severe forms of violence, a psychoanalytic approach may be used by individual counsellors and psychiatrists. It is not widely adopted by clinical psychologists.

In Freudian terms, non-instrumental violence will probably be the consequence of an over-developed or (more likely) under-developed superego (see Chapter 4). As this is something which is central to the first few years of a person's life, redressing any fundamental deficiency that arose during this period is likely to be a long and arduous process, involving regular and extensive therapist–client contact. According to Kline (1987: 69), custodial treatment 'is always too little, too late'. This – together with a growing perception that such an approach does not 'work' – explains its relative demise. The issue of the criteria used to judge the success of psychoanalytic techniques when employed on offenders is a difficult one. Psychiatrists refer to notions such as improved self-awareness or self-control, targets which seem insufficiently precise for politicians and criminal justice professionals, who prefer to think in terms of reconviction rates. This lack of agreement over the aims of treatment has only served to heighten the appeal of the more focused cognitive-behavioural courses.

Cognitive-behavioural approaches

In recent years, there has been a marked shift among psychologists towards a cognitive-behavioural approach as a means of addressing a wide range of

152   Understanding violent crime

psychological problems. This is based on the writings of Bandura (1973) and views aggressive behaviour as a learned phenomenon (see Chapter 4). Both the emotions leading up to the attack and the use of violence as an appropriate way of dealing with them are seen as a result of the individual's distorted thought patterns. Through their attitudes, attributions and expectancies, people respond to their *cognitive perceptions* of the environment rather than to the environment as such. Whereas a psychoanalytic approach will usually look for the underlying causes of behaviour in a person's early life, a cognitive-behavioural approach will locate the problem in the misleading thoughts of the present. Leading researchers in this area include Hollin (1996), Howells (1996) and McGuire (1995).

Work is carried out to change the distortions. Offenders are taught to confront their behaviour and its consequences, to understand their motives, and to develop ways of controlling their behaviour. Social skills training may also be included, particularly for young offenders, where individuals are taught to communicate with others (such as parents) more effectively, and to resist pressure from delinquent peers.

Anger management
Programmes designed to deal with individual violence increasingly contain at least some consideration of how the emotion of anger is dealt with. However, it is important to remember that violence is by no means an inevitable outcome even of extreme angry feelings. Just as it is possible to be angry without resorting to violence, it is possible to be violent without feeling anger. Novaco (see below) has pointed out that anger is neither a necessary nor a sufficient condition for violence. Instrumental violence provides an example of this. Men are not necessarily angry when being violent to their partners; it is often power and control that they are seeking to exercise. Indeed, as an ordinary human emotion, anger can have positive functions, including the communication of disapproval, the energizing of behaviour and the strengthening of a person's feelings of control. Anger only becomes a problem when it has a significantly adverse effect on someone, whether the angered person, the object of the anger, or even bystanders. What is 'significantly adverse' may be a matter for debate, but it is likely to include the infliction of violence.

According to Wessler and Wessler (1980), there are two types of anger – destructive and functional. In both types the angered person considers that another should not have broken a particular rule. Destructive anger leads the person to think that the other should be punished for so doing, and retaliatory measures will be adopted, which may include physical violence. A functionally (or 'non-damning') angry person, although deprecating the behaviour, is likely to respond merely in an assertive fashion.

Novaco's Anger Control Therapy   The involvement of cognitive-behavioural techniques in dealing with destructive anger is most strongly associated with the work of Raymond Novaco (1975). In his Anger Control Therapy, chronic anger is said to be the consequence of cognitive dysfunctions, which take the form of biased expectations or beliefs and distorted automatic thoughts. Novaco referred to these as 'self-statements'. This underlines the fact that anger is not an unthinking or impulsive reaction to a situation; its creation, maintenance and dispersal all result from cognitive processes. Novaco thought that anger is the consequence of a combination of externally aversive events, internal processes such as interpretation, and the behaviours which form the response to these events. The external event alone cannot cause the anger, because there is a range of possible emotional responses. Novaco considered that there are three main aspects of how the individual will view such an event: appraisal; expectation; and private speech.

Appraisal involves cognitive evaluations of the meaning of the event for the person: for example, whether it is threatening of image or status, and what capacity the person has to respond. An event can also be assessed in relation to the individual's expectations. If people anticipate that something will annoy them, they are likely to look for cues which will reinforce the expectancy. Also, arousal may occur when the experience is different from the expectations. Novaco thought that, if a person expects an expression of anger to have a particular consequence, such as the other person's backing down, the level of anger may increase if the outcome fails to materialize.

Private speech, or self-statements, are generally reflections on appraisals and expectations. According to Novaco, these can affect the formation of an anger reaction. If people keep telling themselves that someone is trying to annoy them, this can serve to aggravate the situation.

Of course, resort to violence is only one possible consequence of anger. Other more common responses include the verbal expression of feelings and a physical withdrawal from the situation. The nature of the person's reaction will depend on cognitive processes influenced by past events and the prediction of future outcomes. The process is entirely subjective; it is therefore meaningless to make an objective assessment of an incident as 'trivial'. Although criminal law only allows provocation as a defence when the aggressive response to it has been immediate, in reality the effects of rumination can lead to a 'slow burn' anger, which can result in an outburst of violence some time after the original provoking event. There can also be a series of incidents which can cumulatively reinforce anger.

Novaco developed his Anger Control Therapy on the basis that anger results from a reaction to stressful events. The approach is primarily based on learning, in that it involves the exposure of subjects to controlled, mildly stressful situations which will activate their coping responses, together with guidance on the thought processes which should restrict the development of destructively aggressive responses. The aims of the training are therefore to prevent destructive anger; to control any arousal that does occur; and to cultivate the ability to deal with the provocative circumstances.

Various changes are predicted to result from the Anger Control Therapy programme. In physiological terms, there should be a lowering of arousal when the client is confronted with stressful incidents. In cognitive terms, the client should become more realistic in expectations of both self and others. Private speech should become more positive, and there should be a reduced tendency to ruminate over provocative comments or events. In behavioural terms, there should be an improvement in interpersonal skills, with a less hostile approach to others. Competence in problem-solving should also be enhanced.

Novaco himself realized that the programme would need to be adapted to different types of client, and the wide range of variations on the programme that are now practised makes the overall approach difficult to evaluate. However, one particular version has been reported as having had some success with a group of child-abusing parents (Nomellini and Katz 1983).

Research in a youth custody centre by McDougall *et al.* (1987) compared a group of inmates who had manifested anger control problems within the institution, and who undertook an anger control training programme, with a control group who did not undertake the programme. Several changes to Novaco's scheme were considered necessary to suit the particular group. Relaxation was not incorporated into every session (because some of the boys did not take it seriously) and only group work was used. Attempts to explain the different reasons why people become angry proved too complicated for the inmates. The deliberate creation of real provocative incidents was considered inappropriate in a custodial setting. After three months, there was a statistically significant improvement in the behaviour of the training group, measured in terms of disciplinary reports. No such change occurred in the control group.

Other research has also found that anger management programmes are generally successful at reducing anger levels in the short term, and are particularly effective in reducing disorderly behaviour in institutional settings (Levey and Howells 1990). What is not clear, however, is the effectiveness of such techniques at reducing violence in the longer term (Hollin 1990).

Rational Emotive Behaviour Therapy This is another cognitive-based approach which can be used to address anger. Originally developed in the USA during the 1950s by Albert Ellis, it is now widely used throughout the world (Dryden 1996). Ellis assumed that individuals' main aim is the pursuit of happiness, but that everyone has a biological tendency towards irrationality. This can be demonstrated by the fact that, not only will people inevitably behave irrationally even when it goes against everything they have learned, but that, having conquered existing irrational tendencies, they often develop new ones. The aim of Rational Emotive Behaviour Therapy is to alter people's thought patterns to a more realistic level of attainment. Ellis placed a great deal of emphasis on rationality, and Socratic argument is much used in the therapy. The basis of the approach is that rational beliefs and thoughts lead to functional and desired behaviour or feelings, whereas irrational beliefs and thoughts result in dysfunctional and undesired behaviour or feelings, such as destructive anger or depression.

Relaxation training   Although the research literature is sparse, Howells (1988) concluded that there is some evidence that relaxation training can be successful in reducing anger. McGurk (1980) reported that the use of such procedures resulted in a significant decline of reported rates of aggression in a prison during a six-month follow-up period. However, this was not reflected in subsequent reconviction rates for violent offences. A leading proponent of relaxation training, Deffenbacher, has argued that cognitive and relaxation techniques are equally effective if used in isolation. He has also claimed that some clients are more resistant to cognitive training and find the relaxation approach more helpful (Deffenbacher *et al.* 1988).

Sexual assaults
Approaches to sexual offences based on behavioural conditioning try to reinforce 'desirable' sexual activity – consensual adult heterosexual intercourse – at the expense of 'undesirable' behaviour. Various types of aversion therapy have been employed for this purpose. Electric shocks, although claimed by some to be effective, are increasingly considered unethical. Masturbatory reconditioning, which involves the client obtaining an orgasm to a non-deviant fantasy, is also used. Some researchers have even tried unpleasant odours (usually in the form of a gas) coupled with exposure to the deviant fantasy as a form of aversive treatment. However, these approaches have generally been applied in cases of minor sexual deviance, such as indecent exposure, and there is no firm evidence that they can reduce sexual violence. Moreover, they neither address the motives which arouse or sustain deviant sexuality, nor offer offenders any insight into their behaviour.

Many sex offender programmes have concentrated on social deficits, such as poor social problem-solving techniques, low self-esteem, and weak conversational skills, all of which can lead to an inability to form and maintain close relationships. Cognitive-based programmes involve confronting offenders with the consequences of their actions and highlighting distortions in their cognitive processes. This may include the challenging of beliefs about 'rape myths' (see Chapter 6) and the appropriateness of adult–child sex. Offenders have to increase their ability to empathize with their victims and learn to understand the emotional aspects of sexual activity. Therapy can occur in individual or group settings.

The effectiveness of such programmes is usually judged in terms of reconviction rates, a reduction in which should ideally be shown over a fairly lengthy period. Although the evidence suggests a reasonable level of success for less serious sexual offenders, the picture concerning rapists is far from clear. There is a particular methodological difficulty involving control groups, as the random allocation of offenders for treatment or no treatment for such a serious crime raises ethical problems. Research by Maletzky (1991) involved an extensive follow-up procedure for periods of up to 17 years for 5000 sex offenders who had received outpatient treatment based on behavioural methods. The failure rates were lowest for heterosexual paedophiles (5 per cent) and exposers (7 per cent): rapists had the highest rate (26 per cent). More recently, Marshall and Pithers (1994) have claimed that the results of behavioural treatment for sex offenders are encouraging.

The California Sex Offender Treatment and Evaluation Project, created in 1985, uses cognitive-behavioural techniques for a small number of carefully selected prisoners convicted of child molestation or rape. They are transferred to a state hospital, where they remain for about two years before release on parole, which includes compulsory participation in a 12-month aftercare programme. The inmates receive both individual and group therapy, with a strong emphasis on relapse prevention. Marques *et al.* (1994) have assessed the success of the programme by using comparisons with matched groups of offenders who did not undertake it. Overall, the treatment group had lower reoffending rates for both sex and other violent offences than the comparison groups. The difference was greatest for the child molesters: the treated rapists were less likely to commit sexual offences, but remained just as likely to commit other violent crimes.

Therapeutic communities

The idea of a therapeutic community (TC) first arose in Britain in the 1940s. Although there are several different types, the commonest involves a small community of individuals suffering from various forms of psychological disorder (but especially severe personality disorder), which works to eliminate antisocial behaviour in a relatively informal communal setting. The community, which is run on democratic lines, concentrates on the confrontation of its members' problems in group discussion. Offenders have to discuss their crimes, be open to challenge from other group members, and have their behaviour and reactions constantly monitored by their peers in a way which would be difficult in the outside world.

TCs are usually found in institutional settings, such as prisons or hospitals. In England, Grendon Prison in Buckinghamshire was built in the 1960s to operate such a community (Genders and Player 1995). Offenders, who must already be in the prison system, apply to go to Grendon and are assessed for suitability by Grendon's own psychologists. In America, TCs tend to concentrate on drug and alcohol abusers, and often utilize former addicts as members of staff. Indeed, it is a common aspect of all types of TC that the inmates become involved in each other's therapy. The sharing of day-to-day tasks and decision-making is believed to foster the development of relationships and the articulation of feelings: difficulties in these areas are widely considered as underlying a variety of psychological disorders.

Early evidence of the effectiveness of TCs in reducing offending was mixed. Gunn and Robertson (1987) found there was no decline in reconviction rates after ten years for a group of prisoners released from Grendon. On the other hand, Cooke's (1989) study of a small sample discovered a reduction in violence levels following admission to the former Special Unit at Barlinnie Prison in Scotland, and a lower than expected recidivism rate following release. However, Cooke's results must be treated with a certain amount of caution, as there was no control group.

More recent research into Grendon by Marshall (1997) and Taylor (2000) has been encouraging. In Marshall's study, the reconviction rates after four years of 702 patients admitted between 1984 and 1989 (the admitted group) were compared with those of 142 prisoners who were selected for Grendon, but did not go (the waiting list group), and a larger, matched group of prisoners from the general prison population (the general prison group). The waiting list offenders were more likely to be reconvicted than the admitted group. This was also the case for violent offences, although the results were only statistically significant for offenders aged over 30 on release with two or more previous convictions for violence. The reconviction rate of this group was 28 per cent, compared with 49 per cent for comparable offenders on the waiting list. There was also a lower reconviction rate for repeat sex offenders in the admitted group than in the waiting list group. The length of stay at Grendon had an important impact on the likelihood of reconviction, with inmates who stayed 18 months showing a reduction in the rate of between one-fifth and one-quarter. In a further analysis of the sample, Taylor (2000) discovered that Marshall's findings were still broadly applicable when the reconviction rates were considered after seven years.

These findings suggest that the treatment at Grendon 'works', especially for older violent and for recidivist sex offenders. One important point to emerge from the research may explain why earlier studies failed to arrive at this conclusion. The reconviction rate of the waiting list offenders was substantially worse than that of the general prison group. This shows that Grendon has been selecting inmates with a far higher risk of reconviction, and that earlier comparisons of Grendon prisoners with the general prison population had not compared like with like.

Nevertheless, despite the more recent Grendon research, there is still a degree of scepticism among both psychologists and policy-makers as to the effectiveness of the TC regime. Many people who visit Grendon after viewing an ordinary prison are likely to leave with the view that 'this is how prisons ought to be'. The view somehow lingers that the inmates react positively to being treated in a humane, non-punitive manner, rather than directly benefiting from the challenges posed by group therapy. However, staff and (most) inmates tell a different story, and Marshall's study at last provides them with some supporting evidence.

Lees *et al.* (1999) have reviewed the international literature on the effectiveness of TCs for mentally disordered offenders. The most effective research technique was considered to involve the randomized allocation of patients to treatment or non-treatment groups. Of the ten completed studies using this approach which were identified, seven found better results for the TC.

Pharmacological treatment

Certain drugs can affect mood and influence the parts of the brain that trigger violent acts. Opinion is divided over the desirability of their employment for this purpose, and in practice the use of major tranquillizers tends to be restricted to patients in psychiatric hospitals, particularly when the safety of others is under threat. The danger of such drugs being applied for control purposes strongly militates against their use in prisons. The side-effects can be particularly unpleasant and sometimes harmful (Miczek *et al.* 1994). Any benefits will only last for the course of the treatment. The underlying causes of the violence will therefore never be tackled by this approach. Minor tranquillizers are more widely used, often in conjunction with therapy, but care must be taken as they can actually induce violence in certain types of patient.

The administration of anti-libidinal drugs to effect the 'chemical castration' of violent sex offenders is also, not surprisingly, a deeply controversial issue: many people consider their use to be unethical. In any event, it is by no means clear that such drugs achieve their purpose. The assumption is that rape and other violent sexual attacks are a consequence of a sexual 'drive', and that a reduction of the sex hormone testosterone would thereby reduce such incidents (see Chapter 3). However, it is now widely recognized that rape in particular is not necessarily committed for sexual gratification (Perkins 1991).

A pro-feminist approach

A completely different way of dealing with male violence against women is advocated by some feminists (Hague and Malos 1993). This emphasizes the historical and cultural basis of the behaviour, where men have been placed in a dominant position over women. Such violence is viewed by feminists as intentional rather than pathological, and individualistic explanations are rejected as excuses – men cannot be seen as victims. While accepting the utility of cognitive-behavioural techniques in changing thought processes and improving communication skills, feminists consider that a more urgent requirement is a change in male *attitudes* to women, in particular their expectation of exercising control. Some feminists consider that this change cannot happen without a fundamental shift of power in society and the end of the patriarchal family.

Under the pro-feminist approach, intervention has to involve all the parties concerned, as it is necessary that men be informed at first hand of the harm they have caused. This itself can understandably cause difficulties for some women. Ideally, the meetings should only occur as a result of a court punishment, as the involvement of the criminal justice system is considered necessary to demonstrate the gravity of the situation to the abusive men. In the Scottish research by Dobash *et al.* (1996) discussed below, the women in the Lothian scheme threatened to withdraw their cooperation from the programme if the male violence were to be effectively decriminalized by being dealt with outside the system.

Some women's organizations are opposed to strategies involving the abusive male on the grounds that they allow the perpetrators to offer excuses for their behaviour, and take up valuable resources which could be better utilized in helping abused women (Finkelhor and Yllö 1985). In the research by Scourfield and Dobash (1999) discussed below, 39 per cent of the resistance to male violence groups was judged to come from women's refuge organizations, and was broadly based on these two grounds, although the view was also expressed that violent men are incapable of change. In America, however, women's groups have played a more active role in the development and running of such programmes.

One such approach which has become popular in the USA is the 'Duluth model', which was developed by the Duluth Domestic Abuse Intervention Project (DAIP) in Duluth, Minnesota, during the 1980s. Most of the men are referred by the police or courts, although a small number attend as volunteers. The programme is based on the premise that the battering of women is an attempt by the men to assert power and control. As physical abuse is invariably accompanied by such conduct as emotional abuse, intimidation, coercion, and a general assumption of dominance in the relationship, the 26-week course is designed to eradicate this behaviour and make the men realize that relationships should be based on equality, shared responsibility, mutual trust and support, and respect (Pence and Paymar 1994). In Britain, the Home Office (1999c) has shown interest in the scheme.

Evaluations of the DAIP have found a reported reduction in abusive behaviour. When a sample of 100 men was considered five years after completing the programme, 22 had been convicted of domestic assault and 15 made the subject of civil orders on the grounds of such violence (Shepard 1992).

In Canada, organizations such as New Directions, Vivre sans Violence and Entre Hommes not only provide anti-sexist education for all-male groups, but also offer a telephone 'hotline' for men to call when they feel like assaulting their female partner (DeKeseredy and Ellis 1995).

Sources of treatment

Voluntary agencies

There are various settings in which problems of violence can be confronted. A person whose behaviour has not resulted in criminal proceedings has the freedom to choose whether to seek help. In Britain, this may be available on the National Health Service. Alternatively, individual treatment can be sought privately from a psychiatrist, psychologist or therapist.

In practice, most people in Britain who seek help to overcome their violence outside the criminal justice system obtain it in a group setting. This is largely because such services are often provided free or at a low cost. There is some evidence that group work can have a contaminating effect on less experienced offenders, which can actually increase the likelihood of further offending (McIvor 1992). However, for practical reasons this approach at present seems unavoidable. In North America, however, it is far more common to find individual treatment provided.

Some of the bodies offering such a service are funded by central or local government. Others obtain charitable status or exist without any mainstream funding. For example, in England, The Violence Initiative is a self-help group based in London which gives free or low-cost assistance to such individuals, and the Everyman Centre in Brixton, London, deals with self-referrals from men who physically abuse their partners. In Canada, the John Howard Society provides nationwide voluntary support through a network of local groups. Alternatives to Violence International is an American-based organization operating in many countries. It runs programmes both in prisons and in the community, including workshops for people wanting to deal with their own violence problem.

There is a clear division between violence counsellors who think that, to be effective, attendance should be mandated by a court, and those who feel that voluntarism is necessary. Research by Scourfield and Dobash (1999), based on a telephone survey of 23 agencies providing a service for men who are violent towards their partners, found that 57 per cent of them only took men who had volunteered for the programme, and 13 per cent only took men whose attendance had been ordered by a court.

The criminal justice system

Many violent individuals do not take the opportunity to evaluate their behaviour until they become involved in the criminal justice system. In domestic violence cases, where the police are called but the victim does not subsequently wish to press charges, aggressors may either be encouraged by the police or decide of their own volition to seek help. Where a person is convicted of a violent offence, the question of whether any treatment is forthcoming will depend on the nature of the sentence.

Probation and community sentences
There are two main ways in which the probation service will encounter violent offenders. Some will be placed on probation or given a community sentence, perhaps with the condition that they attend an anti-violence course. Others will be referred to the service when they are released from prison on automatic or discretionary conditional release.

Since the mid-1980s, it has become increasingly common for probation officers to adopt a cognitive-behavioural approach in their courses for violent offenders. This has been encouraged by a growing body of evidence that such intervention can be effective. Hedderman *et al.* (1997) conducted a national survey of probation services' use of the approach. They found that most areas had either developed or bought in programmes involving cognitive or cognitive-behavioural skills. Although two-thirds of the programmes were mainly run for offenders whose presence was required as a condition of a court order, only a few excluded offenders from attending voluntarily. There was a general feeling that the approach 'worked', although very few areas had attempted a rigorous form of evaluation.

One research project which did involve evaluation was a three-year study of two innovative Scottish men's probation programmes, CHANGE and the Lothian Domestic Violence Probation Project, which were designed to deal with violence to partners (Dobash *et al.* 1996). The men had agreed to participate as a condition of a probation order. This involved weekly attendance at the groups for up to seven months. The programmes were based on cognitive-behavioural principles. The study compared participants with a matched sample of offenders who had been given other punishments. Court records showed that 7 per cent of men in the programme and 10 per cent in the control group were convicted of violent offences against their partners during the follow-up period of one year.

These figures could suggest that it was involvement in the criminal justice system that had the strongest impact on such offenders, as the programmes were only slightly more successful than other sanctions. However, when the views of the men's partners were sought, a different picture emerged. They reported that only 33 per cent of the men committed a violent act against them during the 12-month follow-up period: the corresponding figure from the partners of men who received other punishments was 75 per cent. An even greater difference emerged when the overall frequency of violent offending was considered. According to their partners, only 7 per cent of men participating in the programmes – compared with 37 per cent of men dealt with in other ways – started five or more violent incidents during the follow-up period.

Cognitive-behavioural approaches have been used for many years in America and, in particular, Canada, where the Reasoning and Rehabilitation (R & R) programme was developed (Ross *et al.* 1988). This is a cognitive skills approach designed for high-risk offenders. In the original

162 Understanding violent crime

Ontario model, groups of four to six offenders received 80 hours of intensive training designed to change aspects of their thinking, including their impulsiveness and failure to understand other people's views and feelings. Reconviction rates over a nine-month period were impressive: only 18 per cent of the group were reconvicted, compared with 69 per cent of standard probationers and 47 per cent of those receiving life-skills training. The R & R programme is now a core curriculum element for Correctional Services of Canada (Ross and Ross 1995).

By late 1993, the R & R programme was being used by 13 probation services in England and Wales (Hedderman *et al.* 1997). The Mid Glamorgan service has carried out a detailed evaluation, including a comparison of reconviction rates with offenders receiving standard probation supervision or short custodial sentences. Unlike the other groups, those subject to the R & R programme had better than predicted reconviction rates in the 12 months following completion. Although this advantage disappeared during the following 12 months, the researchers felt that this was due to the way the scheme had been organized (Raynor and Vanstone 1996).

Some of the programmes dealing with violent young offenders have sought to include parents and school teachers in their cognitive-based approach. Borduin *et al.* (1995) reported on a study involving such 'multisystemic treatment' (MST). Offenders aged 12–17 were randomly assigned either to MST or individual therapy. Evaluation included measuring arrests for violent crimes during a four-year period. The youths who had been involved in the MST programme were significantly less likely to be arrested than those who had received individual therapy.

In Britain, the Home Office has become interested in Aggression Replacement Training (Goldstein *et al.* 1999), an American programme which uses training in prosocial skills, anger control and moral reasoning to help adolescents understand what makes them feel angry or act aggressively.

Intensive probation
Evidence from America suggests that what is termed 'intensive rehabilitation supervision' can be particularly effective with certain types of offender. These programmes are also run on behavioural principles. They involve extensive contact between probation and parole officers and offenders. There is a high level of surveillance, but care is taken not to over-emphasize the threat of sanctions for non-compliance, as earlier schemes which adopted this approach proved to be unsuccessful. In a survey of the research literature, Gendreau *et al.* (1994) identified the key elements in the best programmes, which in some cases showed a reduction in recidivism levels of 80 per cent. In these schemes, intensive supervision was only used for high-risk offenders. Traditional Freudian psychoanalytic techniques were generally ineffective. The supervision was specifically targeted at offenders' needs, even to the extent of matching them with particular therapists, who should be highly qualified and experienced.

In England, the creation of intensive probation schemes was encouraged from the late 1980s, and the Home Office evaluated several of these between 1990 and 1992 (Mair *et al.* 1994). Although no reconviction rates have been published, the main participants – sentencers and offenders – appear to have been broadly satisfied with the way the programmes ran, and many offenders, who would otherwise have probably been given a custodial sentence, felt that the schemes had prevented them from reoffending.

Examples of intensive probation programmes which were designed to tackle anger and violence in male offenders are the Keep Your Head and Relationships for Men courses run by the Newcastle Intensive Probation Unit (Gardiner and Nesbit 1996). Rather than employing the traditional probation approach of weekly meetings, these programmes involve constant therapy for three or four consecutive days. Yet again, the schemes are operated on cognitive-behavioural principles.

With the increased profile given to sexual offences in recent years, probation services have come under governmental pressure to devise community-based programmes for offenders. Involvement with rapists is far less common than with child abusers, and is most likely to occur following their release from prison on licence. This in itself may have implications for any evaluation of their treatment, as the effects of imprisonment (positive or negative) may be difficult to separate from those of probation schemes. Most of the research has related to paedophiles, and there is evidence that treatment based on cognitive-behavioural principles can be successful both in changing attitudes (Beckett *et al.* 1994) and reducing offending (Hedderman *et al.* 1997).

However, the evidence is less clear concerning rapists. A survey by Barker and Morgan (1993) discovered that reconviction rates following treatment were consistently higher than those of abusers. Such offenders are clearly viewed as problematic by some probation services: a survey by the Association of Chief Officers of Probation (Procter and Flaxington 1996) found that, although all group programmes accepted referrals of men who sexually offended against children, a quarter did not provide for sexual offenders against adults (or, indeed, for any female sexual offenders).

More recent research has indicated that rapists may indeed benefit from community-based treatment programmes. Hedderman and Sugg (1996) compared the two-year reconviction rates of sex offenders who had participated in one of seven special schemes with those of a matched group who had received ordinary probation supervision. Although largely comprising offenders convicted of indecent assault, the 'special group' did include a small number of men convicted of rape or attempted rape. The researchers also pointed to the evidence showing that a high proportion of incidents initially reported as rape result in convictions for indecent assault (Grace *et al.* 1992). The results showed that 5 per cent of the 'special group' and 9 per cent of the control group were reconvicted of a sexual offence within two years. In addition, members of the control group were five times as likely to be convicted of a further non-sexual offence.

Imprisonment

Whatever comments may be made by the sentencing judge concerning the desirability of treatment, a sentence of imprisonment does not incorporate a probability – let alone a legal right – that prisoners will receive any help in addressing psychological or other problems which may have contributed to their offending behaviour. Broadly speaking, the longer the sentence, the more likely that such assistance will be available.

The Prison Department has been encouraged to create inmate programmes which tackle problems causing particular public concern. This has resulted in attention being concentrated on drug use and sex offending. Although violence is arguably a greater social problem than either of these phenomena, it has been given a lower priority for attention. This may be because violence, which has always existed, has not been implicated in a 'moral panic' (see Chapter 4), such as the one which – in the view of some people – has arisen in the case of illegal drugs; or received the publicity which has resulted from the growing discovery of child sexual abuse. Alternatively, it may be a consequence of a 'nothing works' mentality having developed from previous unsuccessful attempts to deal with the problem.

However, it appears that there is now a greater desire to deal with violence, and the Prison Department's Directorate of Inmate Programmes has begun to train prison officers to conduct anger management groups (Towl 1994). Certain prisons, such as Parkhurst on the Isle of Wight, have dedicated special wings to the treatment of violent prisoners. Grendon Prison operates a therapeutic community in an attempt to deal with psychologically disturbed inmates (see above).

The Offending Behaviour Programmes Unit of the Prison Department Offending Behaviour Unit has developed the CALM Programme ('Controlling Anger and Learning to Manage it'). This was devised in Canada, where its use in prisons has resulted in a significant reduction in reconviction rates. The course consists of 24 group sessions, each of two hours, and is based on Novaco's anger management therapy. Another North American approach which is currently interesting the Prison Department is the Cognitive Self-Change programme, which has operated in Vermont since 1988 (Bush 1995). This is based on the view that offenders' cognitive patterns are closely related to their feelings of self-worth. Constraints are seen as an insult and a challenge to individual autonomy, which is broadly defined as being able to have what one wants. Offenders view themselves as victims, those considered responsible stand accused, and violence is one possible reaction. This is reinforced by the sense of gratification resulting from feeling in charge again. The aim of the programme is to challenge the cognitive processes that make violence seem rewarding.

Henning and Frueh (1996) compared two matched groups of prisoners, the majority of whom had been convicted of violent offences. The members of one group had voluntarily participated in the Cognitive Self-Change programme. Only half the offenders in the treatment group were charged with an offence during the two years following release, compared with 71 per cent of the control group.

Mental health legislation

A violent offender (other than one convicted of murder), who is found by a court to be suffering from a mental disorder within the definition of section 1(2) of the Mental Health Act 1983 (see Chapter 3), can be made the subject of a hospital order under s. 37 of the Act, provided that a place for the offender has been arranged in a particular hospital. This is an important requirement because, in practice, beds are often unavailable and mentally disordered offenders are then sentenced to imprisonment. In the case of a person suffering from psychopathic disorder or mental impairment, a hospital order should only be made if treatment is likely to alleviate or prevent a deterioration of the condition. A court can now make a 'hospital direction' stipulating that, on the conclusion of treatment for a psychopathic disorder (or a finding in hospital that the disorder is untreatable), the offender will be transferred to prison rather than released into the community.

A hospital order initially lasts for six months, but can be renewed by medical staff. Where the offender is thought to be particularly dangerous, a court may impose a restriction order under s. 41, the effect of which is that the offender cannot be released without the permission of the Home Secretary or a Mental Health Review Tribunal. There is provision, under s. 47 of the Act, for an offender to be transferred from prison to a mental hospital.

Any, or any combination, of the methods of treating violence which are discussed above are liable to be used in a hospital setting.

A study of all the patients subject to restriction orders who were conditionally discharged from hospitals between 1972 and 1994 showed that those convicted of violent offences, who formed by far the largest proportion at 55 per cent, had the lowest reconviction rate (9 per cent) over a two-year period (Kershaw et al. 1997). It seems unlikely that this can be solely attributed to the success of the treatment adopted. A more plausible explanation is that far more care was taken in authorizing the release of violent offenders than those whose crime was, for example, theft (who had a reconviction rate of 28 per cent).

Conclusion

In both institutional and community settings, treatment based to some extent on cognitive-behavioural principles has come to replace psychoanalysis as the favoured approach of psychologists when dealing with both violent and sexual offenders. This may in part reflect the greater prominence of behavioural psychologists in this area of work. There are also political advantages. Whereas psychoanalysis might appear to some to involve sympathizing with, and trying to 'cure', a 'sick' offender, cognitive-behavioural techniques are more in keeping with the current expectation that such people should be blamed: they must accept that they are fully responsible for their actions, and appreciate the harm that has been caused to their victims.

It is also claimed that cognitive-behavioural methods are more 'successful' than psychoanalytic ones. In the context of the criminal justice system, this translates into the likelihood of reoffending. However, most of the evidence of this success comes from community-based schemes involving relatively minor offenders. The situation regarding seriously violent people in secure institutions is far less clear: for instance, most researchers consider that rapists do not respond well to cognitive-behavioural therapy. It may be that the psychosexual problems experienced by these offenders are far more severe than, for example, the 'inappropriate attitudes' towards women on the part of abusive men, which cognitive-behavioural therapy can show some success in changing.

Further reading

The renewed interest in the treatment of offenders is reflected in the contributions found in *What Works? Reducing Reoffending – Guidelines from Research and Practice* (McGuire 1995). *Applying Psychology to Imprisonment: Theory and Practice* (McGurk *et al.* 1987) discusses a range of approaches that are used in custodial settings. *Dangerous People* (Walker 1996) considers the particular problems that arise in the treatment of serious sexual and violent offenders.

Conclusion

Throughout this book, various theories of violent behaviour have been considered. In some cases, the explanation may appear to be convincing, but only of limited application. Perhaps the best example is the violence that can result from certain forms of mental illness. Other explanations, such as the notion that human violence serves an evolutionary function, seem to be more questionable. There is a large body of research evidence suggesting that violent behaviour patterns can, in some way, be learned from other people. Although this evidence does not reveal what lay behind the violence of the original actor in the chain, in some situations learning theories can provide a plausible account of how a person came to resort to physical aggression. Corporal punishment is supposed to teach children to obey orders. It may also teach them that the use of force is an effective means of imposing one's will on others.

The question whether visual depictions of physical and sexual violence sensitize people to, or encourage, its use in the real world continues to be controversial. Many psychologists argue that there is no proven connection between such exposure and violence. Sociologists, however, are more likely to consider that, as pornography portrays women as sexual objects, it is bound to encourage attacks by men. Whatever the merits of these arguments, the prevailing morality in most countries is still more concerned with the affront caused by portrayals of sexual activity, and far less attention is paid to the production of violent films for entertainment.

The issue of control is often considered important in relation to crime. Gottfredson and Hirschi (1990) argued that offending occurs because of poor socialization in childhood. One of the difficulties with this view is that it does not explain why most offenders (including violent ones) have largely ceased their criminal activities by the time they reach middle age. The control balance theory set out by Tittle (1995) is better able to deal with this: older people have less need than the young to demonstrate control over others.

In recent years, there has been a growing awareness of the high level of violence that occurs within families. The physical and sexual assault of women by their male partners is clearly widespread but, for the reasons explained in Chapter 2, rarely prosecuted. The use of 'reasonable force' by parents to beat their children is still lawful, but is increasingly coming under challenge from provisions designed to protect human rights. There is no evidence that children in Denmark, Austria and Cyprus behave worse than those in other countries, but these are some of the states where hitting children is illegal, whether at home or at school. There is also a growing concern over the use of consensual violence, and the British Medical Association is just one of the organizations that are opposed to boxing.

The sexual assault of children has attracted growing public and police attention, and responses to it are becoming tougher. Whereas the harm that sexual interference can cause is nowadays regarded as self-evident, little attention is given to the vast amount of evidence put forward by psychologists such as Murray Straus indicating that corporal punishment can result in emotional as well as physical scars, and that the victims have an increased likelihood of developing into aggressors themselves. This appears to be an important line to pursue although, as elsewhere, an explanation based on learning theory alone must be incomplete: although more boys are beaten than girls, such an account would still predict a higher level of physically aggressive women.

Anthropological studies indicate that family violence is a good predictor of other forms of violence (Levinson 1989). What distinguishes the few reported societies with little or no violence from those where it is commonplace? One notable difference is that these low-violence communities would be considered very primitive by contemporary Western standards. As there is no prospect of a reversion by the West to a far simpler way of life, this may not appear to be a fruitful line to pursue. Nevertheless, there are other lessons that can be learned. Levinson (1989) highlighted several distinctive features in the family life of the non-violent societies he identified, all of which could be integrated into modern Western culture. There was sexual equality in family decision-making. Couples lived in monogamous relationships and were interdependent on both an economic and emotional level. Disagreements were settled by disengagement or mediation rather than recourse to violence. Other family members and neighbours were prepared to intervene and help where violence was threatened or used.

These factors suggest that the explanations of violence based on the exercise of male power in a patriarchal society merit particular attention. Feminist writers have been studying this, particularly since the 1970s. The work on 'masculinities' goes even further and claims that, among men, there are superior and subordinated masculinities. In other words, some men will play an inferior role to others. Although writers such as Messerschmidt criticized much feminist work for being essentialist, explanations of violence solely based on masculinities are open to the same charge. The question still remains why certain males have to show their dominance through violence, whereas others may, for example, wield economic power in the home or participate in sport. Different answers are possible. It may be that violence is committed by people who feel they have no other effective way of asserting themselves or achieving anything. Another explanation may look back to the earliest experiences of children at the hands of their parents.

Although unfashionable nowadays with academics (but not practitioners), psychoanalytic explanations of violence based on events during early childhood are still of interest. These are increasingly focusing on attachment theory and what de Zulueta (1993: 225) called 'the dehumanisation of the "other"'. According to this view, the seeds of violent behaviour are sown in the failure of proper attachments to form between parent and infant, whether through rejection, neglect or abuse. Inadequate attachments can hinder the development of empathy and altruism, and ultimately result in psychological problems. Whereas proper attachments in infancy will lead to an appropriate sense of self-esteem, poor attachments may cause strong feelings of inadequacy, together with anger against the parents.

The patriarchal nature of society and the resulting differences in the socialization of boys and girls can exacerbate these problems. As boys are expected to become 'manly', they are encouraged to distance themselves from what is arguably their most important early attachment – their mother – and by implication some of the key qualities she embodies. Boys may be brought up to think that they are superior to, and in control of, 'lesser' groups. These have traditionally comprised women, but they now include any males who are 'different' and form 'subordinated masculinities' (such as racial minorities, foreigners and gays). People who experience poor attachments in infancy may split off feelings they cannot cope with and, in extreme cases, form 'multiple personalities'. The self or other may be dehumanized, or viewed as an object. Given the societal pressure on boys in particular to 'prove' themselves, the resultant lack of empathy may, together with the repressed feelings of anger, lead to violence, especially where no other adequate means of being in control are available.

Girls are not expected to assert themselves in this way. They have traditionally been socialized into passivity and conformity to male requirements. Where the anger, misery and frustration which the female victims of poor parental attachment and childhood abuse feel is manifested in violence, it is more likely to be in the form of self-mutilation. It is possible that this different form of expression is encouraged by learned inhibitions against the manifestation of aggressive behaviour towards others.

Societies therefore condone, or even encourage, the desire of some men to establish dominance over other men or women. Life has become far more competitive, whether in the school, the workplace or even recreational activities. It is likely that feelings of detachment from others have grown as people increasingly see themselves in competition. It is many years since sociologists and other writers first warned of the possible consequences of the strain that can arise from rivalry. The sources of strain identified by Merton in the 1930s, and set out in his theory of anomie, are even stronger at the beginning of the twenty-first century. Most instances of physical violence are still perpetrated by the poor and the unsuccessful.

Although the question whether violence is more common than in earlier times will continue to be a matter of debate, it is undeniable (and encouraging) that society's tolerance of it is declining. It is not just the victims of domestic and sexual violence who are increasingly speaking out. However, the important question still remains as to the best way of dealing with the problem. Imprisonment is still the chosen option. With the encouragement of politicians and the popular press, courts are passing more and longer custodial sentences, especially for repeat and violent sexual offenders. There is a widespread assumption that, as societies are becoming more developed, all forms of crime, including violence, should be declining. Growing concern for the victims of violent crime (and, in some cases, the seeking of their views on punishment) has contributed to the adoption of a more punitive approach to offenders.

The fact that many violent offenders could themselves be classed as victims does not fit easily within this approach. In 1998, the British Government stated that police and prosecutors should consider teenage female prostitutes as victims rather than offenders, on the grounds that they are likely to have been sexually abused (Department of Health 1998b). There is now plenty of evidence showing that many other offenders, both male and female, have also suffered abuse. Although it is unlikely that the status of victim will be extended to them in the foreseeable future, perhaps one small step has been taken in the right direction.

The importance of the notion of blame in modern society has been shown repeatedly throughout this book. It is encouraged by the editors of the popular press, and politicians are happy to offer their support. Even the victims of crime are sometimes blamed for not taking more care to protect themselves. Yet a concentration on blame does nothing to tackle the underlying causes of violent crime. Moreover, it is interesting that politicians are prepared to abandon a reliance on blame when it suits their purposes. For example, the Prime Minister, Tony Blair, has said there is no point indulging in 'the blame game' in relation to the political situation in Northern Ireland. The same attitude would be very welcome in the Government's approach to crime. In addition to more help for both the individuals who are prone to violence and their victims, the vast resources at present being channelled into imprisonment should be diverted to addressing such fundamental problems as child neglect and abuse; the pressure on people (especially men) to show they are 'better' than others; and the distrust of individuals who are in any way 'different'. It can be stated with confidence that a significant move towards the attainment of these goals would result in a reduction in violent crime.

Sentencing for violent crime in Australia, Canada, New Zealand and the USA

THE LAW

Australia

Although, as members of a federation, the Australian states have their own separate legal systems, the definitions of non-fatal crimes against the person are similar, being based on the English common law. Queensland, Tasmania and Western Australia have criminal codes which cover all aspects of the criminal law. The other states rely on statutory definitions covering certain areas only. All the states use case law (both Australian and English) either to explain the codes or, in the absence of codes or statutory provision, as the sole repository of the law.

Code jurisdictions

Assaults
The Queensland and Western Australia Codes are identical in providing that any application of force to another person without their consent amounts to an assault, and that any assault (unless authorized, justified or excused by law) constitutes a criminal offence. The Tasmanian Code states that an assault is the intentional application of direct or indirect force to the person of another, or a threat by any person to apply such force, providing that the person threatened has reasonable grounds to believe that the threat will be carried out, or that the threatener may deprive the person of their liberty. Neither words alone nor physical contact 'which is reasonably necessary for the common intercourse of life' constitute an assault.

Indecent assault and rape
The law in Western Australia contains offences of indecent and aggravated indecent assault, together with sexual penetration and aggravated sexual penetration. The term

'sexual assault' in New South Wales is defined in a similar way to 'sexual penetration'. Tasmania and Queensland have retained traditional definitions of indecent assault and rape, but Tasmania has introduced an offence of aggravated sexual assault, which is constituted by any penetration of the vagina, genitalia or anus of another person by any part of the body other than the penis, or any inanimate object. Queensland's offence of sexual assault carries enhanced maximum penalties in two situations: an act involving 'penetrating the vagina, anus or vulva to any extent with an object or a part of the body other than the penis'; and 'bringing into contact any part of the genitalia or the anus with any part of the mouth'.

Non-code jurisdictions

Assaults

Each of the three non-code states – New South Wales, South Australia and Victoria – has a principal Crimes Act which contains provisions governing assaults. There are differences, however, between the first two states and Victoria.

In New South Wales and South Australia, the law is generally either virtually identical with English common law notions of assault, or has formed around concepts which have developed from the common law (as with 'wound' and 'grievous bodily harm') (Gillies 1997). The old distinction between assault and battery therefore remains. It is possible recklessly to commit a battery. Both states have a crime of assault occasioning actual bodily harm. There are provisions involving wounding and grievous bodily harm which are very similar to those in England. A crime which does not exist in England, however, is that of causing grievous bodily harm by a grossly negligent act or omission.

In Victoria, new provisions creating assault-based offences were introduced in 1985. The offences are now simpler – although not more exact (Gillies 1997) – and terms like 'grievous bodily harm' have been abandoned. They are now based on 'injury' and 'serious injury'. The former 'includes unconsciousness, hysteria, pain and any substantial impairment of bodily function'. The new offences include intentionally causing serious injury to another; causing serious injury to another recklessly; and intentionally or recklessly causing injury to another. All the injuries must be caused 'without lawful excuse'. There is also a crime of negligently causing serious injury. The notion of 'assault' has not been abandoned: there are several assault offences including assault or threat to assault a person with intent to commit an indictable (serious) offence.

Indecent assault and rape

Each of the non-code jurisdictions has an offence of indecent assault where the key concepts of 'indecency' and 'assault' are defined in substantially the same way as they are in England. In New South Wales, the crime is committed by an assault where the defendant 'commits an act of indecency on or in the presence of another person'. A similar provision is found in South Australia, where consent cannot be a defence for a guardian or teacher if the victim is under 18. Victoria creates an offence where the assailant 'is aware that the person is not consenting or might not be consenting'.

There have also been extensive changes to the traditional concept of rape in the non-code jurisdictions. A common theme is that rape can now be committed by a person of either sex against a person of either sex. New South Wales has followed the Canadian example (see below) by abolishing the specific offence of rape. The main new offences, sexual assault and aggravated sexual assault, are based on a widened definition of sexual intercourse. This term now includes penetration of the genitalia or anus by an object; the insertion of any part of the penis into another's mouth; and cunnilingus. A sexual assault occurs when a person has sexual intercourse with another, knowing that the other does not consent or being reckless as to the matter. Aggravated sexual assault occurs when there is any one of a series of aggravating factors, including the use or threat of violence; the attacker's being accompanied by another person; and the physical or mental disability of the victim.

The term 'rape' has survived the changes made in South Australia. The former rule that only a woman could be raped has been abolished. Sexual intercourse is defined as including any activity involving '(a) the penetration of the labia majora or anus of a person by any part of the body of another person or by any object; (b) fellatio; or (c) cunnilingus'. Knowledge of lack of consent, or indifference to consent, is required for a conviction.

Victoria's changes to the law in this area, while also keeping the term 'rape', are similar to the more fundamental reforms made in New South Wales. Rape is broadly defined as sexual penetration of another person. Sexual penetration is defined in terms of the insertion by a person of his penis into the vagina, anus or mouth of another person, or the insertion of an object or part of the body (other than the penis) into the vagina or anus of another person.

Canada

Assaults

In Canada, the basic offence of assault (which includes battery) is defined in the Criminal Code as occurring where someone '(a) without the consent of another person, applies force intentionally to the person of the other, directly or indirectly; (b) attempts or threatens, by an act or gesture, to apply force to another, if he has, or causes that other person to believe on reasonable grounds that he has, present ability to effect his purpose; or (c) while openly wearing or carrying a weapon or an imitation thereof, accosts or impedes another person or begs'. In England (c) would not necessarily amount to an assault.

Any person who unlawfully causes bodily harm is guilty of an offence. This includes the causing of such harm by negligence. It is an aggravated assault to wound, maim, disfigure or endanger the life of a person. The prosecution must prove intention to assault in circumstances where a reasonable person would have realized that any of the prohibited consequences would result: it is unnecessary to prove that the accused intended the consequence.

There is also an offence of threatening to cause serious bodily harm. The Supreme Court of Canada has held that the psychological harm resulting from the receipt of a letter threatening rape can amount to serious bodily harm for this purpose (*R v McCraw* (1991) 7 Canada Reports (4th) 314).

Indecent assault and rape
The Canadian Criminal Code does not make a distinction between sexual and non-sexual assaults in terms of liability; the definition of assault applies to both. However, the distinction is still valid for sentencing purposes. A sexual assault is one committed in circumstances of a sexual nature, so that the sexual integrity of the victim was violated. The test is whether the sexual nature of the assault would be visible to a reasonable observer. The maximum punishment is double that for a non-sexual assault. There is an aggravated form of this crime with similar requirements to those of an aggravated (non-sexual) assault (above). This now includes the crime of rape, which has been abolished as a specific offence.

New Zealand

Assaults
In New Zealand, the common law offences of 'assault' and 'battery' have been unified into a single crime of 'assault'. Although, in most respects, the constituent elements of this offence are the same as those in English law, there are differences (Simester and Brookbanks 1998). In New Zealand, it is not possible to commit an assault recklessly; it is necessary that intention is proved. The threat of an assault can amount to a crime even if the person threatened is unaware of the threat. The use of words alone unaccompanied by any physical manifestation of a threat cannot amount to an assault.

There are also offences based on wounding, maiming, disfiguring, or causing grievous bodily harm to a person. The most serious crime requires proof of an intention to cause grievous bodily harm. The less serious crimes require proof either of intent to injure, or that the accused acted with reckless disregard for the safety of others.

In *R v Mwai* [1995] 3 New Zealand Law Reports 149, the New Zealand Court of Appeal approved the approach adopted by the English and Canadian courts whereby serious bodily harm can be constituted by psychological injury (but not by distress, fear or panic).

There are two other notable differences between the English and New Zealand law on assaults. In New Zealand, negligent conduct resulting in injury which would have resulted in liability for manslaughter had death ensued will itself amount to a criminal offence. In England, no criminal liability can generally arise from non-fatal injury that was caused through negligence. New Zealand also has a separate offence of aggravated assault by a male on a female.

Indecent assault and rape
Major changes were made to the law relating to sexual offences in 1985. The crime of rape has been replaced by a broader offence of 'sexual violation'. This is a gender-neutral offence in that, in addition to the rape of a woman, it includes 'unlawful sexual connection' between any two people. Sexual connection is defined as 'penetration of the genitalia or anus of another person by any part of the body, or any object held or manipulated by another person, otherwise than for bona fide medical purposes' or 'connection between the mouth and tongue of any person and any part

of the genitalia of any other person'. The law makes it clear that the crime of sexual violation can still be committed where the parties are married to each other. The word 'genitalia' replaced 'vagina' in 1994, and consequently rape can now be committed by any penetration of the vulva.

Although the term 'rape' retains its historic exclusive application to female victims, it is otherwise more broadly defined and now forms only one possible means of committing the new offence of sexual violation.

Another new sexual offence has been created – inducing sexual connection by coercion. It is a crime to have sexual connection with a person, knowing that the other has been induced to consent by a threat to commit a non-violent imprisonable offence (which presumably could embarrass the person); to make an 'accusation or disclosure' about misconduct likely to damage another's reputation; or to make improper use of any power or authority to the detriment of another. This would typically apply to coercion exercised by people in managerial positions at work.

The definition of the crime of indecent assault appears to be the same as in England: a battery committed in circumstances that ordinary people would consider indecent. The purpose of the accused may be relevant in determining whether an equivocal act is indecent, but this is unnecessary where ordinary people would not consider it indecent.

USA

With some 50 criminal jurisdictions, it is only possible here to provide the briefest of outlines of non-fatal offences against the person applicable in most American states.

Assaults

Assault and battery, which were common law crimes, now exist as statutory offences in all American jurisdictions. In general, English common law definitions are still fairly closely adhered to. Unlike in Canada, the assault–battery distinction still applies in many states. On the question of whether a battery can be committed negligently (as opposed to recklessly), a substantial majority of states require at least recklessness, although it is also common to attribute criminal liability on the basis of negligence if the harm is caused with a deadly weapon. The justification for this exception is that the use of any such dangerous implement should be accompanied by a higher standard of care than is usually required.

All the states have laws which deal with aggravated forms of battery. There are offences such as 'assault with intent to commit grievous bodily harm', but the modern tendency is for the aggravating factor to be the means of committing the offence, such as the use of a weapon, or the status of the victim (for example, police officers, fire fighters, teachers and bus drivers).

Indecent assault and rape

The traditional common law requirement for rape was that sexual intercourse was performed by a male on a female who was not his wife, either (a) by force; (b) by means of certain types of deception; (c) while the victim was asleep or unconscious; or (d) under certain circumstances where the victim was not competent to give consent (such as mental disability, the influence of alcohol, or youth) (Dressler 1995). Nowadays, around three-quarters of the states have a gender-neutral definition of what has traditionally been termed rape, and more than half the states do not have a specific offence of rape, preferring such terms as sexual assault (Scarce 1997).

Most prosecutions have traditionally been on the basis of forcible rape, and a conviction was highly unlikely without clear evidence that the victim had resisted or been physically threatened. However, an increasing number of states are either reducing or abolishing the resistance requirement. In some, 'force' has been redefined as the physical act required for penetration. The New Jersey Supreme Court has been in the vanguard of rape law reform: it has held that a person is guilty of 'forcible sexual assault' if they commit an act of sexual penetration of another person in the absence of freely-given permission, either express or implied (*State in the Interest of M.T.S.* 609 A.2d 1266).

Although the common law rule that a husband could not rape his wife has been abolished in most countries (see above), many American states retain the rule in a modified form, although it would generally not apply if the parties were living apart at the time of the rape.

The Model Penal Code (see Chapter 1) generally follows the common law definition of rape. The crime can only be committed by males against females and cannot result from sexual intercourse between spouses or persons living together 'as husband and wife'. However, 'sexual intercourse' includes anal, genital and oral sexual penetration by the male of the female. The offence is defined in terms of the male's aggressive conduct rather than the female's lack of consent. Resistance by the victim is not required.

THE PRACTICE

Australia

Dangerous offenders

All the jurisdictions have introduced provisions allowing the extended incarceration of dangerous offenders. For example, in Queensland a court cannot make a parole recommendation where the offender has been convicted of a serious violent offence. In the Northern Territory, a prison sentence (immediate or suspended) must be imposed for a sexual offence or a second conviction for violence. In Western Australia, a court can order indefinite imprisonment if it is satisfied that an offender would be a danger to society on release.

Early release

By the mid-1980s, the jurisdictions were starting to abolish automatic remission and restrict parole. For example, for prison sentences in Queensland, and those over six months in New South Wales (NSW) and 12 months in the Northern Territory (subject to special cases), a minimum term of custody is specified by the sentencer during which the offender cannot be released on parole. In NSW, a minimum of two-thirds of the sentence should normally be served. In the Northern Territory, the period is half, except for serious sexual offences, where it increases to 70 per cent. In Western Australia, parole can be granted after one-third of a term of six years or less, and two years less than two-thirds of a longer term. In Victoria, a non-parole period is optional for sentences of between 12 and 24 months and mandatory for longer ones.

Sentencing practice

Assaults
As in England, simple assaults are usually dealt with by fines or community penalties. However, prison sentences are upheld on appeal in more serious cases. In *Traeger* (1992) 63 Australian Criminal Reports 424 (South Australia), the appeal court held that a six-month sentence was appropriate where the defendant had entered his wife's home in defiance of a restraint order and struck her across the face, causing one ear to bleed. In *Griffin* (1997) 94 A Crim R 26 (Q), a sentence of one year was upheld for a defendant who had disciplined his son by applying electric shocks. Assaults against police officers, even of a minor nature, are often punished by imprisonment. However, in *Warrell v Kay* (1995) 83 A Crim R 493 (WA) probation was substituted for a 24-week custodial sentence where the defendant had thrown a piece of concrete which narrowly missed an officer.

Aggravated assaults
This intermediate category covers a range of offences which are more serious than simple assaults, but lack the intention to cause really serious harm. Custodial sentences are common, but not inevitable. In *Rowe* (1991) 52 A Crim R 196 (WA), the appeal court refused to interfere with a sentence of community service, imposed after the defendant had smashed a glass into an innocent bystander's face, causing permanent scarring. The defendant had shown impressive signs of rehabilitation. Three months' imprisonment followed by 400 hours' community service was considered appropriate in *Kurungaiyi v Garner* (1991) 54 A Crim R 465 (NT), where the defendant had stabbed his brother in the back with a screwdriver after the latter had sworn at him.

In *Melano* (1994) 75 A Crim R 392 (Q), a sentence of 15 months, with 12 suspended, was upheld on a defendant who left his victim requiring 38 stitches and scarred after an argument at a club. The sentence of ten months imposed in *Watterson v Kulmer* (1994) 76 A Crim R 440 (SA), where the victim suffered significant loss of sight in one eye, was considered so low 'that it would shock the public': a period of two and a half years was the appropriate starting point before any allowance was made for youth. In *Amituanai* (1995) 78 A Crim R 588 (Q), the appeal court refused to reduce a three-year sentence where the drunken defendant had inflicted a martial arts kick on the head of the victim, causing brain damage.

Physical harm resulting from 'off the ball' attacks in Australian Rules football matches will not inevitably incur custodial penalties. In *McAvaney v Quigley* (1992) 58 A Crim R 457 (SA), the appeal court, in rejecting a prosecution appeal against the leniency of a $400 fine following a conviction for assault occasioning actual bodily harm, considered the fact that the incident occurred during a football match to be an extenuating factor. In *Abbott* (1995) 81 A Crim R 55 (WA), an 18-month sentence for inflicting grievous bodily harm was varied to enable the immediate release of the defendant (who had served three months).

Serious assaults

Substantial terms of imprisonment can be upheld or imposed on appeal. The three-year sentence for intentionally causing serious injury in *Clarke* (1996) 85 A Crim R 114 (V) was increased on appeal to five years, even though the defendant had learning difficulties. In *Fletcher-Jones* (1994) 75 A Crim R 381 (NSW), a sentence of just under three years imposed on the defendant, who severely attacked his wife for the purpose of sexual intercourse, was increased on appeal to six years. In *Stone* (1996) 85 A Crim R 436 (NSW), the defendant, who said he had AIDS and would kill the police officer with whom he was struggling, inflicted two needle injuries. The officer suffered severe psychological harm. The appeal court refused to alter the sentence of six years and eight months. In *Stokes and Difford* (1990) 51 A Crim R 25 (NSW), the 25-year sentence imposed on Stokes for maliciously inflicting grievous bodily harm with intent on another prisoner was not considered excessive by the appeal court.

Sexual assaults

Custodial sentences are likely to be short for what are considered minor incidents. In *Lancaster and Touhy* (1991) 58 A Crim R 290 (NSW), a six-month sentence for indecent assault for two soldiers who had conducted 'initiation rights' on new recruits was varied on appeal to allow their immediate release (they had served three months). The wishes of the victim may be taken into account: in *H* (1995) 81 A Crim R 88 (WA), the appeal court substituted probation for a sentence of just under three years where the victim of her husband's sexual assault asked for clemency.

Where there has been sexual interference with a minor, imprisonment is the usual sentence. However, in *Roadley* (1990) 51 A Crim R 336 (V) a six-year sentence imposed on a man with a mental age of 5 or 6, following an isolated act of sexual penetration, was replaced on appeal with a binding-over order conditional on compliance with social workers' directions. In *Brazier v Police* (1994) 75 A Crim R 404 (SA), a two-year sentence on a priest for indecently assaulting a 16-year-old male was suspended on appeal. However, the appeal against a three-and-a-half-year sentence in *Dick* (1994) 75 A Crim R 303 (WA) for indecent assaults against boys in a Roman Catholic home 30 years earlier was unsuccessful.

Longer terms of imprisonment are approved for sustained abuse. In *Lane* (1995) 80 A Crim R 208 (SA), the appeal court doubled a three-year sentence where a teacher had engaged in sexual intercourse with one of his pupils between the ages of 9 and 16. In *Ridsdale* (1995) 78 A Crim R 486 (V), an appeal against an 18-year sentence for the sexual abuse of children between 1961 and 1982 was rejected.

The normal starting point for punishing a rape without any aggravating circumstances appears to be five years' imprisonment – the same as recommended in the English case of *Billam*. In *Athanasiadis* (1990) 51 A Crim R 292 (SA), a seven-year sentence was lowered on appeal to five years for this reason. The appeal court refused to reduce a sentence of four years and three months in *Attard* (1999) 105 A Crim R 431 (V), describing it as a 'most lenient one'. The fact that the parties knew each other should not affect the level of punishment (*Stephens* (1994) 76 A Crim R 5 (Q)). In *Daniel* (1997) 94 A Crim R 96 (Q), the appeal court rejected claims that an eight-year sentence should be reduced on the grounds that the defendant came from a deprived community where alcohol abuse and violence were more generally tolerated than elsewhere.

Canada

Dangerous offenders

Under the Criminal Code, a person convicted of a serious personal injury offence, who is considered by a court to constitute a danger to the life, safety or well-being (physical or mental) of others, may be deemed a dangerous offender and sentenced to an indeterminate prison sentence. A 'serious personal injury offence' is one involving violence, attempted violence or a sexual offence, which could inflict mental or physical injury on another. To be considered 'serious', the offence must be subject to a maximum sentence of at least ten years' imprisonment.

Early release

Offenders sentenced to less than two years' imprisonment can apply for parole after serving one-third of their sentence. Even if parole is not granted, they will normally be released after serving two-thirds. For longer sentences, the situation is more complicated. Such offenders are usually eligible for parole after serving a third of their sentence or seven years, whichever is less. However, for certain convictions, if the sentencer thinks that either society's denunciation or the grounds of deterrence so require, an order can be made prohibiting release before half the sentence has been served (or ten years, if that is less). Furthermore, offenders sentenced for any one of a range of crimes which are considered dangerous – including violent and sexual offences – will not be released after serving two-thirds of their sentence if the Parole Board considers that it is reasonably likely that they will commit an offence causing death or serious harm during the remaining third of the sentence.

Sentencing practice

Assault (maximum sentence 5 years)

A discharge was given for hugging a female stranger from behind in the street (*Croft* (1978) 22 Alberta Reports 224). Discharges can also be found in cases of minor assaults with a hockey stick during a game and provoked assaults by teachers on pupils. Fines are common for brawls in bars. Custodial sentences are imposed for a variety of reasons, including the defendant's tendency to violence, the context of the assault, and the harm caused. In *Brown* (1992) 73 C.C.C. (3d)) 242, the Alberta Court of Appeal considered the principles for sentencing in cases of wife assault. The sentence should be the same as if the victim had been a stranger. If the assault was a serious one, considerations of general deterrence and denunciation should be of particular importance. Applying these principles, a sentence of two years less a day was imposed in *Bonneteau* (1994) 93 C.C.C. (3d) 385 for three assaults on a spouse. Deterrence is also considered a strong factor in the sentencing of hate crimes. In

Simms (1990) 60 C.C.C. (3d) 499, the two accused were sentenced respectively to 12 months for simple assault and 18 months for aggravated assault for a 'neo-Nazi' attack which caused the victim to lose an eye.

Assault with a weapon or causing bodily harm (maximum sentence, 10 years)

In *Sanipas* (1992) 125 New Brunswick Reports, a suspended prison sentence was considered appropriate for an aboriginal convicted of threatening to use a knife in a domestic argument.

However, a more serious view is taken where the charge is based on the causing of bodily harm; indeed, this resulted in the previous maximum sentence of five years being doubled in an amendment to the Criminal Code. The Alberta Court of Appeal has stated that non-custodial sentences may sometimes be appropriate (*Casey* (1982) 26 C.R. (3d) 332) and suspended sentences have been approved in cases involving fairly serious violence where the attack was, at least in part, attributable to the accused's use of alcohol or mental disturbance. On the other hand, sentences of six months or more are often found when the harm results from drunken brawls. In *Parsons* (1985) 66 Nova Scotia Reports (2d) 322, a sentence of six months was approved for a defendant with a prior criminal record, who had assaulted a bouncer while another had held his arms. A 12-month sentence was confirmed in *Downey* (1979) 31 N.S.R. (2d) 181, where a defendant with a substantial criminal record committed an assault during the course of a robbery.

Longer terms of imprisonment may be upheld by appeal courts. Attacks against vulnerable people are viewed seriously, and this includes partners and children. In *Petrovic* (1984) 4 Ontario Appeal Cases 29, the appeal court imposed a two-year sentence for an assault on a wife as a deterrent measure, even though the injuries were not serious. In *Atkinson, Ing and Roberts* (1978) 43 C.C.C. (2d) 342, the same court gave two-year sentences for the severe beating of three gay men. It was stressed that the sentence needed to reflect the public abhorrence of such attacks. A five-year sentence was imposed in *Fraser* (1982) 37 A.R. 23, where a taxi-diver had been stabbed several times during a robbery.

Aggravated assault (maximum sentence 14 years)

This offence applies when the violence has been extreme, and a custodial sentence will nearly always result.

At the lower end of the scale, a six-month sentence was imposed in *Augustine* (1992) 125 N.B.R. (2d) 382 where the defendant stabbed her brother with a knife, which required his admission to hospital. In *Coleman* (1992) 110 N.S.R. (2d) 65, a 12-month sentence was considered appropriate where the defendant kicked and hit his girlfriend, fracturing her nose and injuring her eye. Generally, the higher sentences will be found in the cases of the most severe violence. A five-year sentence was upheld in *Khan* (1991) 49 O.A.C. 42 where the defendant seriously injured a stranger in a knife attack. In *T. (R.)* (1992) 17 C.R. (4th) 247, the defendant removed eight of the victim's teeth, impaled her hand on a table with a knife, and cut off her arm. The Ontario Court of Appeal approved a sentence of ten years. The same punishment was upheld in *Szpala* (1998) 39 O.R. (3d) 97, where the defendant threw acid in the face of the victim, rendering her blind and scarring one of her breasts.

Sexual assaults (maximum sentence 10 years, or life for an aggravated sexual assault)

Sentences for what was formerly termed indecent assault will be aggravated by factors such as whether the attacker broke into the victim's home and, in particular, whether the incident is close to attempted rape. In such cases, two years' imprisonment has been upheld. There is some variation in the approach to sentencing in rape cases among the different provinces. In *Glassford* (1988) 42 C.C.C. (3d) 259, the Ontario Court of Appeal rejected the notion of a fixed 'starting point' for sentencing in this area. In *M. (T.E.)* (1997) 114 C.C.C. (3d) 436, the Supreme Court stated that appellate courts should not create specific categories of assault and assign certain penalties to them. An appellate court could advise starting points for sentencing but, unless there had been a key error of principle, deviation from them should not mean that the sentence must be altered.

The sort of aggravating and mitigating factors that should be considered for rape are broadly similar to those discussed in the English case *Billam*. Sentences may be reduced where the victim has been in the accused's company during the course of an evening (*Kozy* (1990) 58 C.C.C. (3d) 500). However, it should not be relevant that the victim unwisely placed herself in danger by agreeing to accompany the accused (*Seaboyer* (1991) 66 C.C.C. (3d) 321). In *T. (J.C.)* (1998) 39 O.R.(3d) 26, the Ontario Court of Appeal upheld a conditional (suspended) prison sentence on a severely stressed husband, who had engaged in non-consensual intercourse with his cohabiting wife.

New Zealand

Dangerous offenders

An offender who, in the course of committing an offence punishable with a maximum of at least two years' imprisonment, used serious violence against, or caused serious danger to the safety of, another, will receive a non-suspended and non-periodic custodial sentence in the absence of any special circumstances. Where a court sentences an offender to imprisonment for two years or more (including an indeterminate sentence) for a serious violent offence, it may order that the offender serve a minimum period of imprisonment. This should not exceed three months before the expiry of the sentence, or ten years, whichever is the lesser.

Early release

Parole eligibility for a sentence of one year or more for any crime other than a serious violent offence arises after one-third has elapsed. For a period of 15 years or more for a serious violent offence, or for an indeterminate sentence, eligibility arises after ten years. Otherwise, no offender who has been convicted of a serious violent offence shall be eligible for parole. Offenders imprisoned for 12 months or less will be released after half their sentence. Other offenders will be released after two-thirds, unless they have received a minimum sentence for committing a serious violent offence which takes them past the two-thirds mark.

Sentencing practice

Assault (maximum sentence 1 year)

In *Tevaga* [1991] 1 NZLR 296, the defendant had been sentenced to four months' periodic detention for assault, having run 20 yards to involve himself in a fight during a rugby match and delivered a punch which broke the victim's jaw. The Court of Appeal, noting the accused's previous good character, felt able to reduce the sentence to one of 100 hours' community service. In *Saifiti* [1989] 3 NZLR 53, the Court of Appeal refused to replace a sentence of six months' periodic detention with community service where the accused had punched a man he had been talking to. However, the accused had previous convictions for assault.

Injuring a person with intent to cause grievous bodily harm (maximum sentence 10 years)

In *Waters* [1979] 1 NZLR 375, a four-year sentence was upheld on a defendant who caused abrasions and bruises to the victim, having entered her house on a pretext and threatened her with a knife. The fact that the attack occurred in her home was a clear aggravating factor.

Wounding or causing grievous bodily harm with intent to cause grievous bodily harm (maximum sentence 14 years)

In *Wikiriwhi* [1985] 2 NZLR 501, the Court of Appeal reduced from four years to three a prison sentence imposed on the defendant who, during a consensual fight, kicked the victim so severely that he sustained severe fractures to, and depression of, his facial bones. The fact that no weapon was used was stated to be a mitigating factor. On the other hand, the Court of Appeal has taken a strong line against inter-gang warfare, particularly where weapons were used and serious injury ensued. In *Hereora* [1986] 2 NZLR 164, the Court substantially increased the sentences (in Hereora's case, from two to six years) on a group men who attacked and stabbed members of a rival gang.

Sexual violation (maximum sentence 20 years)

In *A* [1994] 2 NZLR 129, the Court of Appeal set out a new series of guidelines for sentencing in rape cases. Previously, the English guidelines in *Billam* (see above) had been followed. However, the Court now felt that, as the New Zealand parliament had recently increased the maximum prison term, this should be reflected in the general level of sentencing, and eight years should be the starting point in contested cases. The aggravating and mitigating factors listed in *Billam* should still apply.

Where children are the victims of sexual violation or indecency, the Court is likely to insist on a custodial sentence, even where there is mitigation. In *N* [1998] 2 NZLR 272, the defendant had committed a series of acts against victims under 10 when he was 14 and 15. He himself had been seriously sexually abused by his elder brother. The Court replaced the two-year suspended sentence with a three-and-a-half-year immediate sentence. The defendant's own experience of abuse could not be regarded as a special circumstance.

References

Adams, D. (1988) Treatment models of men who batter: a profeminist analysis, in K. Ylló and M. Bograd (eds) *Feminist Perspectives on Wife Abuse.* Beverly Hills, CA: Sage.

Adler, F. and Laufer, W. S. (eds) (1995) *Advances in Criminological Theory: The Legacy of Anomie Theory,* Vol. 6. New Brunswick, NJ: Transaction Press.

Adler, P. A. (1985) *Wheeling and Dealing: An Ethnography of an Upper-Level Dealing and Smuggling Community.* New York: Columbia University Press.

Agnew, R. (1992) Foundation for a general strain theory of crime and delinquency, *Criminology,* 30(1): 47–87.

Agnew, R. and White, H. R. (1992) An empirical test of general strain theory, *Criminology,* 30(4): 475–99.

Allport, G. (1954) *The Nature of Prejudice.* Cambridge, MA: Addison-Wesley.

Amir, M. (1971) *Patterns of Forcible Rape.* Chicago: University of Chicago Press.

Angermeyer, M. C. and Matschinger, H. (1996) The effect of violent attacks by schizophrenic persons on the attitude of the public towards the mentally ill, *Social Science and Medicine,* 43(12): 1721–8.

Appleby, L., Shaw, J., Amos T. *et al.* (1999) *Safer Services. Report of the National Confidential Inquiry into Suicide and Homicide by People with Mental Illness.* London: Stationery Office.

Archer, D. and Gartner, R. (1984) *Violence and Crime in Cross-National Perspective.* New Haven, CT: Yale University Press.

Ashworth, A. (1993) Victim impact statements and sentencing, *Criminal Law Review,* 498–509.

Ashworth, A. (2000) *Sentencing and Criminal Justice,* 3rd edn. London: Butterworths.

Ashworth, A. and Gostin, L. (1985) Mentally disordered offenders and the sentencing process, in L. Gostin (ed.) *Secure Provision.* London: Tavistock.

Athens, L. (1997) *Violent Criminal Acts and Actors Revisited.* Chicago: University of Illinois Press.

Australian Bureau of Statistics (1994) *Crime and Safety, Australia 1993,* ABS Cat. No. 4509.0. Canberra: Australian Bureau of Statistics.

Australian Bureau of Statistics (1996) *Women's Safety Survey,* ABS Cat. No. 4128. Canberra: Australian Bureau of Statistics.

Aye Maung, N. and Mirrlees-Black, C. (1994) *Racially Motivated Crime: A British Crime Survey Analysis*, Home Office Research and Planning Unit Paper 82. London: Home Office.

Bailey, S. (1993) Fast forward to violence: violent visual imaging and serious juvenile crime, *Criminal Justice Matters*, 11: 6–7.

Baldassare, M. (ed.) (1994) *The Los Angeles Riots: Lessons for the Urban Future.* Boulder, CO: Westview Press.

Baldwin, J. D. (1990) The role of sensory stimulation in criminal behaviour, with special attention to the age peak in crime, in L. Ellis and H. Hoffman (eds) *Crime in Biological, Social and Moral Contexts.* New York: Praeger.

Bandura, A. (1973) *Aggression: A Social-Learning Analysis.* Englewood Cliffs, NJ: Prentice Hall.

Bandura, A. (1976) Social learning analysis of aggression, in E. Ribes-Inesta and A. Bandura (eds) *Analysis of Delinquency and Aggression.* Hillsdale, NJ: Erlbaum.

Bandura, A. and Huston, A. (1961) Identification as a process of incidental learning, *Journal of Abnormal and Social Psychology*, 63: 311–18.

Barclay, G. C. (ed.) (1993) *A Digest of Information on the Criminal Justice System in England and Wales.* London: Home Office Research and Statistics Department.

Barclay, G. C. and Tavares, C. (2000) *International Comparisons of Criminal Justice Statistics 1998*, Home Office Statistical Bulletin 04/00. London: Home Office.

Barker, M. and Morgan, R. (1993) *Sex Offenders: A Framework for the Evaluation of Community-Based Treatment.* London: Home Office.

Bartlett, P. and Sandland, R. (2000) *Mental Health Law Policy and Practice.* London: Blackstone Press.

Bartol, C. R. (1991) *Criminal Behavior: A Psychosocial Approach*, 3rd edn. Englewood Cliffs, NJ: Prentice Hall.

Becker, H. S. (1963) *Outsiders.* New York: Free Press.

Beckett, R., Beech, A., Fisher, D. and Fordham, A. S. (1994) *Community-Based Treatment for Sex Offenders: An Evaluation of Seven Treatment Programmes.* London: Home Office.

Beirne, P. (1993) *Inventing Criminology: The Rise of 'Homo Criminalis'.* Albany, NY: State University of New York Press.

Belsky, J. (1988) The 'effects' of infant day care reconsidered, *Early Childhood Research Quarterly*, 3: 235–72.

Benzvy Miller, S. H. (1999) Federal sentencing in America, in J. V. Roberts and D. P. Cole (eds) *Making Sense of Sentencing.* Toronto: University of Toronto Press.

Best, J. (1999) *Random Violence: How We Talk about New Crimes and New Victims.* Berkeley: University of California Press.

Birmingham, L., Mason, D. and Grubin, D. (1996) Prevalence of mental disorder in remand prisoners. Consecutive case study, *British Medical Journal*, 313: 1521–4.

Bjorkqvist, K., Nygren, T., Bjorklund, A. and Bjorkqvist, S. (1994) Testosterone intake and aggressiveness: real effect or anticipation, *Aggressive Behavior*, 20(1): 17–26.

Blackburn, R. (1968) Personality in relation to extreme aggression in psychiatric offenders, *British Journal of Psychiatry*, 114: 821–8.

Blair, I. (1999) Patrolling provision, *Policing Today*, 5(2): 16–18.

Blumenthal, M. D., Kahn, R. L., Andrews, F. M. and Head, K. B. (1972) *Justifying Violence: Attitudes of American Men*. Ann Arbor, MI: Institute for Social Research, The University of Michigan.

Bonger, W. (1916) *Criminality and Economic Conditions*. Boston: Little, Brown.

Borduin, C. M., Mann, B. J., Cone, L. T. *et al.* (1995) Multisystemic treatment of serious juvenile offenders: long-term prevention of criminality and violence, *Journal of Consulting and Clinical Psychology*, 63(4): 569–78.

Bottomley, A. K. and Pease, K. (1986) *Crime and Punishment: Interpreting the Data*. Milton Keynes: Open University Press.

Bottoms, A. E. (1995) The philosophy and politics of punishment and sentencing, in C. M. V. Clarkson and R. Morgan (eds) *The Politics of Sentencing Reform*. Oxford: Oxford University Press.

Bourgois, P. (1996) *In Search of Respect: Selling Crack in El Barrio*. Cambridge: Cambridge University Press.

Bowling, B., Graham, J. and Ross, A. (1994) Self-reported offending among young people in England and Wales, in J. Junger-Tas, G. Terlouw and M. Klein (eds) *Delinquent Behaviour Among People in the Western World*. Amsterdam: Kugler.

Box, S. (1983) *Power, Crime and Mystification*. London: Tavistock.

Box, S. (1987) *Recession, Crime and Punishment*. Basingstoke: Macmillan.

Braithwaite, J. (1979) *Inequality, Crime and Public Policy*. London: Routledge & Kegan Paul.

Braithwaite, J. (1981) The myth of social class and criminality reconsidered, *American Sociological Review*, 46(1): 36–57.

Braithwaite, J. (1989) *Crime, Shame and Reintegration*. Cambridge: Cambridge University Press.

Bratton, W. with Knobler, P. (1998) *Turnaround: How America's Top Cop Reversed the Crime Epidemic*. New York: Random House.

Breier, A. B., Kelsoe, J. R., Kirwin, P. D. *et al.* (1988) Early parental loss and development of adult psychopathology, *Archives of General Psychiatry*, 45(11): 987–93.

Brooke, D., Taylor, C., Gunn, J. and Maden, A. (1996) Point prevalence of mental disorder in unconvicted male prisoners in England and Wales, *British Medical Journal*, 313: 1524–7.

Brown, G. and Anderson, B. (1991) Psychiatric morbidity in adult inpatients with childhood histories of sexual and physical abuse, *American Journal of Psychiatry*, 148(1): 55–61.

Brown, M. (1996) Serious offending and the management of public risk in New Zealand, *British Journal of Criminology*, 36(1): 18–36.

Brownmiller, S. (1975) *Against Our Will*. New York: Bantam.

Buchholz, E. S. and Korn-Bursztyn, C. (1993) Children of adolescent mothers: are they at risk for abuse?, *Adolescence*, 28(110): 361–82.

Buruma, I. (1994) *The Wages of Guilt. Memories of War in Germany and Japan*. New York: Farrar Straus Giroux.

Bush, J. (1995) Teaching self-risk management to violent offenders, in J. McGuire (ed.) *What Works? Reducing Reoffending – Guidelines from Research and Practice*. Chichester: Wiley.

Cadoret, R. J. (1986) Epidemiology of anti-social personality, in W. Reid, D. Door,

J. Walker and J. Bonne (eds) *Unmasking the Psychopath*. London: W. W. Norton.

Campbell, A. (1984) *The Girls in the Gang*. New York: Basil Blackwell.

Carlen, P. (1985) *Criminal Women*. Oxford: Polity Press.

Carlen, P. (1988) *Women, Crime and Poverty*. Milton Keynes: Open University Press.

Carter, D. L., Prentky, R. A., Knight, R. A., Vanderveer, P. L. and Boucher, R. J. (1987) Use of pornography in the criminal and developmental histories of sex offenders, *Journal of Interpersonal Violence*, 2(2): 196–211.

Centerwall, B. S. (1989) Exposure to television as a cause of violence, in G. Gomstock (ed.) *Public Communication and Behavior*. New York: Academic Press.

Chambliss, W. J. (1995) Crime control and ethnic minorities: legitimizing racial oppression by creating moral panics, in D. E. Hawkins (ed.) *Ethnicity, Race, and Crime: Perspectives across Time and Place*. Albany: State University of New York Press.

Chappell, D., Grabosky, P. and Strang, H. (1991) *Australian Violence: Contemporary Perspectives*. Canberra: Australian Institute of Criminology.

Charlton, T. and Gunter, B. (1999) TV-violence effects: exceptionally vulnerable viewers, *Emotional and Behavioural Difficulties*, 4(1): 36–45.

Chiricos, T. G. (1987) Rates of crime and unemployment: an analysis of aggregate research evidence, *Social Problems*, 34(2): 187–211.

Choudry, S. (1996) *Pakistani Women's Experience of Domestic Violence in Great Britain*, Home Office Research Findings No. 43. London: Home Office.

Christiansen, K. O. (1974) Seriousness of criminality and concordance among Danish twins, in R. Hood (ed.) *Crime, Criminology and Public Policy*. London: Heinemann.

Christiansen, K. O. (1977) A preliminary study of criminality among twins, in S. A. Mednick and K. O. Christiansen (eds) *Biosocial Bases of Criminal Behaviour*. New York: Gardiner Press.

Christie, M., Marshall, W. and Lanthier, R. (1979) *A Descriptive Study of Incarcerated Rapists and Pedophiles*. Report to the Solicitor General of Canada, Ottawa.

Cicchetti, D. (1990) A historical perspective on the discipline of developmental psychopathology, in J. Rolf, A. Masten, D. Cicchetti, K. Neuchterlein and S. Weintraub (eds) *Risk and Protective Factors in the Development of Psychopathology*. New York: Cambridge University Press.

Cicchetti, D. and Olsen, K. (1990) The developmental psychopathology of child maltreatment, in M. Lewis and S. Miller (eds) *Handbook of Developmental Psychopathology*. New York: Plenum.

Clarkson, C. M. V. (in press) *Understanding Criminal Law*, 3rd edn. London: Sweet & Maxwell.

Cloward, R. A. and Ohlin, L. E. (1960) *Delinquency and Opportunity*. New York: Free Press.

Cohen, A. K. (1955) *Delinquent Boys: The Culture of the Gang*. New York: Free Press.

Cohen, L. E. and Felson, M. (1979) Social change and crime rate trends: a routine activities approach, *American Sociological Review*, 44(4): 588–608.

Cohen, P. (1972) *Subcultural Conflict and Working Class Community*, Working

Papers in Cultural Studies No. 2. Birmingham: Centre for Contemporary Studies, University of Birmingham.

Cohen, S. (1972) *Folk Devils and Moral Panics*. Oxford: Martin Robertson.

Cohen, S. (1996) Crime and politics: spot the difference, *British Journal of Sociology*, 47(1): 1–21.

Coid, J. (1982) Alcoholism and violence, *Drug and Alcohol Dependence*, 9(1): 1–13.

Coleman, C. and Moynihan, J. (1996) *Understanding Crime Data*. Buckingham: Open University Press.

Coleman, D. H. and Straus, M. A. (1983) Alcohol abuse and family violence, in E. Gottheil, K. A. Druley, T. E. Skoloda and H. M. Waxman (eds) *Alcohol, Drug Abuse, and Aggression*. Springfield, IL: Charles C. Thomas.

Collier, R. (1998) *Masculinities, Crime and Criminology*. London: Sage.

Collins, J. J. (1986) The relationship of problem drinking in individual offending sequences, in A. Blumstein, J. Cohen, J. Roth and C. A. Visher (eds) *Criminal Careers and 'Career Criminals'*, Vol. 2. Washington, DC: National Academy Press.

Collins, J. J. and Bailey, S. L. (1990) Traumatic stress disorder and violent behavior, *Journal of Traumatic Stress*, 3: 203–20.

Connell, R. W. (1987) *Gender and Power*. Oxford: Polity.

Cooke, D. (1989) Containing violent prisoners: an analysis of the Barlinnie Special Unit, *British Journal of Criminology*, 29(2): 129–43.

Cortés, J. B. (1972) *Delinquency and Crime: A Biological Approach*. New York: Seminar Press.

Court, J. H. (1984) Sex and violence: a ripple effect, in N. M. Malamuth and E. Donnerstein (eds) *Pornography and Sexual Aggression*. New York: Academic Press.

Cowie, J., Cowie, V. and Slater, E. (1968) *Delinquency in Girls*. London: Heinemann.

Crawford, A., Jones, T., Woodhouse, T. and Young, J. (1990) *Second Islington Crime Survey*. London: Middlesex Polytechnic.

Cretney, A. and Davis, G. (1995) *Punishing Violence*. London: Routledge.

Crown Prosecution Service (1994) *Annual Report for the Period April 1993 – March 1994*, HC 444. London: HMSO.

Curran, D. J. and Renzetti, C. M. (1994) *Theories of Crime*. Boston: Allyn & Bacon.

Curtis, L. A. (1974) Victim precipitation and violent crime, *Social Problems*, 21: 594–605.

Cuthbert, M., Lovejoy, F. and Fulde, G. (1991 Investigation of the incidence and analysis of cases of alleged violence reporting to St Vincent's Hospital, in D. Chappell, P. Grabosky and H. Strang (eds) *Australian Violence: Contemporary Perspectives*. Canberra: Australian Institute of Criminology.

Davis, G. (1992) *Making Amends: Mediation and Reparation in Criminal Justice*. London: Routledge.

de Waal, F. (1989) *Peacemaking among Primates*. London: Penguin.

de Zulueta, F. (1993) *From Pain to Violence: The Traumatic Roots of Destructiveness*. London: Whurr Publishers.

Deehan, A. (1999) *Alcohol and Crime: Taking Stock*, Crime Reduction Research Series Paper 3. London: Home Office.

Deffenbacher, J. L., Story, D. A., Brandon, A. D., Hogg, J. A. and Hazaleus, S. L. (1988) Cognitive and cognitive-relaxation treatments of anger, *Cognitive Therapy and Research*, 12(2): 167–84.

DeKeseredy, W. S. and Ellis, D. (1995) Intimate male violence against women, in J. I. Ross (ed.) *Violence in Canada: Sociopolitical Perspectives*. Toronto: Oxford University Press.

Delgado, J. M. R. (1971) The neurological basis of violence, *International Social Science Journal*, 23(1): 27–35.

Department of Health (1998a) *Modernising Mental Health Services: Safe, Sound and Supportive*. London: Stationery Office.

Department of Health (1998b) *The Government's Response to the Children's Safeguards Review*, Cm 4105. London: Stationery Office.

Department of Health (2000) *Protecting Children, Supporting Parents. A Consultation Paper on the Physical Punishment of Children*. London: Department of Health.

Ditton, J., Bannister, J., Gilchrist, E. and Farrall, S. (1999) Afraid or angry? Recalibrating the 'fear' of crime, *International Review of Victimology*, 6(2): 83–99.

Dobash, R. E. and Dobash, R. P. (1979) *Violence against Wives: A Case against Patriarchy*. New York: Free Press.

Dobash, R. E. and Dobash, R. P. (1984) The nature and antecedents of violent acts, *British Journal of Criminology*, 24(2): 269–88.

Dobash, R. E. and Dobash, R. P. (1992) *Women, Violence and Social Change*. London: Routledge.

Dobash, R. E. and Dobash, R. P. (1998) Violent men and violent contexts, in R. E. Dobash and R. P. Dobash (eds) *Rethinking Violence against Women*. Thousand Oaks, CA: Sage.

Dobash, R. P., Dobash, R. E., Cavanagh, K. and Lewis, R. (1996) *Research Evaluation of Programmes for Violent Men*. Edinburgh: HMSO.

Doob, A. N. (1995) The United States Sentencing Commission Guidelines: if you don't know where you are going, you might not get there, in C. M. V. Clarkson and R. Morgan (eds) *The Politics of Sentencing Reform*. Oxford: Oxford University Press.

Doob, A. N. and Roberts, J. V. (1988) Public punitiveness and public knowledge of the facts: some Canadian surveys, in N. D. Walker and M. Hough (eds) *Public Attitudes to Sentencing: Surveys from Five Countries*. Aldershot: Gower.

Dressler, J. (1995) *Understanding Criminal Law*, 2nd edn. New York: Matthew Bender.

Dryden, W. (1996) Rational Emotive Behaviour Therapy, in W. Dryden (ed.) *Handbook of Individual Therapy*. London: Sage.

Dunning, E., Murphy, P. and Williams, J. (1988) *The Roots of Football Hooliganism: An Historical and Sociological Study*. London: Routledge & Kegan Paul.

Durkheim, E. (1951) *Suicide*. Glencoe, IL: Free Press. (First published 1897.)

Dworkin, A. (1987) *Intercourse*. New York: Free Press.

Egeland, B., Jacobvitz, D. and Papatola, K. (1987) Intergenerational continuity of parental abuse, in R. J. Gelles and J. B. Lancaster (eds) *Child Abuse and Neglect*. New York: Aldine de Gruyter.

Ehrlich, H. J. (1992) The ecology of anti-gay violence, in G. M. Herek and K. T. Berrill (eds) *Hate Crimes: Confronting Violence against Lesbians and Gay Men*. Newbury Park, CA: Sage.

Elias, R. (1993) *Victims Still: The Political Manipulation of Crime Victims*. London: Sage.

Elliott, D. S. (1994) Serious violent offenders: onset, developmental course, and termination, *Criminology*, 32(1): 1–21.

Elliott, D. S., Hamburg, B. A. and Williams, K. R. (eds) (1998) *Violence in American Schools: A New Perspective*. Cambridge: Cambridge University Press.

Engels, F. (1993) *The Condition of the Working Class in England*. Oxford: Oxford University Press. (First published 1845.)

Erez, E. (1999) Who's afraid of the big bad victim? Victim impact statements as victim empowerment *and* enhancement of justice, *Criminal Law Review*, 545–56.

ESRC Violence Research Programme (1998) *Taking Stock: What Do We Know about Violence?* Uxbridge: ESRC Violence Research Programme.

Farrell, G., Phillips, C. and Pease, K. (1995) Like taking candy: why does repeat victimization occur?, *British Journal of Criminology*, 35(3): 384–99.

Farrington, D. P. (1978) The family background of aggressive youths, in L. Hersov, M. Berger and D. Schaffer (eds) *Aggression and Antisocial Behaviour in Childhood and Adolescence*. Oxford: Pergamon.

Farrington, D. P. (1989) Early predictors of adolescent aggression and adult violence, *Violence and Victims*, 4(2): 79–100.

Fattah, E. A. (1979) Some recent theoretical developments in victimology, *Victimology*, 4(2): 198–213.

Feeley, M. and Simon, J. (1992) The new penology: notes on the emerging strategy of corrections and its implications, *Criminology*, 30(4): 449–74.

Felson, R. B. (1993) Sexual coercion: a social interactionist approach, in R. B. Felson and J. T. Tedeschi (eds) *Aggression and Violence*, Washington, DC: American Psychological Association.

Fergusson, D. M., Horwood, L. J. and Lynskey, M. T. (1992) Family change, parental discord and early offending, *Journal of Child Psychology and Psychiatry*, 33(6): 1059–75.

Finkelhor, D. (1984) *Child Sexual Abuse: New Theories and Research*. New York: Free Press.

Finkelhor, D. and Yllö, K. (1985) *License to Rape*. New York: Holt, Rinehart and Winston.

Fishbein, D. H. (1992) The psychobiology of female aggression, *Criminal Justice and Behavior*, 19(2): 99–126.

FitzGerald, M. and Hale, C. (1996) *Ethnic Minorities, Victimisation and Racial Harassment*, Home Office Research Study No. 154. London: Home Office.

Fletcher, J. (1997) *Violence and Civilization: An Introduction to the Work of Norbert Elias*. Cambridge: Polity Press.

Frankel, M. (1973) *Criminal Sentences: Law without Order*. New York: Hill and Wang.

Frase, R. S. (1995) Sentencing guidelines in Minnesota and other American states: a progress report, in C. M. V. Clarkson and R. Morgan (eds) *The Politics of Sentencing Reform*. Oxford: Oxford University Press.

Freedman, J. L. (1992) Television violence and aggression: what psychologists should tell the public, in P. Suedfeld and P. Tetlock (eds) *Psychology and Public Policy*. New York: Hemisphere.

Freud, S. (1955) Beyond the pleasure principle, in J. Strachey (ed. and trans.) *The*

Standard Edition of the Complete Psychological Works of Sigmund Freud, Vol. 18. London: Hogarth Press. (First published 1920.)

Frude, N. (1994) Marital violence: an interactional perspective, in J. Archer (ed.) *Male Violence*. London: Routledge.

Gardiner, D. and Nesbit, D. (1996) Cognitive behavioural groupwork with male offenders: the Newcastle-upon-Tyne Intensive Probation Unit, in T. Newburn and G. Mair (eds) *Working with Men*. Lyme Regis: Russell House Publishing.

Geen, R. G. and Gange, J. J. (1977) Drive theory of social facilitation: twelve years of theory and research, *Psychological Bulletin*, 84(6): 1267–88.

Genders, E. and Player, E. (1995) *Grendon: A Study of a Therapeutic Prison*. Oxford: Oxford University Press.

Gendreau, P. and Ross, R. R. (1979) Effective correctional treatment: bibliotherapy for cynics, *Crime and Delinquency*, 25(4): 463–89.

Gendreau, P., Cullen, F. T. and Bonta, J. (1994) Intensive rehabilitation supervision: the next generation in community corrections? *Federal Probation*, 58(1): 72–8.

Genn, H. (1988) Multiple victimization, in M. Maguire and J. Pointing (eds) *Victims of Crime: A New Deal?* Milton Keynes: Open University Press.

Giancola, P. and Zeichner, A. (1994) Neuropsychological performance on tests of frontal-lobe functioning and aggressive behavior in men, *Journal of Abnormal Psychology*, 103(4): 832–5.

Gillies, P. (1997) *Criminal Law*, 4th edn. Sydney: LBC Information Services.

Godenzi, A. (1994) What's the big deal? We are men and they are women, in T. Newburn and E. A. Stanko (eds) *Just Boys Doing Business? Men, Masculinities and Crime*. London: Routledge.

Goldhagen, D. J. (1996) *Hitler's Willing Executioners: Ordinary Germans and the Holocaust*. London: Little, Brown and Co.

Goldstein, A. P., Glick, B. and Gibbs, J. C. (1999) *Aggression Replacement Training: A Comprehensive Intervention for Aggressive Youth*, Revised Edition. Champaign, IL: Research Press.

Goldstein, P. J. (1985) The drugs/violence nexus: a tripartite conceptual framework. *Journal of Drug Issues*, 15: 493–506.

Goodman, A., Johnson, P. and Webb, S. (1997) *Inequality in the UK*. Oxford: Oxford University Press.

Goodwin, D. W., Schulsinger, F., Hermansen, L., Guze, S. B. and Winokur, G. (1973) Alcohol problems in adoptees raised apart from alcoholic biological parents, *Archives of General Psychiatry*, 28: 238–43.

Gottfredson, M. R. (1984) *Victims of Crime: The Dimensions of Risk*, Home Office Research Study No. 81. London: HMSO.

Gottfredson, M. R. and Hirschi, T. (1990) *A General Theory of Crime*. Stanford, CA: Stanford University Press.

Gove, W. R. and Wilmoth, C. (1990) Risk, crime, and neurophysiologic highs: a consideration of brain processes that may reinforce delinquent and criminal behavior, in L. Ellis and H. Hoffman (eds) *Crime in Biological, Social, and Moral Contexts*. New York: Praeger.

Grace, S., Lloyd, C. and Smith, L. (1992) *Rape: From Recording to Conviction*. Home Office Research and Planning Unit Paper No. 71. London: Home Office.

Graham, J. and Bowling, B. (1995) *Young People and Crime*, Home Office Research Study No. 145. London: Home Office.

Gramsci, A. (1971) *Selection from the Prison Notebooks*. London: Lawrence and Wishart.

Groth, A. N. (1979) *Men who Rape: The Psychology of the Offender*. New York: Plenum.

Groth, A. N. and Burgess, A. W. (1977) Rape: a sexual deviation, *American Journal of Orthopsychiatry*, 47(3): 400–6.

Groth, A. N., Longo, R. E. and McFadin, J. B. (1982) Undetected recidivism among rapists and child molesters, *Crime and Delinquency*, 28(3): 450–8.

Gulbenkian Foundation (1995) *Children and Violence*. London: Calouste Gulbenkian Foundation.

Gunn, J. (1993) Human violence: a biological perspective, in P. Taylor (ed.) *Violence in Society*. London: Royal College of Physicians.

Gunn, J. and Robertson, G. (1987) A ten-year follow-up of men discharged freom Grendon prison, *British Journal of Psychiatry*, 151: 674–8.

Gurr, T. R. (1970) *Why Men Rebel*. Princeton, NJ: Princeton University Press.

Hagan, J. (1994) *Crime and Disrepute*. Thousand Oaks, CA: Pine Forge Press.

Hagan, J., Gillis, A. R. and Simpson, J. H. (1985) The class structure of gender and delinquency: toward a power-control theory of common delinquent behaviour, *American Journal of Sociology*, 90(6): 1151–78.

Hagan, J., Simpson, J. H. and Gillis, A. R. (1979) The sexual stratification of social control: a gender-based perspective on crime and delinquency, *British Journal of Sociology*, 30(1): 25–38.

Hagedorn, J. M. (1988) *People and Folks: Gangs, Crime and the Underclass in a Rustbelt City*. Chicago: Lakeview.

Hagedorn, J. M. (1994) Neighborhoods, markets, and gang drug organization, *Journal of Research in Crime and Delinquency*, 31(3): 264–94.

Hagell, A. and Newburn, T. (1994) *Young Offenders and the Media*. London: Policy Studies Institute.

Hague, G. and Malos, E. (1993) *Domestic Violence: Action for Change*. Cheltenham: New Clarion Press.

Hall, G. (1999) *Hall's Sentencing*. Auckland: Butterworths.

Hanks, S. E. and Rosenbaum, C. D. (1977) Battered women: a study of women who live with violent alcohol-abusing men, *American Journal of Orthopsychiatry*, 47(2): 291–306.

Hare, R. D. (1986) Twenty years of experience with the Cleckley psychopath, in W. H. Reid, D. Dorr, J. I. Walker and J. W. Bonner (eds) *Unmasking the Psychopath: Antisocial Personality and Related Syndromes*. New York: Norton.

Harlow, H. and Mears, C. (1979) *Primate Perspectives*. New York: Wiley.

Harries, R. (1999) *The Cost of Criminal Justice*, Home Office Research Findings No. 103. London: Home Office.

Harris, J. and Grace, S. (1999) *A Question of Evidence? Investigating and Prosecuting Rape in the 1990s*, Home Office Research Study No. 196. London: Home Office.

Harris, M. (1985) *Bikers: Birth of a Modern-Day Outlaw*. London: Faber and Faber.

Harry, J. (1992) Conceptualizing anti-gay violence, in G. M. Herek and K. T. Berrill (eds) *Hate Crimes: Confronting Violence against Lesbians and Gay Men*. Newbury Park, CA: Sage.

Harvey, E. (1999) Short-term and long-term effects of early parental employment on children of the National Longitudinal Survey of Youth, *Developmental Psychology*, 35(2): 445–59.

Haskett, M., Johnson, C. and Miller, J. (1994) Individual differences in risk of child abuse by adolescent mothers: assessment in the perinatal period, *Journal of Child Psychology and Psychiatry and Allied Disciplines*, 35(3): 461–76.

Hearn, J. (1996) Is masculinity dead? A critique of the concept of masculinity, in M. Mac an Ghaill (ed.) *Understanding Masculinities*. Buckingham: Open University Press.

Hedderman, C. and Sugg, D. (1996) *Does Treating Sex Offenders Reduce Reoffending?*, Home Office Research Findings No. 45. London: Home Office.

Hedderman, C., Sugg, D. and Vennard, J. (1997) *Changing Offenders' Attitudes: What Works?*, Home Office Research Study No. 171. London: Home Office.

Heelas, P. (1982) Anthropology, violence and catharsis, in P. Marsh and A. Campbell (eds) *Aggression and Violence*. Oxford: Basil Blackwell.

Heidensohn, F. (1991) Women and crime in Europe, in F. Heidensohn and M. Farrell (eds) *Crime in Europe*. London: Routledge.

Heimer, K. and Matsueda, R. L. (1994) Role-taking, role commitment, and delinquency: a theory of differential social control, *American Sociological Review*, 59(3): 365–90.

Henderson, M (1983) Self-reported assertion and aggression among violent offenders with high or low levels of overcontrolled hostility, *Personality and Individual Differences*, 4: 113–15.

Henning, K. R. and Frueh, B. C. (1996) Cognitive-behavioral treatment of incarcerated offenders: an evaluation of the Vermont Department of Corrections' Cognitive Self-Change Program, *Criminal Justice and Behavior*, 23(4): 523–41.

Herek, G. M. (1992) The social context of hate crimes: notes on cultural heterosexism, in G. M. Herek and K. T. Berrill (eds) *Hate Crimes: Confronting Violence against Lesbians and Gay Men*. Newbury Park, CA: Sage.

Hinde, R. A. (1991) Aggression and the institution of war, in R. A. Hinde (ed.) *The Institution of War*. Basingstoke: Macmillan.

Hindelang, M. J., Dunn, C., Sutton, L. and Aumick, A. (1975) *Sourcebook of Criminal Justice Statistics, 1974*, Washington, DC: US Government Printing Office.

Hindelang, M. J., Gottfredson, R. and Garofalo, J. (1978) *Victims of Personal Crime*. Cambridge, MA: Ballinger.

Hindelang, M. J., Hirschi, T. and Weis, J. G. (1979) Correlates of delinquency: the illusion of discrepancy between self-report and official measures, *American Sociological Review*, 44(6): 995–1014.

Hindelang, M. J., Hirschi, T. and Weis, J. G. (1981) *Measuring Delinquency*. Beverly Hills, CA: Sage.

Hirschi, T. (1969) *Causes of Delinquency*. Berkeley: University of California Press.

Hobbs, D. (1997) Criminal collaboration: youth gangs, subcultures, professional criminals, and organized crime, in M. Maguire, R. Morgan and R. Reiner (eds) *The Oxford Handbook of Criminology*, 2nd edn. Oxford: Oxford University Press.

Hodge, J. (1993) Alcohol and violence, in P. Taylor (ed.) *Violence in Society*. London: Royal College of Physicians.

Hollin, C. R. (1990) *Cognitive-Behavioral Interventions with Young Offenders*. New York: Pergamon.

Hollin, C. R (1996) Young offenders, in C. R. Hollin (ed) *Working with Offenders: Psychological Practice in Offender Rehabilitation*. Chichester: Wiley.

Hollitscher, W. (1947) *Sigmund Freud: An Introduction*. London: Routledge & Kegan Paul.

Home Office (1990) *Crime, Justice and Protecting the Public*, Cm 965. London: HMSO.

Home Office (1999a) *The Government's Proposals for Regulation of the Private Security Industry in England and Wales*, Cm 4254. London: Stationery Office.

Home Office (1999b) *Statistics on Women and the Criminal Justice System*, Home Office Research, Development and Statistics Directorate. London: Home Office.

Home Office (1999c) *What Works? Reducing Reoffending: Evidence-Based Practice*. London: Home Office.

Home Office (2000) *Criminal Statistics, England and Wales 1998*, Cm 4649. London: Stationery Office.

Hough, M. (1986) Victims of violent crime: findings from the first British Crime Survey, in E. Fattah (ed) *From Crime Policy to Victim Policy*. London: Macmillan.

Hough, M. and Roberts, J. V. (1998) *Attitudes to Punishment: Findings from the British Crime Survey*, Home Office Research Study No. 179. London: Home Office.

House of Commons (1993) *Memorandum of Evidence to Home Affairs Select Committee on Domestic Violence*, p. 25.

Hovland, C. I. and Sears, R. R. (1969) Minor studies of aggression: Correlations of lynchings with economic indices, in A. Grimshaw (ed.) *Racial Violence in the United States*. Chicago: Aldine.

Howells, K. (1983) Social constructing and violent behaviour in mentally abnormal offenders, in J. Hinton (ed.) *Dangerousness: Problems of Assessment and Prediction*. London: Allen & Unwin.

Howells, K. (1988) The management of angry aggression: a cognitive behavioural approach, in W. Dryden and P. Trower (eds) *Developments in Cognitive Psychotherapy*. London: Sage.

Howells, K. (1996) The psychological management of violence in clinical and forensic settings: pitfalls and remedies, *Psychiatry, Psychology and Law*, 3: 71–6.

Howitt, D. (1998) *Crime, the Media and the Law*. Chichester: Wiley.

Howitt, D. and Owusu-Bempah, J. (1994) *The Racism of Psychology*. Hemel Hempstead: Harvester Wheatsheaf.

Hoyle, C. and Sanders, A. (2000) Police response to domestic violence: from victim choice to victim empowerment? *British Journal of Criminology*, 40(1): 14–36.

Hsieh, C-C. and Pugh, M. (1983) Poverty, income inequality, and violent crime: a meta-analysis of recent aggregate data studies, *Criminal Justice Review*, 18(2): 182–202.

Huesmann, L. R. and Eron, L. D. (1986) *Television and the Aggressive Child: A Cross-National Comparison*. Hillsdale, NJ: Erlbaum.

Hulsman, L. H. C. (1986) Critical criminology and the concept of crime, *Contemporary Crises*, 10(1): 63–80.

Hurley, D. (1994) Imminent danger, *Psychology Today*, 27(4): 54–62.

Ito, K. (1993) Research on the fear of crime: perceptions and realities of crime in Japan, *Crime and Delinquency*, 39(3): 385–92.

Jefferson, T. (1994) Theorizing masculine subjectivity, in T. Newburn and E. A.

Stanko (eds) *Just Boys Doing Business? Men, Masculinities and Crime*. London: Routledge.

Jefferson, T. (1996) Introduction, in T. Jefferson and P. Carlen (eds) *Masculinities, Social Relations and Crime*, special issue of the *British Journal of Criminology*, 36(3): 337–47.

Johnson, B., Goldstein, P. J., Preble, E. *et al.* (1985) *Taking Care of Business: The Economics of Crime by Heroin Abusers*. Lexington, MA: Lexington Books.

Johnston, M. E. (1988) Correlates of early violence experience among men who are abusive toward female mates, in G. T. Hotaling, D. Finkelhor, J. T. Kirkpatrick and M. A. Straus (eds) *Family Abuse and Its Consequences: New Directions in Research*. Beverly Hills, CA: Sage.

Jones, A. (1999) *Out of Sight, Out of Mind? The Experiences of Homeless Women*. London: Crisis.

Jones, T. and Newburn, T. (1998) *Private Security and Public Policing*. Oxford: Oxford University Press.

Jones, T., Maclean, B. and Young, J. (1986) *The Islington Crime Survey*. Aldershot: Gower.

Jonkers, J. (1986) *Victims of Violence*. London: Fontana.

Junger-Tas, J., Terlouw, G. J. and Klein, M. (1994) *Delinquent Behaviour Among Young People in the Western World: First Results of the International Self-Report Delinquency Study*. Amsterdam: Kugler.

Kagan, J. (1984) *The Nature of the Child*. New York: Basic Books.

Kanarek, R. (1994) Nutrition and violent behavior, in A. Reiss, K. Miczek and J. Roth (eds) *Understanding and Preventing Violence*, Vol. 2. Washington, DC: National Academy Press.

Kandel, E. and Mednick, S. A. (1991) Parental complications predict violent offending. *Criminology*, 29(3): 519–29.

Kandel-Englander, E. (1992) Wife-battering and violence outside the family, *Journal of Interpersonal Violence*, 7(4): 462–70.

Kang, S., Magura, S. and Shapiro, J. L. (1994) Correlates of cocaine/crack use among inner-city incarcerated adolescents, *American Journal of Drug and Alcohol Abuse*, 20(4): 413–29.

Karsten, P. (1978) *Law, Soldiers, and Combat*. Westport, CT: Greenwood Press.

Katz, J. (1988) *Seductions of Crime*. New York: Basic Books.

Kenny, R. G. (1999) *An Introduction to Criminal Law in Queensland and Western Australia*, 5th edn. Sydney: Butterworths.

Kerner, O. (1968) *Report of the National Advisory Commission on Civil Disorder*. New York: Bantam.

Kershaw, C., Dowdeswell, P. and Goodman, J. (1997) *Restricted Patients – Reconvictions and Recalls by the End of 1995: England and Wales*. Home Office Statistical Bulletin 1/97. London: Home Office.

Kersten, J. (1996) Culture, masculinities and violence against women, *British Journal of Criminology*, 36(3): 381–95.

Kilpatrick, D. G., Best, C. L., Veronen, L. J. *et al.* (1985) Mental health correlates of criminal victimization: a random community survey, *Journal of Consulting and Clinical Psychology*, 53(6): 866–73.

Kinsey, R. (1984) *Merseyside Crime Survey*. Edinburgh: Centre for Criminology, University of Edinburgh.

Klaus, K. (1994) Crime statistics, *Congressional Digest*, 73(6–7): 167–9.

Klein, M. (1995) *The American Street Gang: Its Nature, Prevalence, and Control.* New York: Oxford University Press.

Kline, P. (1987) Psychoanalysis and crime, in B. J. McGurk, D. M. Thornton and M. Williams (eds) *Applying Psychology to Imprisonment: Theory and Practice.* London: HMSO.

Kolvin, I., Miller, F. J. W., Fleeting, M. and Kolvin, P. A. (1988) Social and parenting factors effecting criminal-offence rates: findings from the Newcastle Thousand Family Study (1947–1980), *British Journal of Psychiatry*, 152: 80–90.

Koss, M. P. and Gaines, J. A. (1993) The prediction of sexual aggression by alcohol use, athletic participation, and fraternity affiliation, *Journal of Interpersonal Violence*, 8(1): 94–108.

Koss, M. P., Gidycz, C. A. and Wisniewski, N. (1987) The scope of rape: incidence and prevalence of sexual aggression and victimization in a national sample of higher education students, *Journal of Consulting and Clinical Psychology*, 55(2): 162–70.

Kraemer, G. (1985) Effects of differences in early social experience on primate neuro-biological-behavioural development, in M. Reite and T. Field (eds) *The Psychobiology of Attachment and Separation.* London: Academic Press.

Kuper, L. (1981) *Genocide.* Harmondsworth: Penguin.

Lacey, N. and Wells, C. (1998) *Reconstructing Criminal Law: Critical Perspectives on Crime and the Criminal Process*, 2nd edn. London: Butterworths.

Laidler, K. A. J. and Hunt, G. (1997) Violence and social organization in female gangs, *Social Justice*, 24(4): 148–69.

Lamb, S. (1996) *The Trouble with Blame: Victims, Perpetrators, and Responsibility.* Cambridge, MA: Harvard University Press.

Land, K. C., Cantor, D. and Russell, S. T. (1995) Unemployment and crime rate fluctuations in the post-World War II United States, in J. Hagan and R. D. Peterson (eds) *Crime and Inequality.* Stanford, CA: Stanford University Press.

Lang, A. R., Goeckner, D. J., Adesso, V. J. and Marlatt, G. A. (1975) Effects of alcohol on aggression in male social drinkers, *Journal of Abnormal Psychology*, 84(5): 508–18.

Lau, M., Pihl, R. and Peterson, J. (1995) Provocation, acute alcohol intoxication, cognitive performance, and aggression, *Journal of Abnormal Psychology*, 104(1): 150–5.

Law Commission (1992) *Domestic Violence and Occupation of the Family Home*, Law Commission Report No. 207. London: HMSO.

Laws, D. R. and Marshall, W. L. (1990) A conditioning theory of the etiology and maintenance of deviant sexual preference and behavior, in W. L. Marshall, D. R. Laws and H. E. Barbaree (eds) *Handbook of Sexual Assault: Issues, Theories and Treatment of the Offender.* New York: Plenum.

Le Bon, G. (1952) *The Crowd.* London: Ernest Benn. (First published 1895.)

Lees, J., Manning, N. and Rawlings, B. (1999) *Therapeutic Community Effectiveness.* York: NHS Centre for Reviews and Dissemination, University of York.

Lees, S. (1996) *Carnal Knowledge: Rape on Trial.* London: Hamish Hamilton.

Lees, S. (1997) *Ruling Passions: Sexual Violence, Reputation and the Law.* Buckingham: Open University Press.

Lemert, E. M. (1967) *Human Deviance, Social Problems and Social Control*. Englewood Cliffs, NJ: Prentice Hall.

Levey, S. and Howells, K. (1990) Anger and its management, *Journal of Forensic Psychiatry*, 1: 305–27.

Levi, M. (1997) Violent crime, in M. Maguire, R. Morgan and R. Reiner (eds) *The Oxford Handbook of Criminology*, 2nd edn. Oxford: Oxford University Press.

Levinson, D. (1989) *Family Violence in Cross-Cultural Perspective*. Newbury Park, CA: Sage.

Lindqvist, P. (1986) Criminal homicide in Northern Sweden, 1970–1981 – alcohol intoxication, alcohol abuse and mental disease, *International Journal of Law and Psychiatry*, 8: 19–37.

Lindqvist, P. and Allebeck, P. (1990) Schizophrenia and crime: a longitudinal follow-up of 644 schizophrenics in Stockholm, *British Journal of Psychiatry*, 157: 345–50.

Lipton, D. N., McDonel, E. C. and McFall, R. M. (1987) Heterosocial perception in rapists, *Journal of Consulting and Clinical Psychology*, 55(1): 17–21.

Livingstone, S. (1996) On the continuing problem of media effects, in J. Curran and M. Gurevitch (eds) *Mass Media and Society*. London: Arnold.

Lloyd, C. and Walmsley, R. (1989) *Changes in Rape Offences and Sentencing*, Home Office Research Study No. 105. London: HMSO.

Loftin, C. and Hill, R. H. (1974) Regional subculture and homicide: an examination of the Gastil–Hackney thesis, *American Sociological Review*, 39(5): 714–24.

Loftus, E. and Ketcham, K. (1994) *The Myth of Repressed Memory: False Memories and Allegations of Sexual Abuse*. New York: St Martin's.

Lombroso, C. (1876) *L'Uomo Delinquente*. Milan: Hoepli.

Lombroso, C. and Ferrero, G. L. (1895) *The Female Offender*. London: Unwin.

Lonsway, K. A. and Fitzgerald, L. F. (1994) Rape myths: in review, *Psychology of Women Quarterly*, 18(2): 133–64.

Lorenz, K. (1966) *On Aggression*. London: Methuen.

Lyons, M. J., True, W. R., Eisen, S. A. *et al.* (1995) Differential heritability of adult and juvenile antisocial traits, *Archives of General Psychiatry*, 52(11): 906–15.

MacAndrew, C. and Edgerton, R. B. (1969) *Drunken Comportment: A Social Explanation*. Chicago: Aldine.

McBurnett, K., Lahey, B. B., Rathouz, P. J. and Loeber, R. (2000) Low salivary cortisol and persistent aggression in boys referred for disruptive behavior, *Archives of General Psychiatry*, 57(1): 38–43.

McCord, J. (1979) Some child-rearing antecedents of criminal behavior in adult men, *Journal of Personality and Social Psychology*, 37(9): 1477–86.

McDougall, C., Barnett, R. M., Ashurst, B. and Willis, B. (1987) Cognitive control of anger, in B. J. McGurk, D. M. Thornton and M. Williams (eds) *Applying Psychology to Imprisonment: Theory and Practice*. London: HMSO.

McGuire, J. (ed.) (1995) *What Works? Reducing Reoffending – Guidelines from Research and Practice*. Chichester: Wiley.

McGuire, R. J., Carlisle, J. M. and Young, B. G. (1965) Sexual deviations as conditioned behaviour: a hypothesis, *Behaviour Research and Therapy*, 2: 185–90.

McGurk, B. J. (1980) *An Attempt to Evaluate the Efficiency of Relaxation Training, Desensitisation and Biofeedback in the Treatment of Violent Behaviour*. Directorate of Psychological Services Report, II, 81.

McGurk, B. J. and McGurk, R. E. (1979) Personality types among prisoners and prison officers, *British Journal of Criminology*, 19(1): 31–49.

McGurk, B. J., Thornton, D. M. and Williams, M. (eds) (1987) *Applying Psychology to Imprisonment: Theory and Practice*. London: HMSO.

McIvor, G. (1992) Intensive probation; does more mean better? *Probation Journal*, 39(1): 2–6.

MacKinnon, C. A. (1979) *Sexual Harassment of Working Women*. New Haven, CT: Yale University Press.

MacMillan, H. L., Boyle, M. H., Wong, M. Y-Y. *et al.* (1999) Slapping and spanking in childhood and its association with lifetime prevalence of psychiatric disorders in a general population sample, *Canadian Medical Association Journal*, 161(7): 805–9.

Macpherson, W. (1999) *The Stephen Lawrence Inquiry*, Cm 4262. London: Stationery Office.

Magnusson, D. (1988) Antisocial behavior of boys and autonomic reactivity, in T. E. Moffitt and S. A. Mednick (eds) *Biological Contributions to Crime Causation*. Dordrecht: Martinus Nijhoff.

Maguire, M. (ed.) (1996) *Street Crime*. Aldershot: Dartmouth.

Maguire, M. (1997) Crime statistics, patterns, and trends: changing perceptions and their implications, in M. Maguire, R. Morgan and R. Reiner (eds) *The Oxford Handbook of Criminology*, 2nd edn. Oxford: Oxford University Press.

Maguire, M. and Corbett, C. (1987) *The Effects of Crime and the Work of Victim Support Schemes*. Aldershot: Gower.

Maguire, M. and Pointing, J. (eds) (1988) *Victims of Crime: A New Deal?* Milton Keynes: Open University Press.

Maguire, M., Kemshall, H., Noaks, L., Sharpe, K. and Wincup, E. (2000) *Risk Assessment and Management of Sexual and Dangerous Offenders*. London: Home Office.

Main, M. and George, C. (1985) Responses of abused and disadvantaged toddlers to distress in agemates: a study in the day care setting, *Developmental Psychology*, 21(3): 407–12.

Mair, G., Lloyd, C., Nee, C. and Sibbitt, R. (1994) *Intensive Probation in England and Wales: An Evaluation*, Home Office Research Study No. 133. London: Home Office.

Maletzky, B. M. (1991) *Treating the Sex Offender*. Newbury Park, CA: Sage.

Markowitz, S. (1999) *The Price of Alcohol, Wife Abuse, and Husband Abuse*, NBER Working Paper No. 6916. Cambridge, MA: National Bureau of Economic Research.

Marques, J. K., Day, D. M., Nelson, C. and West, M. A. (1994) Effects of cognitive-behavioral treatment on sex offender recidivism: preliminary results of a longitudinal study, *Criminal Justice and Behavior*, 21(1): 28–54.

Marshall, P. (1997) *A Reconviction Study of HMP Grendon Therapeutic Community*, Home Office Research Findings No. 53. London: Home Office.

Marshall, W. L. and Pithers, W. D. (1994) A reconsideration of treatment outcome with sex offenders, *Criminal Justice and Behavior*, 21(1): 10–25.

Martinson, R. (1974) What works? Questions and answers about prison reform, *Public Interest*, 10: 22–54.

Martinson, R. (1979) New findings, new views: a note of caution regarding sentencing reform, *Hofstra Law Review*, 7: 243–58.

Matsueda, R. L. (1988) The current state of differential association theory, *Crime & Delinquency*, 34(3): 277–306.

Mattinson, J. and Mirrlees-Black, C, (2000) *Attitudes to Crime and Criminal Justice: Findings from the 1998 British Crime Survey*, Home Office Research Study No. 220. London: Home Office.

Maxfield, M. G. and Widom, C. S. (1996) The cycle of violence: revisited 6 years later, *Archives of Pediatrics and Adolescent Medicine*, 150(4): 390–5.

Mayhew, P. and Elliott, D. (1990) Self-reported offending, victimization and the British Crime Survey, *Violence and Victims* 5(2): 83–96.

Mayhew, P. and van Dijk, J. J. M. (1997) *Criminal Victimisation in Eleven Industrialised Countries: Key Findings from the 1996 International Crime Victims Survey*. Leiden: Ministry of Justice WODC.

Mayhew, P., Aye Maung, N. and Mirrlees-Black, C. (1993) *The 1992 British Crime Survey*, Home Office Research Study No 132. London: HMSO.

Mayhew, P., Elliott, D. and Dowds, L. (1989) *The 1988 British Crime Survey*, Home Office Research Study No. 111. London: HMSO.

Mead, G. H. (1934) *Mind, Self, and Society*. Chicago: University of Chicago Press.

Mednick, S. A., Moffitt, T. E. and Stack, S. A. (eds) (1987) *The Causes of Crime: New Biological Approaches*. New York: Cambridge University Press.

Mednick, S. A., Pollock, V., Volavka, J. and Gabrielli, W. F. (1982) Biology and violence, in M. E. Wolfgang and N. A. Weiner (eds) *Criminal Violence*. Beverly Hills, CA: Sage.

Megargee, E. I. (1966) Undercontrolled and overcontrolled personality types in extreme antisocial aggression, *Psychological Monographs*, 80: Whole No. 611.

Menard, S. (1995) A developmental test of Mertonian anomie theory, *Journal of Research in Crime and Delinquency*, 32(2): 136–74.

Mental Health Foundation (1999) *Bright Futures: Promoting Children and Young People's Mental Health*. London: Mental Health Foundation.

Merton, R. K. (1938) Social structure and anomie, *American Sociological Review*, 3(5): 672–82.

Merton, R. K. (1968) *Social Theory and Social Structure*. New York: Free Press.

Messerschmidt, J. W. (1993) *Masculinities and Crime*. Lanham, MD: Rowman and Littlefield.

Messerschmidt, J. W. (1997) *Crime as Structured Action*. Thousand Oaks, CA: Sage.

Messner, S. F. (1983) Regional and racial effects on the urban homicide rate: the subculture of violence revisited, *American Journal of Sociology*, 88(5): 997–1007.

Messner, S. F. and Rosenfeld, R. (1994) *Crime and the American Dream*. Belmont, CA: Wadsworth.

Mewett, A. W. and Manning, M. (1994) *Mewett & Manning on Criminal Law*, 3rd edn. Markham, Ont.: Butterworths.

Miczek, K. A., Haney, M., Tidey, J., Vivian, J. and Weerts, E. (1994) Neurochemistry and pharmacotherapeutic management of aggression and violence, in A. K. Reiss, K. A. Miczek and J. A. Roth (eds) *Biobehavioral Influences*. Washington, DC: National Academy Press.

Miers, D. (1992) The responsibilities and the rights of victims of crime, *Modern Law Review*, 55: 482–505.

Milgram, S. (1974) *Obedience to Authority: An Experimental View*. London: Harper & Row.

Miller, A. (1983) *For Your Own Good: Hidden Cruelty in Child Rearing and the Roots of Violence*. London: Virago.

Miller, W. B. (1958) Lower class culture as a generating milieu of gang delinquency, *Journal of Social Issues*, 14: 5–19.

Milner, J., Halsey, L. and Fultz, J. (1995) Empathic responsiveness and affective reactivity to infant stimuli in high- and low-risk for physical child abuse mothers, *Child Abuse and Neglect*, 19(6): 767–80.

Mirrlees-Black, C. (1999) *Domestic Violence: Findings from a New British Crime Survey Self Completion Questionnaire*, Home Office Research Study No. 191. London: Home Office.

Mirrlees-Black, C., Budd, T., Partridge, S. and Mayhew, P. (1998) *The 1998 British Crime Survey*, Home Office Statistical Bulletin 21/98. London: Home Office.

Mirrlees-Black, C., Mayhew, P. and Percy, A. (1996) *The 1996 British Crime Survey*, Home Office Statistical Bulletin 19/96. London: Home Office.

Monahan, J. (1992) Mental disorder and violent behaviour. Perceptions and evidence, *American Psychologist*, 47(4): 511–21.

Monahan, J. (1997) Clinical and actuarial predictions of violence, in D. Faigman, D. Kaye, M. Saks and J. Sanders (eds) *West's Companion to Scientific Evidence*. St Paul, MN: West.

Mooney, J. (1993) *The North London Domestic Violence Survey*. Enfield: Middlesex University Centre for Criminology.

Morris, A. (1987) *Women, Crime and Criminal Justice*. Oxford: Blackwell.

Mott, J. (1990) *Young People, Alcohol and Crime*, Home Office Research Bulletin, 28: 24–8.

Mott, J. and Taylor, M. (1974) *Delinquency amongst Opiate Users*, Home Office Research Study No. 23. London: HMSO.

Muehlenhard, C. L. and Hollabaugh, L. C. (1988) Do women sometimes say no when they mean yes? The prevalence and correlates of women's token resistance to sex, *Journal of Personality and Social Psychology*, 54(5): 872–9.

Muehlenhard, C. L., Powch, I. G., Phelps, J. L. and Giusti, L. M. (1992) Definitions of rape: scientific and political implications, *Journal of Social Issues*, 48(1): 23–44.

Mueller, C. W. (1983) Environmental stressors and aggressive behaviour, in R. G. Geen and E. I. Donnerstein (eds) *Aggression: Theoretical and Empirical Reviews*, Vol. 2. New York: Academic Press.

Mullen, P. E., Burgess, P., Wallace, C., Palmer, S. and Ruschena, D. (2000) Community care and criminal offending in schizophrenia, *Lancet* 355: 614–17.

Murugason, R. and McNamara, L. (1997) *Outline of Criminal Law*. Sydney: Butterworths.

MVA Consultancy (1997) *The 1996 Scottish Crime Survey: First Results*, Scottish Office Central Research Unit Crime and Criminal Justice Research Findings No. 16. Edinburgh: The Scottish Office.

Needleman, H. L., Riess, J. A., Tobin, M. J., Biesecker, G. E. and Greenhouse, J. B. (1996) Bone lead levels and delinquent behavior, *Journal of the American Medical Association*, 275(5): 363–9.

Newburn, T. (1995) *Crime and Criminal Justice Policy*. London: Longman.

Newburn, T. and Stanko, E. A. (eds) (1994) *Just Boys Doing Business? Men, Masculinities and Crime*. London: Routledge.

Nietzel, M. (1979) *Crime and Its Modification: A Social Learning Perspective.* New York: Pergamon.

Nomellini, S. and Katz, R. C. (1983) Effects of anger control training on abusive parents, *Cognitive Therapy and Research*, 7(1): 57–67.

Novaco, R. W. (1975) *Anger Control.* Lexington, MA: Heath.

O'Connor, T. G., McGuire, S., Reiss, D., Hetherington, E. M. and Plomin, R. (1998) Co-occurrence of depressive symptoms and antisocial behavior in adolescence: a common genetic liability, *Journal of Abnormal Psychology*, 107(1): 27–37.

Olweus, D. (1986) Aggression and hormones: behavioural relationship with testosterone and adrenaline, in D. Olweus, J. Block and M. Radke-Yarrow (eds) *Development of Antisocial and Prosocial Behaviour.* New York: Academic Press.

Olweus, D. (1987) Testosterone and adrenaline: aggressive and antisocial behaviour in normal adolescent males, in S. A. Mednick, T. E. Moffitt and S. A. Stack (eds) *The Causes of Crime: New Biological Approaches.* Cambridge: Cambridge University Press.

Ontario Ministry of Community and Social Services (1990) *Children First: Report of the Advisory Committee on Children's Services.* Toronto: MCSS.

Painter, K. and Farrington, D. P. (1998) Marital violence in Great Britain and its relationship to marital and non-marital rape, *International Review of Victimology*, 5: 257–76.

Parent, D. G. (1988) *Structuring Criminal Sentences: The Evolution of Minnesota's Sentencing Guidelines.* Stoneham, MA: Butterworths.

Parker, H. and Bottomley, T. (1996) *Crack Cocaine and Drugs-Crime Careers*, Home Office Research and Statistics Directorate. Paper 34. London: Home Office.

Paternoster, R. and Mazerolle, P. (1994) General strain theory and delinquency: a reception and extension, *Journal of Research in Crime and Delinquency*, 31(3): 235–63.

Patrick, J. (1973) *A Glasgow Gang Observed.* London: Eyre Methuen.

Pearson, G. (1983) *Hooligan: A History of Respectable Fears.* London: Macmillan.

Pease, K. (1998) *Repeat Victimisation: Taking Stock*, Crime Detection and Prevention Series Paper 90. London: Home Office.

Peay, J. (1997) Mentally disordered offenders, in M. Maguire, R. Morgan and R. Reiner (eds) *The Oxford Handbook of Criminology*, 2nd edn. Oxford: Oxford University Press.

Pence, E. and Paymar, M. (1993) *Education Groups for Men who Batter.* New York: Springer.

Percy, A. and Mayhew, P. (1997) *Estimating Sexual Victimisation in a National Crime Survey: A New Approach*, Studies on Crime and Crime Prevention, 6: 125–50.

Perkins, D. (1991) Clinical work with sex offenders in secure settings, in C. R. Hollin and K. Howells (eds) *Clinical Approaches to Sex Offenders and their Victims.* Chichester: John Wiley.

Pernanen, K. (1991) *Alcohol in Human Violence.* New York: Guilford Press.

Perse, E. (1994) Uses of erotica and acceptance of rape myths, *Communication Research*, 21(4): 488–515.

Petersilia, J., Greenwood, P. and Lavin, M. (1978) *Criminal Careers of Habitual Felons.* Washington, DC: US Department of Justice, National Institute of Law Enforcement and Criminal Justice.

Phillips, D. P. and Hensley, J. E. (1984) When violence is rewarded or punished: the impact of mass media stories on homicide, *Journal of Communication*, 34(3): 101–11.

Platt, T. (1978) Street crime – a view from the Left, *Crime and Social Justice*, 9: 26–34.

Pollak, O. (1950) *The Criminality of Women*. Philadelphia: University of Pennsylvania Press.

Povey, D. and Prime, J. (1998) *Notifiable Offences England and Wales April 1997 to March 1998*, Home Office Statistical Bulletin 22/98. London: Home Office.

Povey, D. and Prime, J. (1999) *Recorded Crime Statistics England and Wales, April 1998 to March 1999*, Home Office Statistical Bulletin 18/99. London: Home Office.

Power, A. and Tunstall, R. (1997) *Dangerous Disorder: Riots and Violent Disturbances in 13 Areas of Britain*. York: York Publishing Services.

Pratt, J. (2000) The return of the wheelbarrow men; or, the arrival of postmodern penality? *British Journal of Criminology*, 40(1): 127–45.

Procter, E. and Flaxington, F. (1996) *Community-Based Interventions with Sex Offenders Organised by the Probation Service: A Survey of Current Practice*. London: Association of Chief Officers of Probation.

Quinney, R. (1977) *Class, State, and Crime*. New York: McKay.

Quinsey, V. L. (1984) Sexual aggression: studies of offenders against women, in D. Weisstub (ed.) *Law and Mental Health: International Perspectives*, Vol. 1. New York: Pergamon.

Rada, R. T. (1975) Alcoholism and forcible rape, *American Journal of Psychiatry*, 132(4): 444–6.

Rada, R. T. (1978) *Clinical Aspects of the Rapist*. New York: Grune and Stratton.

Rafter, N. H. (1997) Psychopathy and the evolution of criminological knowledge, *Theoretical Criminology*, 1(2): 235–59.

Raine, A. (1993) *The Psychopathology of Crime*. San Diego, CA: Academic Press.

Raine, A., Lencz, T., Bihrle, S., LaCasse, L. and Colletti, P. (2000) Reduced prefrontal gray matter volume and reduced autonomic activity in antisocial personality disorder, *Archives of General Psychiatry*, 57(2): 119–27.

Raine, A., Reynolds, C., Venables, P. H., Mednick S. A. and Farrington, D. P. (1998) Fearlessness, stimulation-seeking, and large body size at age 3 years as early predispositions to childhood aggression at age 11 years, *Archives of General Psychiatry*, 55(8): 745–51.

Raper, A. F. (1970) *The Tragedy of Lynching*. New York: Dover. (First published in 1933.)

Raynor, P. and Vanstone, M. (1996) Reasoning and Rehabilitation in Britain: the results of the Straight Thinking on Probation (STOP) programme, *International Journal of Offender Therapy and Comparative Criminology*, 40(4): 272–84.

Redl, F. and Toch, H. (1979) The psychoanalytic perspective, in H. Toch (ed.) *Psychology of Crime and Criminal Justice*. New York: Holt, Rinehart & Winston.

Reicher, S. S. (1984) The St Paul's Riot: an explanation of the limits of crowd action in terms of a social identity model, *European Journal of Social Psychology*, 14: 1–21.

Reiner, R. (2000) *The Politics of the Police*, 3rd edn. Oxford: Oxford University Press.

Reiss, A. J. and Roth, J. A. (eds) (1993) *Understanding and Preventing Violence*. Washington, DC: National Academy Press.

Reiss, A. J., Miczek, K. A. and Roth, J. A. (eds) (1994) *Biobehavioral Influences*. Washington, DC: National Academy Press.

Rice, M. E. and Harris, G. T. (1992) A comparison of criminal recidivism among schizophrenic and non-schizophrenic offenders, *International Journal of Law and Psychiatry*, 15(4): 397–408.

Rice, M. E., Chaplin, T. C., Harris, G. T. and Coutts, J. (1994) Empathy for the victim and sexual arousal among rapists and nonrapists, *Journal of Interpersonal Violence*, 9(4): 435–49.

Roberts, J. V. and Cole, D. P. (eds) (1999) *Making Sense of Sentencing*. Toronto: University of Toronto Press.

Roberts, J. V. and Stalans, L. J. (1997) *Public Opinion, Crime, and Criminal Justice*. Boulder, CO: Westview Press.

Robertson, G. and Taylor, P. (1993) Psychosis, violence and crime, in J. Gunn and P. Taylor (eds) *Forensic Psychiatry: Clinical, Ethical, and Legal Issues*. Oxford: Butterworth-Heinemann.

Robins, D. and Cohen, P. (1978) *Knuckle Sandwich: Growing Up in the Working-Class City*. Harmondsworth: Penguin.

Rock, P. (1990) *Helping Victims of Crime: The Home Office and the Rise of Victim Support in England and Wales*. Oxford: Oxford University Press.

Ross, R. R. and Ross, D. R. (eds) (1995) *Thinking Straight: The Reasoning and Rehabilitation Program for Delinquency Prevention and Offender Rehabilitation*. Ottawa: AIR Training and Publications.

Ross, R. R., Fabiano, E. A. and Ewles, C. D. (1988) Reasoning and rehabilitation, *International Journal of Offender Therapy and Comparative Criminology*, 32(1): 29–35.

Rothbaum, B. O., Foa, E. B., Riggs, D. S., Murdock, T. and Walsh, W. (1992) A prospective examination of post-traumatic stress disorder in rape victims, *Journal of Traumatic Stress*, 5(3): 455–75.

Rowe, D. (1990) Inherited dispositions toward learning delinquent and criminal behaviour: new evidence, in L. Ellis and H. Hoffman (eds) *Crime in Biological, Social, and Moral Contexts*. New York: Praeger.

Ruby, C. C. (1999) *Sentencing*, 5th edn. Markham, Ont.: Butterworths.

Rudé, G. (1964) *The Crowd in History*. New York: John Wiley.

Russell, D. E. H. (1982) *Rape in Marriage*. New York: Macmillan.

Russell, D. E. H. (1984) *Sexual Exploitation: Rape, Child Sexual Abuse, and Workplace Harassment*. Beverly Hills, CA: Sage.

Russell, D. E. H. (ed.) (1993) *Making Violence Sexy: Feminist Views on Pornography*. Buckingham: Open University Press.

Rutter, M. L. (1981) *Maternal Deprivation Reassessed*, 2nd edn. London: Penguin.

Rutter, M. L. (1997) Nature–nurture integration: the example of antisocial behavior, *American Psychologist*, 52(4): 390–8.

Sampson, R. J. and Laub, J. H. (1993) *Crime in the Making: Pathways and Turning Points through Life*. Cambridge, MA: Harvard University Press.

Sampson, R. J. and Lauritsen, J. L. (1994) Violent victimization and offending: individual-, situational-, and community-level risk factors, in A. J. Reiss and J. A. Roth (eds) *Social Influences*. Washington, DC: National Academy Press.

Sanday, P. R. (1981) The socio-cultural context of rape: a cross-cultural study, *Journal of Social Issues*, 37(4): 5–27.

Scarce, M. (1997) *Male on Male Rape: The Hidden Toll of Stigma and Shame*. New York: Insight.

Schubart, R. (1995) From desire to deconstruction: horror films and audience reactions, in D. Kidd-Hewitt and R. Osborne (eds) *Crime and the Media*. London: Pluto Press.

Schwendinger, H. and Schwendinger, J. (1985) *Adolescent Subcultures and Delinquency*. New York: Praeger.

Scourfield, J. B. and Dobash, R. P. (1999) Programmes for violent men: recent developments in the UK, *Howard Journal*, 38(2): 128–43.

Scully, D. (1990) *Understanding Sexual Violence*. London: Harper Collins.

Shah, R. and Pease, K. (1992) Crime, race and reporting to the police, *Howard Journal*, 31(3): 192–9.

Shapland, J., Willmore, J. and Duff, P. (1985) *Victims and the Criminal Justice System*. Aldershot: Gower.

Sheldon, W. H. (1949) *Varieties of Delinquent Youth*. New York: Harper.

Shepard, M. (1992) Predicting batterer recidivism 5 years after community intervention, *Journal of Family Violence*, 7(3): 167–78.

Shepherd, J. P., Qureshi, R., Preston, M. S. and Levers, B. G. H. (1990) Psychological distress after assaults and accidents, *British Medical Journal*, 301: 849–50.

Sheridan, M. (1995) A proposed intergenerational model of substance abuse, family functioning, and abuse/neglect, *Child Abuse and Neglect*, 19(5): 519–30.

Sherwood, M. (1999) Lynching in Britain, *History Today*, 49(3): 21–3.

Shichor, D. and Sechrest, D. K. (eds) (1996) *Three Strikes and You're Out: Vengeance as Public Policy*. Thousand Oaks, CA: Sage.

Sibbitt, R. (1997) *The Perpetrators of Racial Harassment and Racial Violence*, Home Office Research Study No. 176. London: Home Office.

Simester, A. P. and Brookbanks, W. J. (1998) *Principles of Criminal Law*. Wellington: Brooker's.

Sims, A. and Gray, P. (1993) *The Media, Violence and Vulnerable Viewers*. Evidence presented to the Broadcasting Group, House of Lords.

Singleton, N., Meltzer, H. and Gatward, R. with Coid, J. and Deasy, D. (1998) *Psychiatric Morbidity Among Prisoners in England and Wales*. London: Stationery Office.

Sivarajasingam, V. and Shepherd, J. P. (1999) Effect of closed circuit television on urban violence, *Journal of Accident and Emergency Medicine*, 16: 255–7.

Skogan, W. G. (1986) Methodological issues in the study of victimization, in E. A. Fattah (ed.) *From Crime Policy to Victim Policy*. London: Macmillan.

Skolnick, J. H., Bluthenthal, R. and Correl, T. (1993) Gang organization and migration, in S. Cummings and D. Monti (eds) *Gangs: The Origins and Impact of Contemporary Youth Gangs in the United States*. Albany: State University of New York Press.

Smart, C. (1976) *Women, Crime and Criminology*. London: Routledge & Kegan Paul.

Smith, J. C. and Hogan, B. (1999) *Criminal Law*, 9th edn. London: Butterworths.

Smith, S. L. and Donnerstein, E. (1998) Harmful effects of exposure to media violence: learning of aggression, emotional desensitization, and fear, in R. G. Geen and E. Donnerstein (eds) *Human Aggression: Theories, Research, and Implications for Social Policy*. San Diego, CA: Academic Press.

Snyder, H. N. and Sickmund, M. (1995) *Juvenile Offenders and Victims*. Washington, DC: National Center for Juvenile Justice.

Sommers, C. H. (1994) *Who Stole Feminism? How Women Have Betrayed Women*. New York: Simon and Schuster.

Sparks, R. (1992) *Television and the Drama of Crime*. Buckingham: Open University Press.

Sparks, R. F. (1981) Surveys of victimization: an optimistic assessment, in M. Tonry and N. Morris (eds) *Crime and Justice: An Annual Review of Research*, Vol. 3, London: University of Chicago Press.

Sparks, R. F., Genn, H. and Dodd, D. J. (1977) *Surveying Victims*. Chichester: Wiley.

Spergel, I. A. (1995) *The Youth Gang Problem: A Community Approach*. New York: Oxford University Press.

Sroufe, L., Cooper, R. and DeHart, G. (1996) *Child Development: Its Nature and Course*. New York: McGraw-Hill.

Stack, S. (1983) Homicide and property crime: the relationships to anomie, *Aggressive Behavior*, 9: 339–44.

Stanko, E. A. (1987) Typical violence, normal precaution: men, women and interpersonal violence in England, Wales, Scotland and the USA, in J. Hanmer and M. Maynard (eds) *Women, Violence and Social Control*. Basingstoke: Macmillan.

Stanko, E. A. and Hobdell, K. (1993) Assault on men: masculinity and male victimization, *British Journal of Criminology*, 33(3): 400–15.

Steadman, H. J., Cocozza, J. J. and Melick, M. E. (1978) Explaining the increased arrest rate among mental patients: the changing clientele of state hospitals, *American Journal of Psychiatry*, 135(7): 816–20.

Stoller, R. (1968) *Sex and Gender*. London: Hogarth Press.

Stonewall (1996) *Violence Survey*. London: Stonewall.

Storr, A. (1968) *Human Aggression*. Harmondsworth: Penguin.

Straus, M. A. (1983) Ordinary violence, child abuse, and wife-beating: what do they have in common?, in D. Finkelhor, R. J. Gelles, G. T. Hotaling and M. A. Straus (eds) *The Dark Side of Families: Current Family Violence Research*. Beverly Hills, CA: Sage.

Straus, M. A. (1991) Discipline and deviance: physical punishment of children and violence and other crime in adulthood, *Social Problems*, 38(2): 133–54.

Straus, M. A. and Gelles, R. J. (1990) *Physical Violence in American Families*. New Brunswick, NJ: Transaction.

Surgeon General's Scientific Advisory Committee on Television and Social Behavior (1972) *Television and Growing Up: The Impact of Televised Violence*. Washington, DC: United States Government Printing Office.

Sutherland, E. H. (1947) *Criminology*, 4th edn. Philadelphia: Lippincott.

Tarde, G. (1910) *L'Opinion et la Foule*. Paris: Alcan.

Tarling, R. (1993) *Analysing Offending: Data, Models and Interpretation*. London: HMSO.

Taylor, E. (1991) Toxins and allergens, in M. Rutter and P. Casaer (eds) *Biological Risk Factors for Psychosocial Disorders*. Cambridge: Cambridge University Press.

Taylor, P. J. (1986) Psychiatric disorders in London's life-sentenced offenders, *British Journal of Criminology*, 26(1): 63–78.

Taylor, P. J. (1993a) Mental illness and violence, in P. J. Taylor (ed.) *Violence in Society*. London: Royal College of Physicians.

Taylor, P. J. (1993b) Schizophrenia and crime: distinctive patterns of association, in S. Hodkins (ed.) *Mental Disorder and Crime*. Newbury Park, CA: Sage.

Taylor, R. (2000) *A Seven-Year Reconviction Study of HMP Grendon Therapeutic Community*, Home Office Research Findings No. 115. London: Home Office.

Taylor, S. P. and Hulsizer, M. R. (1998) Psychoactive drugs and human aggression, in R. G. Geen and E. Donnerstein (eds) *Human Aggression: Theories, Research, and Implications for Social Policy*. San Diego, CA: Academic Press.

Thomas, W. I. (1923) *The Unadjusted Girl*. New York: Harper & Row.

Thornberry, T. P. (1989) Panel effects and the use of self-reported measures of delinquency in longitudinal studies, in M. W. Klein (ed.) *Cross-National Research in Self-Reported Crime and Delinquency*. Dordrecht: Kluwer.

Thrasher, F. M. (1927) *The Gang*. Chicago: University of Chicago Press.

Tiger, L. and Fox, R. (1974) *The Imperial Animal*. London: Paladin.

Tittle, C. R. (1995) *Control Balance: Toward a General Theory of Deviance*. Boulder, CO: Westview Press.

Tomsen, S., Homel, R. and Thommeny, J. (1991) The causes of public violence: situational and other factors, in D. Chappell, P. Grabosky and H. Strang (eds) *Australian Violence: Contemporary Perspectives*. Canberra: Australian Institute of Criminology.

Tong, R. (1989) *Feminist Thought: A Comprehensive Introduction*. London: Unwin Hyman.

Towl, G. (1994) Anger-control groupwork in prisons, in E. A. Stanko (ed.) *Perspectives on Violence*. London: Quartet.

Trasler, G. B. (1986) Situational crime control and rational choice: a critique, in K. Heal and G. Laycock (eds) *Situational Crime Prevention: From Theory into Practice*. London: HMSO.

Unnithan, N. P., Huff-Corzine, L., Corzine, J. and Whitt, H. P. (1994) *The Currents of Lethal Violence: An Integrated Model of Suicide and Homicide*. Albany: State University of New York Press.

US Department of Justice (1990) *Drugs and Crime Facts, 1990*. Washington, DC: US Department of Justice.

US Department of Justice (1998) *Uniform Crime Reports 1997*. Washington, DC: US Department of Justice.

van Eyken, A. (1987) Aggression: myth or model? *Journal of Applied Philosophy*, 4(2): 165–76.

van Goozen, S., van de Poll, N. and Frijda, N. (1994) Anger and aggression in women: influence of sports choice and testosterone administration, *Aggressive Behavior*, 20(3): 213–22.

van Ness, S. (1984) Rape as instrumental violence: a study of youthful offenders, *Journal of Offender Counselling, Service, and Rehabilitation*, 9: 161–70.

van Reyk, P. (1996) Homophobia, hate and violence against lesbians and gays in NSW: an overview, in C. Sumner, M. Israel, M. O'Connell and R. Sarre (eds) *International Victimology: Selected Papers from the 8th International Symposium*. Canberra: Australian Institute of Criminology.

Virkkunen, M. and Linnoila, M. (1993) Brain-serotonin, Type-II alcoholism and impulsive violence, *Journal of Studies on Alcohol*, 11: 163–9.

Vold, G. B. (1958) *Theoretical Criminology*. New York: Oxford University Press.

von Hentig, H. (1948) *The Criminal and His Victim*. New Haven, CT: Yale University Press.

Waddington, D., Jones, K. and Critcher, C. (1989) *Flashpoints: Studies in Public Disorder*. London: Routledge.

Waldorf, D. and Lauderback, D. (1993) *Gang Drug Sales in San Francisco: Organized or Freelance?* Alameda, CA: Institute for Scientific Analysis.

Walker, J., Collins, M. and Wilson, P. (1988) How the public sees sentencing: an Australian survey, in N. D. Walker and M. Hough (eds) *Public Attitudes to Sentencing: Surveys from Five Countries*. Aldershot: Gower.

Walker, L. E. (1988) The battered woman syndrome, in G. T. Hotaling, D. Finkelhor, J. T. Kirkpatrick and M. A. Straus (eds) *Family Abuse and Its Consequences: New Directions in Research*. Beverly Hills, CA: Sage.

Walker, N. (ed.) (1996) *Dangerous People*. London: Blackstone Press.

Walklate, S. (1989) *Victimology: The Victim and the Criminal Justice Process*. London: Unwin Hyman.

Walklate, S. (1995) *Gender and Crime*. Hemel Hempstead: Harvester Wheatsheaf.

Walklate, S. (1998) *Understanding Criminology*. Buckingham: Open University Press.

Walters, G. D. (1992) A meta-analysis of the gene–crime relationship, *Criminology*, 30(4): 595–613.

Weissberg, M. P. (1983) *Dangerous Secrets: Maladaptive Response to Stress*. New York: W. W. Norton.

Wessler, R. A. and Wessler, R. L. (1980) *The Principles and Practice of Rational-Emotive Therapy*. San Francisco: Jossey-Bass.

West, D. J. and Farrington, D. P. (1977) *The Delinquent Way of Life*. London: Heinemann.

White, R. and van der Velden, J. (1995) Class and criminality, *Social Justice*, 22(1): 51–74.

Wilkins, L. (1964) *Social Deviance*. London: Tavistock.

Willems, H. (1995) Right-wing extremism, racism or youth violence? Explaining violence against foreigners in Germany, *New Community*, 21(4): 501–23.

Williams, P. and Dickinson, J. (1993) Fear of crime: read all about it? *British Journal of Criminology*, 33(1): 33–56.

Wilson, E. O. (1978) *On Human Nature*. New York: Bantam.

Wilson, J. Q. and Herrnstein, R. J. (1985) *Crime and Human Nature*. New York: Simon & Schuster.

Wilson, J. Q. and Kelling, G. (1982) Broken windows, *Atlantic Monthly*, March, 29–38.

Wilson, W. J. (1987) *The Truly Disadvantaged*. Chicago: University of Chicago Press.

Witkin, H. A., Mednick, S. A., Schulsinger, F. et al. (1976) Criminality in XYY and XXY men. *Science*, 193: 547–55.

Wolfgang, M. E. (1958) *Patterns in Criminal Homicide*. Philadelphia: University of Pennsylvania Press.

Wolfgang, M. E. and Ferracuti, F. (1981) *The Subculture of Violence*. Beverly Hills, CA: Sage.

Wright, R. and West, D. J. (1981) Rape – a comparison of group offences and lone assaults, *Medicine, Science and the Law*, 21(1): 25–30.

Yablonsky, L. (1962) *The Violent Gang*. New York: Macmillan.

Young, D. (1995) The economic costs of domestic violence in Greater Glasgow. Unpublished MSc thesis, University of York. See also www.engender.org.uk

Zawitz, M. W., Klaus, P. A., Bachman, R. *et al.* (1993) *Highlights from 20 Years of Surveying Crime Victims: The National Crime Victimization Survey, 1973–92.* Washington, DC: Bureau of Justice Statistics.

Zedner, L. (1997) Victims, in M. Maguire, R. Morgan and R. Reiner (eds) *The Oxford Handbook of Criminology*, 2nd edn. Oxford: Oxford University Press.

Zillmann, D. (1979) *Hostility and Aggression*. Hillsdale, NJ: Erlbaum.

Zimring, F. E. and Hawkins, G. (1997) *Crime Is Not the Problem: Lethal Violence in America*. New York: Oxford University Press.

Index

UNDERSTANDING CRIME PREVENTION
SOCIAL CONTROL, RISK AND LATE MODERNITY

Gordon Hughes

- How can criminological, sociological and historical perspectives illuminate the elusive concept of crime prevention?
- Are we witnessing a new governance of crime control?
- What are the futures of crime prevention in late modernity?

This book offers a comprehensive overview of current and historical debates about crime prevention in particular and social control more generally. It moves beyond the traditional boundaries of criminology and offers an original re-framing of the field of crime prevention based on a synthesis of exciting new thinking in social theory. In particular, recent theorizing around late modernity, risk society, communitarianism and globalization are put forward as important ways of linking trends in crime prevention to wider social transformations.

This innovative text looks at the contested history of crime prevention in the modern era and considers present and future trends in social control in late modernity. Hughes focuses on the question of the managerialization of crime prevention in recent decades, the extent to which crime control may become dominated by privatized security and insurance against risks, and the attractions and pitfalls of informal community-based approaches. *Understanding Crime Prevention* will be essential reading for students and researchers in the field as well as many professional and lay people interested in crime prevention and community safety.

Contents
Introduction – Mapping the terrain of crime prevention – Classicism and the deterrent presences of the modern state – Positivism and the cure of 'criminal man' – Situational crime prevention: the pragmatics of crime control – Multi-agency partnerships: managing corporate crime prevention – Communitariansim: bringing 'the social' back into crime prevention? – The futures of crime control in late modernity – Postscript: beyond crime prevention? Glossary – References – Index.

192pp   0 335 19940 2 (Paperback)   0 335 19941 0 (Hardback)

UNDERSTANDING YOUTH AND CRIME
LISTENING TO YOUTH?

Sheila Brown

- How and why have young people been marginalized by popular and academic opinion?
- Why is it that young people are increasingly seen as offenders?
- Is there room for a broader view of youth and crime based on recent research?

Youth has long been a central focus of the sociologies of crime, deviance and popular culture. This lively and accessible text reassess the growing body of writing and research about crime and young people. It provides a critical introduction to the study of youth, crime and punishment within the context of a social construction of 'youth' which is continually defined as outside of society.

Key features include an overview of the field, an examination of developments in policy and practice, and an assessment of 'new' trends in research and theory. Sheila Brown provides a resource for undergraduate students in criminology, sociology, social policy, and cultural studies in a format which repeatedly poses questions to the reader and offers signposts to further enquiry. At the same time she offers a critical treatment of the marginalization of young people in popular, policy and academic analysis and calls for a criminology that 'listens to youth'.

Contents
Constructing the other: childhood and youth – Problem youth meets criminology: the formative decades – Representing problem youth: the repackaging of reality – In whose interests? Politics and policy – 'Punishing youth': victims or villans? Youth and crime: beyond the boy zone – Conclusion: listening to youth? – Glossary – References – Index.

160pp   0 335 19505 9 (Paperback)   0 335 20004 4 (Hardback)

UNDERSTANDING WHITE COLLAR CRIME

Hazel Croall

- What is the extent and impact of white collar crime?
- How can white collar crime be explained?
- How is white collar crime controlled?

This comprehensive overview of white collar crime begins by introducing the concept, looking at its definition, its identification with class and status, and its development within criminology. The problems of estimating the vast extent of white collar and corporate crime are explored, and some of its major forms are outlined, including fraud, corruption, employment, consumer and environmental crime.

Hazel Croall looks at the kinds of offenders who are convicted for white collar offences and at patterns of victimization which involve class, gender and age. She examines the various ways in which white collar crime has been explained and analysed, including individual, organizational and social structural perspectives. The issues surrounding regulation and punishment are explored, focusing on the contrast between white collar and other crimes, and on alternative approaches to its control.

This new book is a revised, updated and readily accessible replacement for the author's highly successful *White Collar Crime*. It includes expanded coverage of corporate crime, and provides an essential text for undergraduate courses in criminology, sociology and law.

Contents
Series editor's foreword – Acknowledgements – Conceptualizing white collar crime – Exposing white collar crime – White collar offenders – White collar crime and victimization – Explaining white collar crime – Regulating white collar crime: law and policing – Regulating white collar crime: punishment – White collar crime and criminology – References – Glossary – Index.

c.192pp   0 335 20427 9 (Paperback)   0 335 20428 7 (Hardback)

CRIME AND JUSTICE
Series editor: Mike Maguire
Cardiff University

Crime and Justice is a series of short introductory texts on central topics in criminology. The books in this series are written for students by internationally renowned authors. Each book tackles a key area within criminology, providing a concise and up-to-date overview of the principal concepts, theories, methods and findings relating to the area. Taken as a whole, the *Crime and Justice* series will cover all the core components of an undergraduate criminology course.

Published titles

Understanding youth and crime
Sheila Brown

Understanding crime data
Clive Coleman and Jenny Moynihan

Understanding justice
Barbara A. Hudson

Understanding crime prevention
Gordon Hughes

Understanding violent crime
Stephen Jones

Understanding criminology
Sandra Walklate

Understanding violent crime